THE CORPORATE BUY-SELL HANDBOOK

An Essential Guide to
Business Succession Planning

Stephan R. Leimberg
Morey S. Rosenbloom
Joseph M. Yohlin

Dearborn
Financial Publishing, Inc.

While a great deal of care has been taken to provide accurate and current information, the ideas, suggestions, general principles and conclusions presented in this text are subject to local, state and federal laws and regulations, court cases and any revisions of same. The reader is thus urged to consult legal counsel regarding any points of law—this publication should not be used as a substitute for competent legal advice.

Publisher: Kathleen A. Welton
Associate Editor: Karen A. Christensen
Senior Project Editor: Jack L. Kiburz
Interior Design: Lucy Jenkins
Cover Design: The Publishing Services Group

Published by Dearborn Financial Publishing, Inc.

Printed in the United States of America

94   10   9   8   7   6   5   4   3   2

Library of Congress Cataloging-in-Publication Data

Leimberg, Stephan R.
   The corporate buy-sell handbook : an essential guide to business succession planning / Stephan R. Leimberg, Morey S. Rosenbloom, Joseph M. Yohlin.
      p. cm.
   Includes index.
   ISBN 0–79310–405–X (pbk.)
   1. Sale of business enterprises—United States.   2. Corporations—United States—Purchasing.   3. Stock purchase agreements (Close corporations)—United States.   4. Estate planning—United States.   5. Inheritance and succession—United States.   I. Rosenbloom, Morey S.   II. Yohlin, Joseph M.   III. Title.
HD2747.L45   1992
658.1′6—dc20   92–14257
                                                                  CIP

DEDICATION

Stephan R. Leimberg:

To some very special aunts and uncles who have always been there for me:

> "Hen" and "Mutt"
> Sylvia and Milt
> June and Harry
> Lee and Marty

Morey S. Rosenbloom:

To my wife, Marsha, and sons, Brett and Eric, whom I love very much.

Joseph M. Yohlin:

To my wife, Pam, and daughters, Hilary and Elizabeth, whose love and support make all things possible.

CONTENTS

PREFACE AND ACKNOWLEDGMENTS

At no time in the history of business has the buy-sell agreement been more important. A whole generation of entrepreneurs who started closely held businesses in the late 1940s and through the 1950s will be retiring and dying within the next decade. The business lifework of those who have made plans will survive them, but the efforts of many of those who have not will die with them. The forces that threaten survival of the closely held business are merciless toward those who have not prepared for an orderly business transfer. It is therefore essential that planners understand the problems and solutions in this most important business and estate planning area.

This book is the third edition of what began as a master's in taxation paper at Temple University School of Law for the inspirational Philadelphia attorney and teacher Selwyn A. Horvitz and has become the most comprehensive reference on the subject currently in print. This latest revision is accompanied by a name change from *Funding Corporate Buy-Sell Agreements with Life Insurance*, reflecting its much wider scope and breadth.

To make and keep a book of this scope up to date and as accurate and authoritative as possible is a major task in the light of rapidly changing tax law. The addition of my coauthors, business and estate planning experts Morey S. Rosenbloom in the second edition and Joseph M. Yohlin in this latest effort, has significantly helped to improve the quality and enhance the creativity in the final product.

The thrust of the text is toward the sophisticated life insurance practitioner who must communicate the problems and make the clients aware of the urgency and significance of action. But *The Corporate Buy-Sell Handbook* will be an invaluable tool for law students as well as legal, accounting and financial planning professionals seeking an easy-to-access source of information on the tax and other implications of buy-sell planning.

Our goal was to create the best source of up-to-date, pragmatic and transferable information available to help you convey to clients highly complex concepts in a clear and simple manner. We have attempted to identify problem areas, state our opinions on how to handle problem situations and decide on the most efficient and effective course of action (see Chapter 33 on a systems approach to buy-selling planning).

The authors express appreciation to Rosemary Cataldi, Esq., of CMS Companies and Mathew Whitehorn, Esq., and Kit Boyle of Blank, Rome, Comisky & McCauley for their tireless help in researching and updating this text.

Stephan R. Leimberg

CHAPTER 1

Why a Buy-Sell

This book is about stabilizing and maximizing the value of a closely held business and transferring it to the parties desired under specified, controlled circumstances. It is designed for professionals to help their clients, families or business associates retain control of a closely held business and to assure them the full value of the business will be available to provide the maximum financial security in the event of retirement, death, disability or other severance of relationship with the business. This book is very much about controlling the shift in control.[1]

Owners of closely held businesses will find this book an invaluable guide to keeping their corporations "close" and to ensuring the transfer in the most secure manner or to creating a profitable market for what might otherwise be an unmarketable business.

This book will cover how a buy-sell can be used and the tax and nontax problems and opportunities it creates. Although the use of life insurance as a funding mechanism will be emphasized, *The Corporate Buy-Sell Handbook* will be useful to any estate or business planning practitioner.

Chapter 1 points out the problems inherent in closely held businesses, the inevitable conflicts that occur when no buy-sell is created and the advantages of creating a binding arm's-length bona fide agreement.

As you read, keep the buy-sell in context, because it cannot be formed in a vacuum. Business continuation planning must be executed through a systematic process that considers not only the business and its survival but also the personal needs and desires of each of the firm's owners, as well as the needs and desires of their loved ones. In other words, buy-sell planning must be incorporated into a larger picture of estate planning for each of the owners.

THE NATURE OF A CLOSELY HELD CORPORATION

Certain characteristics are common to almost every closely held corporation. To understand the importance of a buy-sell in solving potential problems, the professional must know the problems inherent in the following five characteristics:

1. The majority shareholders are active in the operation of the business.
2. The majority shareholders receive most of their income in the form of salaries or fringe benefits rather than as dividends on their investment.
3. The majority shareholders have limited liability to corporate creditors, except to the extent they have personally guaranteed corporate indebtedness.
4. At the death or disability of a majority shareholder, the legal structure of the business generally remains intact.
5. At the death or long-term disability of a shareholder, the personnel structure changes dramatically.

These five characteristics have a significant impact on the business, its owners, their families and their creditors when ownership changes hands because of death, disability, retirement, divorce, bankruptcy, on a sale to an outside purchaser or termination of a stockholder's employment. Although each of these contingencies must be considered by the professional (and will be covered in detail in separate chapters in this book), the most troublesome circumstances warrant the lion's share of our attention: death or the long-term disability of an owner/worker.

Why are death and disability such traumatic events? While a shareholder is alive, he or she can sell the business interest, give it away or keep it. But at death or disability the choice is gone. If no buy-sell exists, the shareholder's stock will be distributed—either by will or under state intestacy laws. The stock is held and voted, at first by the decedent's executor and later by his or her heirs or the party that purchases the stock from those heirs. Bluntly stated, the death or long-term disability of a shareholder in a closely held business may signal the death of the enterprise. In the authors' experience, the business and the business owner often die on the same day!

At the death or disability of a working owner, no asset tends to deteriorate in value as quickly or as completely as a business.[2] Although the value of a car or home or almost any other asset will remain relatively unchanged one month after its owner dies, the same cannot be said for the value of a business, especially a service-oriented business. If a restaurant doesn't reopen for a month, a doctor's practice is closed for a month or a manufacturing plant produces no goods for a month, what happens to the value of the enterprise? In many cases the precipitous drop in value is staggering!

The following scenarios have been played out many times:

> Across from my dad's jewelry store was Meyer's Shoe Store. Both stores were there since I was a kid. Meyer ran the business with the help of a longtime manager, Eddie, and two part-time summer employees. The business provided a good living for both Meyer and his wife, Miriam, and their two daughters, as well as for Eddie and his growing family.
>
> Meyer was from the old school; he worked night and day in his business but never took the time to make sure the business would survive him. When Meyer had a heart attack and died within three days, his family was hit with the immediate emotional trauma of his unexpected death. They were also confronted with economic problems that soon seemed insurmountable.
>
> At first Miriam tried to run the business. But she had never been involved while Meyer was alive. When she realized she needed help, she offered Eddie a significant raise in pay to keep the business going. But when she had to take out most of the firm's working capital to pay state death taxes and medical expenses not covered by Meyer's insurance, essential summertime business inventories dropped, and inevitably sales plummeted.
>
> Eddie, figuring it was only a matter of time until his job was lost, quickly accepted a position with one of Meyer's former competitors. Miriam had to sell the remaining inventory for less than 30 cents on the dollar.

The problems faced by unrelated co-workers are often compounded when all the owners are family members. Attorney Charles K. Plotnick of Elkins Park,

Pennsylvania, a frequently quoted authority on family-held businesses, related the story of two brothers, Joe and Paul, who during their lifetime could not have been closer.[3]

> They had been in business together for almost thirty years. Business responsibilities were divided down the middle: Joe ran the day-to-day operation of the business while Paul, the younger brother, was a super salesman and worked night and day to build up company profits. Even though the business enjoyed several million dollars a year in sales and was highly profitable, Joe's lifestyle was very conservative. Joe lived in a modest home with his (second) wife Mary and four young children. Paul, a bachelor, lived in a downtown apartment on a much higher scale.
>
> Joe died at age 53 after a six-month battle with cancer. Paul was more than a little shocked when he was invited to the office of his late brother's wife's new attorney. The attorney said that since Joe had owned half the business, Mary, his widow, was entitled to the same income Joe had been bringing home before his death. Mary insisted it was urgent that she receive at least that much since the twins had just started college and the other two children were in their freshman and sophomore years of high school.
>
> Paul, of course, felt a deep moral obligation to his late brother's wife and children. He wanted to do "what was right" and as much as possible. But he knew very little about how the business was actually run. He did know he'd have to hire at least one and probably two people to do the work that Joe had done. He also knew it would put quite a strain on the business to pay—in essence—three salaries.
>
> Paul's accountant cautioned that even Paul's salary might have to be cut back until a competent replacement for Joe was found and properly trained. Mary became distraught. But Paul's accountant told Mary that if the pressure became too much for Paul and his health suffered, the entire value of the business would be jeopardized. He suggested that she should try to find a job to provide for her children's education.

The physical and emotional drain on the surviving partner who tries to do the right thing often ruins that person's health. Regardless of intent, an after-the-fact solution almost always becomes unsatisfactory to some, and often all, of the parties.

THE ALMOST INEVITABLE CONFLICTS OF INTEREST

The interest of the surviving stockholders and the decedent/shareholder's heirs inevitably will conflict. At best the beneficiaries of the deceased shareholder often find that the principal asset of the estate has a value that is substantially less than its intrinsic value, because it is subject to the control of other persons whose interests differ from theirs. At worst, these conflicts of interest can threaten the very life of the corporation and ruin long-term business and personal relationships.[4]

The surviving stockholders typically

- seek to maintain (or increase) their salaries, fringe benefits and other advantages as employees;
- advocate reinvesting corporate earnings and profits in the business;
- favor expansion, growth and other steps that will build up the survival capacity and financial strength of the business;
- support reinvestment of money that might otherwise be paid out in dividends to build up a strong cash reserve for emergencies, opportunities or cyclical working capital needs;
- wish to retain their jobs, although those jobs may be jeopardized if controlling shareholder heirs sell their business interests to outsiders or decide the active shareholders are no longer productive;
- attempt to prevent outsiders from interfering with the management and seizing control of the business and its affairs (yet who would purchase an interest in a business that has just lost a key individual if the money that had to be invested, no matter how much it was, wouldn't buy a controlling voice in corporate decisions?);
- wish to ensure that the ownership of a corporation does not move outside the agreed-on group of entrepreneurs/investors/workers;
- want to keep a family-owned business within the family (many business owners are willing to be in business with a child but not with his or her spouse, ex-spouse, new spouse or lawyer or the creditor of a child who might obtain stock by attachment);
- seek to prevent the loss of an "S" (subchapter S) election;[5]
- attempt to prevent a former shareholder from competing with the business (in the case of a shareholder selling during his or her lifetime); and
- wish to protect against shifts in proportionate ownership.[6]

The decedent/shareholder's family has different problems and goals:

- Dividends are of primary importance to the decedent/shareholder's heirs. If the heirs are not capable of earning a meaningful salary or, for any reason, do not go into the business, dividends often become their major source of income. Heirs may need large amounts of capital to pay estate administration expenses or death taxes and for education expenses.
- Often the heirs can't or don't want to take an active role in the business; they sometimes lack a technical understanding of the business, have little training and experience or are unwilling or unable to handle the severe emotional punishment entailed in modern business management. They may just be too young; minors have a legal disability. Surviving parents may be occupied by raising children or pursuing their own careers. Survivors may be injured and physically incapacitated in the same accident that killed or permanently disabled the shareholder.
- Although surviving stockholders will seldom want to share corporate control or decision making with individuals who have not worked in the business at length, the decedent/shareholder's heirs will want as much control and voice as possible. Remaining inactive means placing their fate in the hands of the surviving shareholders, which is often undesirable because the dividends inactive and nonvocal heirs are likely to receive will probably provide inadequate income.
- It is usually difficult for the heirs (especially minority shareholder heirs) to sell their stock, because the price they want (and often need) is more than most buyers can afford or are willing to pay. Buyers who are aware of the heirs' pressing needs for estate liquidity, capital security or day-to-day income often use this knowledge to their advantage and to the heirs' disadvantage.

Many times the heirs are totally unfamiliar with the true value of the stock and have no objective means of evaluating it. They often erroneously assume that the value of the stock should be a multiple of the shareholder/employee's gross salary. Such misguided expectations often lead to forced sales of stock or other property at depressed prices to raise cash for basic living needs. Finally, finding a buyer (i.e., creating a viable market for the business interest) is itself a difficult task, especially if the heirs are minority shareholders.

- Heirs will want to minimize the cost, time expenditure and aggravation involved with the federal and state death tax valuation process.
- Heirs often want, expect and need for the business to provide them with (high-paying) jobs and to replace valuable fringe benefits (such as medical coverage) lost when the family member/shareholder died.
- Heirs have pressing needs for both income and capital. Income will be

needed to replace lost salaries and provide food, clothing and shelter and to continue the family's standard of living. Capital will be needed in unexpectedly high amounts to pay estate administration costs, death taxes and debts, and for special needs such as college education.

THIRD PARTIES TO THE BUSINESS

Every business deals with third parties: individuals or entities that are not formally part of the business or its legal structure but are essential to the success and sometimes even survival of the business. For instance, consider what would happen to a manufacturing company if one of its three partners was killed in an airplane crash and the bank making loans to the firm was no longer so sure the survivors could maintain the level of success necessary to service present debt or justify future loans.[7]

Consider also the employees who had confidence in and gratefully followed the deceased shareholder, who was the founder of the firm, but who are unsure of their future under the new leadership. If morale suffered and they began to look to the firm's competition for employment, while cash flow tightened, the business's ability to fulfill orders would drop.

The point is: Whenever a business has more than one owner and each is important to the success of the venture, third parties to the business can accelerate the sinking process when triggering events occur, unless there is adequate preparation.

THE INEVITABLE REORGANIZATION

When a working shareholder dies or is disabled for a long period of time, a reorganization of the business personnel is inevitable. Sooner or later the remaining shareholders *must*

- buy out the heirs,
- sell out to the heirs,
- accept the purchasers of the heirs' stock as business associates,
- take the heirs into the business and share profits and decisions or
- do nothing and accept the heirs as silent partners.

Here are some questions clients must be able to answer. Their responses will indicate to you (and illustrate to them) the need for a buy-sell agreement:

- How would the business's creditors react if you or another shareholder died or became disabled for a long period of time?
- If you died or became disabled for a long period of time, would you want your family to retain the business or sell it? To whom? At what price? Under what terms? Could the executor you've named in your will sell your business at a profit? What would your strongest competitor offer your executor for the business the week after you died?
- Would you consider selling your business to key employees? Are there any that would want to buy it? Can they afford to buy it?
- Are there outsiders, such as friendly competitors, who might be interested in securing an interest in your business?
- When was the last time your advisers measured the federal estate tax ("going concern") value of your business? How did they arrive at that figure? Is it realistic today? How realistic will it be five years from now?
- What would be the income-producing ability of the business, assuming you weren't here to direct it?
- Who would control your business at your death or disability? Can or will that person run the business? If not, what have you done to avoid or reduce conflicts of interest between the parties? Who are those persons?
- What members of your family are in the business now or are likely to enter it in the near future? How long will it be before they are capable of earning a decent salary and contributing in a meaningful way to the profits of the business? What part of your business is your son or daughter interested in? Are the members of your family who will be working in the business not only physically but also emotionally able to run the business as well as work in it?
- Who will operate the business until your child is ready to take over? What have you done to keep that person in the business and in a position to willingly build someone else's financial future?
- What have you done to provide security or even things out for those members of your family who will not be coming into the business?
- How comfortable would you feel being in business with your coshareholder's widow? How comfortable would your coshareholder feel being in business with your widow?
- If your business partner was disabled for four to six months, would you want to continue his or her full salary during that time? Would you be able to? If that disability became permanent, how long could you afford to pay that salary? What have you done to offset that potential cost and the cost of hiring a replacement? How long could you handle the business alone?

- What percentage of your salary, after your death or during a long-term disability, will be paid by the business to your family or to you? For how long?
- How important is it to you to guarantee that your business will be controlled by the parties you desire after your death or long-term disability?

If a coshareholder dies and you buy out the decedent's heirs:

- Where will you get the cash?
- What price will you pay, and will the terms of the loan be fair to both parties?

If a coshareholder dies and you sell out to the decedent's heirs:

- Where will they get the cash, and how much will such a loan cost?
- What price will you receive, and will that price be fair to both parties?
- What will you do for work once you have sold yourself out of a job?

If a coshareholder dies and you accept the purchasers of his or her stock in the business:

- Will they be capable of doing their share of the work?
- Will they be willing to do their share of the work?
- Will you get along with them and they with you?
- Will you be willing to allow them to vote on major business decisions?
- Will the heirs obtain a fair and adequate price for their stock? Will they know what a fair price is?
- Will you have a choice if the departed shareholder held a majority interest? (Where does that leave you?)

If a coshareholder dies and you take the heirs into the business:

- Will they be capable of doing their share of the work? Do they have the training and experience to carry their load and earn their salaries?
- Will they be willing to do their share of the work?
- Will you get along with them, and they with you?
- Will you be willing to share major decisions with them?

If a coshareholder dies and you do nothing and the heirs remain inactive:

- Will they trust you to run the business?
- Will the dividends you pay them be sufficient to meet their needs and their expectations? How realistic are their expectations?
- Will the heirs panic if you need to invest business income in the business rather than declare dividends?
- What will happen to the heirs if you sell your stock to an outsider?
- What will the heirs do if you die or become disabled?

Particular Problems of a Professional Practice

A professional in practice with other professionals faces almost all of the problems business owners face and many more. An article in *Medical Economics* started by stating: "If you are in practice with one or more colleagues, the departure, disablement, or death of a stockholder or partner can lead to bitter disputes and unforeseen complications. And if you're the one leaving, you can lose your shirt."[8]

Here are some problems faced by professionals in the absence of a properly drafted and fully funded buy-sell:

- How will patients or clients be divided up if one or more practitioners leave the firm?
- Who keeps the office if one or more practitioners depart? What will the departing practitioner receive for his or her share of the office or office building?
- What happens to office furniture, equipment and art? What will the departing practitioner receive for his or her share of those items?
- How will accounts receivable be apportioned among former coshareholders?
- Should a departing practitioner lose all the money in a nonvested retirement plan?
- Who pays the malpractice tail coverage? The practice? The remaining or the departing professional?
- What happens if a professional loses his or her license or board certification?
- Should you require shareholders to sign a restrictive covenant (agreement not to compete)?
- Will the firm or the other professionals pay a practitioner who is disabled and unable to work for a long period of time? What about permanent disability? What if the practitioner wants to come back to work full-time

but because of mental, emotional, alcohol or drug problems can't perform at the same level as before? At what point would the other practitioners want a buyout?[9]

- At what age should a practitioner be required to retire?[10] How will the firm figure what is due to that person? How will it be paid? Can the professional carry out any insurance owned by the practice on his or her life (such as life or disability insurance)?[11]

WHAT IS A BUY-SELL AGREEMENT?

By this point it should be obvious that

> When a corporate business owner dies or becomes permanently disabled, his or her business may die or be permanently stricken and disabled the same day—not because something wrong was done but because nothing was done!

Most professional advisers recommend a buy-sell agreement (also called a *business continuation* or *shareholders' agreement*) as a solution to these problems. A buy-sell agreement is a legally binding contract that places certain restrictions on the transfer of stock and requires certain actions on given events.

Typically, at the death of a shareholder (or at one of the other specified triggering events such as retirement or long-term disability) a buy-sell agreement will require the surviving shareholders (or the corporation or a combination of both) to buy and the owner of the stock (such as the estate of the deceased shareholder or a retiring or permanently disabled shareholder) to sell the ownership interest represented by the stock. Three types of buy-sell agreements are as follows:

1. *Cross-purchase agreement.* If the remaining shareholders are to be the purchasers, the agreement is called a *cross-purchase* (or *crisscross*) *plan.* Upon the occurrence of the specified event each remaining shareholder buys the agreed-on portion of the stock of the departing shareholder. The seller receives cash and/or notes, and the buyer receives the stock in exchange. For example, on the death of shareholder X, the other shareholders Y and Z would be required to purchase X's stock, and X's estate would be required to sell it at the price (or according to the formula) specified in the agreement.

2. *Stock redemption agreement.* If the corporation is to be the purchaser, the agreement is called a *stock redemption* (or *entity purchase*) *plan.* Upon the occurrence of the specified event the corporation itself buys the agreed-on number of shares of the departing shareholder. The seller receives cash and/or notes, and the corporation receives the stock in exchange.[12] For example, on the death of shareholder *X,* the corporation would be required to purchase *X*'s stock, and *X*'s estate would be required to sell it to the corporation at the price (or according to the formula) provided in the agreement.

3. *Wait-and-See buy-sell.* Besides the cross-purchase and stock redemption type of agreement, there is a hybrid type of buy-sell called the Wait-and-See buy-sell. The term comes from the title of the book by the authors, Stephan R. Leimberg and Morey S. Rosenbloom, called the *Wait and See Buy-Sell.*[13] This unique and highly flexible tool allows the parties to wait until the triggering event occurs to see which buyer—or combination of buyers—would serve the objectives of the parties best. The Wait-and-See buy-sell is covered in more detail in Chapter 29.

The purchase is typically triggered on the occurrence of specified events, such as a shareholder's retirement, death, long-term disability, divorce, bankruptcy or receipt of an outside offer to buy.

The agreement, which should (and in some states must[14]) be in writing, can also be incorporated into the corporate charter, the bylaws of the corporation or both.[15] It is extremely important that restrictions placed on the transfer of stock be documented on the stock certificates themselves.[16]

The agreement, regardless of whether it takes the form of a cross-purchase, stock redemption or Wait-and-See buy-sell, should specify a purchase price for the shares. That price should be established by (1) a stated fixed-dollar amount, (2) a formula or (3) a required appraisal. The pros and cons of each option will be discussed in detail in Chapter 11.

WHY DOES THE BUY-SELL MAKE SENSE?

The buy-sell makes a good deal of financial sense for many reasons. It answers many of the concerns of the surviving shareholders and heirs presented earlier in the chapter.

From the viewpoint of the active surviving shareholder:

- The corporation is protected against inactive, uninformed and potentially dissident shareholders, who often cause conflict over management policies such as the size of dividends relative to the level of salaries, fringe benefits or other perks provided to working shareholders and risks the corporation should take for growth.
- Active shareholders can be assured that the profits produced by their efforts benefit them rather than inactive shareholders (or the purchasers of their stock), and they can receive a salary commensurate with increased work load and responsibilities.
- Surviving shareholders are assured of all or the bulk of the cash needed to purchase the heirs' interests.
- Surviving shareholders know they will not have to pay more than a fair price for the stock.
- Only a buy-sell agreement can guarantee a smooth and complete management transition and consolidation of corporate control in the hands of the agreed-on group.
- The buy-sell agreement can be used to effect changes in ownership percentages that may be appropriate at a stockholder's death.
- A properly drawn buy-sell can protect an S corporation election.
- The buy-sell agreement gives the surviving shareholders a convenient means of fulfilling the obligation they naturally feel toward a deceased comrade's family.
- Minority shareholders are protected against a "lockout" of their salaries. A buyout arranged during the shareholder's lifetime prevents a new majority shareholder from firing the minority shareholder, cutting his or her pay or fringe benefits or making work so aggravating that it becomes intolerable.
- Perhaps one of the least appreciated benefits of a buy-sell agreement is the ability to prevent involuntary coshareholdership with unexpected outsiders, such as the creditors of a shareholder, who obtain stock through a legal judgment in satisfaction of debt (for example, when a lender forecloses on a loan and takes the shares of stock pledged as collateral). Shareholders are from time to time forced into personal bankruptcy. The trustee in bankruptcy automatically becomes the successor to any stock held by the bankrupt party. Finally, a divorce court may award stock to an ex-spouse. A buy-sell can prevent involuntary coshareholdership with an ex-spouse (and his or her new spouse or lawyer) who obtains stock through divorce proceedings.

From the viewpoint of the deceased shareholder's heirs:

- A binding and properly funded buy-sell agreement not only helps provide a market for what might otherwise be an unmarketable asset, it also helps ensure that the decedent's heirs will receive a reasonable price for the stock, especially if the decendent held only a minority interest.
- After the agreement is executed, the heirs' economic futures will no longer be tied to the fate of the business, and they will be free from worry about the financial success of the business.
- The payout of buy-sell proceeds will reduce the pressure to liquidate other estate assets and provide the cash to pay estate taxes and other settlement costs.
- A properly drafted buy-sell agreement will help establish the value of the stock for death tax purposes and therefore avoid costly and aggravating IRS litigation, as well as the legal and emotional costs of a valuation dispute with the surviving shareholders.
- A buy-sell provides a means for withdrawing funds from a family corporation income-tax-free at death and with capital gains treatment (which may include lower tax rates and a tax-free return of the stockholder's tax basis) during the stockholder's lifetime.
- A buy-sell may increase the cash flow of the heirs as well as reduce their financial risk. Even if the business can afford to pay out a dividend—and in fact does so—the decedent's survivors will have only the after-tax income to use for living expenses. Worse, all their income will be from one source—the business—and will be lost if the business goes bankrupt. The buy-sell replaces stock with cash, which can be reinvested to produce income.
- If the deceased shareholder held a controlling interest, a buy-sell can avoid the problem that arises when a key employee (including a minority shareholder employee) ends up operating the business. Without a buy-sell the family may be at that person's mercy. On the other hand, that person may be hamstrung by a family that knows little about how the business actually must be operated. With a funded buy-sell the family has cash and the operator of the business can run it without interference.
- The 50 percent stalemate is broken through a buy-sell. A 50 percent shareholder's interest is more like a minority than a majority shareholder's stock in some ways: there is a loss of salary at his or her death, his or her heirs have no right or ability to force the corporation to pay dividends and—at least temporarily—as a practical matter the surviving shareholder controls the board of directors until the next annual meeting.

- A buy-sell prevents the lockout of income flow to minority shareholders. Without a buy-sell the minority shareholder may be without a means of recovering his or her investment in the business.

WHERE DO WE GO FROM HERE?

The balance of this book focuses on a comparison of the stock redemption (corporation purchases the decedent/shareholder's stock), cross-purchase (each surviving shareholder purchases a portion of the decedent/shareholder's interest) and wait-and-see (combination of redemption and cross-purchase) approaches and considers various ways that such agreements may be funded and the tax implications of each. Many of the issues that must be considered with respect to special problems—such as election of S corporation tax treatment or operation as a partnership or sole proprietorship—are covered. You will also find provisions or other solutions that address those unique problems.

Endnotes

1. See Gatewood, "Shifting Shareholder Control—Why? When? How?", *Life Association News*, August 1991: 140.
2. See Nelson, "What's Missing in Buy-Sell Agreements?", *Best's Review*, August 1991: 27.
3. This story taken with permission from a client-oriented brochure entitled *Don't Give the IRS the Business!* It is available from Financial Data Center, PO Box 1332, Bryn Mawr, PA 19010 in quantities of 100 copies for $40. Call 215-525-6957.
4. Donald, "Corporate Buy-Out Agreements," 106-5th *T.M.*: A-1.
5. See Chapter 26 for more details. The S election can be lost through a transfer of stock to an ineligible shareholder. IRC §1362(d)(2). A transfer of S corporation stock will also cause the termination of the election when the total number of shareholders exceeds 35. See Leimberg, et al., *Tools and Techniques of Estate Planning* (Cincinnati: National Underwriter Co., 1992), call 800-543-0874. For these reasons it is essential that the shareholders of an S corporation enter into an agreement that imposes restrictions on any transfer that could jeopardize the tax election. One such restriction may be to require the consent of shareholders owning more than a specified percentage of the corporation's stock before a disqualifying transaction may be made.
6. Donald, "Corporate Buy-Out Agreements," 106-5th *T.M.*: A-1.
7. See Kraus, "Using Life Insurance To Fund Buy-Sell Agreements," *Personal Financial Planning*, Nov–Dec. 1989: 57.
8. Hodes, "Why You Need a Buy-Sell Agreement Now," *Medical Economics*, Nov. 26, 1990: 172.
9. See Chapter 32.

10. Absent such a provision, younger professionals would have no way to ease out aging colleagues gracefully and make room for new practitioners.

11. Absent such a provision, the coverage could be canceled and the retiring professional could be uninsured or forced to seek more expensive coverage.

12. This sale would be subject to any state law limitations on the corporation's ability to purchase its own shares. See Chapter 34.

13. This book has recently been reprinted and may be obtained by sending $10 per copy to Financial Data Center, PO Box 1332, Bryn Mawr, PA 19010 or by calling 215-525-6957.

14. FLA. STAT. §607.107(1) and Del. Gen. Corp Law §218(c). Courts have, however, enforced oral buy-sells. See *Merlino v. West Coast Macaroni Mfg. Co.*, 202 P.2d 748 (Cal. Dist. Ct. App. 1949) and *Shubin v. Surchin*, 27 A.D.2d 452 (1967). The Uniform Commercial Code (§8-318) may require the agreement to be in writing if it is viewed as a contract to sell securities. See also *Thomas v. Prewitt*, 355 So. 2d 657 (Miss. 1978); and *Fisher v. C. J. Laurence and Co., Inc.*, 481 F. Supp. 357 (S.D.N.Y. 1979).

15. Compare *In re Brophy*, 179 A. 128 (S. Ct. N.J. 1935), which held that a bylaw granting cumulative voting rights was invalid where there was no similar provision in the company's charter, and *Fromkin v. Merrall Realty, Inc.*, 30 Misc. 2d 288, 215 N.Y.S.2d 525 (1961), aff'd 15 A.D.2d 288, 215 N.Y.S.2d 632 (1962), which held that the requirement of unanimity for the sale of certain real estate was unenforceable because it was not in the corporation's charter. See, however, *Sansabaugh v. Polson Plywood Company*, 342 P.2d 1064 (Mont. 1959), which held that although a bylaw could not override the state constitution's requirement for cumulative voting in the election of directors, the stockholders could contract among themselves as to how they would vote.

16. The Uniform Commercial Code (§8-204) provides that restrictions on the transfer of stock must be evidenced on the security itself, or they will not be effective against subsequent transferees without actual notice.

It would be quite difficult to change bylaws and charters whenever the agreement among the shareholders was modified. Furthermore, there is a possibility that fewer than all of the stockholders can change the bylaws or charter. But see *Cowles v. Cowles Realty Company*, 201 A.D. 460, 194 N.Y.S. 546 (N. Y. App. Div. 1922); and *Bechtold v. Coleman Realty Co.*, 79 A.2d 661 (Pa. 1951), where the court held that the charter and the bylaws restricting stock transfers result in a contract that cannot be amended without the consent of all the affected parties.

C H A P T E R 2

Funding the Buyer's Obligation

PLANNING OBJECTIVES

A corporate buy-sell agreement should be funded by a method that will facilitate a trouble-free transfer of a business interest in the following four contingencies:

1. At the withdrawal of an owner before retirement
2. At normal retirement age
3. In the event of a stockholder's long-term disability[1]
4. At a stockholder's death

Ideally the method used to provide funds to meet these contingencies would

- have a relatively low cost,
- be simple to understand,
- be easy to administer and
- not adversely affect the working capital or credit position of the business.

Although a properly drafted buy-sell agreement should consider the possibility of a buyout at a number of events (which are covered later in the book), this chapter focuses primarily on the income tax ramifications of funding a purchase that will be triggered by a shareholder's death or long-term disability.

PROBABILITY OF DEATH

The probability of the death of at least one of two male business owners before age 65 is surprisingly high.[2] Expressed as the number of chances out of 100 that at least one or two business owners in relatively good health (able to qualify for standard insurance rates) will die before age 65, the figures are as follows:

Chances of Death before 65	Ages of Business Owners
41.1	30/30
40.2	35/35
38.9	40/40
36.8	45/45
33.3	50/50
40.6	30/35
39.5	35/40
37.8	40/45
35.1	45/50
30.4	50/55

ALTERNATIVES

Although most buy-sells are funded with life insurance, there are, of course, alternative methods for creating such funds. Professionals should consider each of these options carefully.

Cash

The first alternative is cash, which has the apparent advantages of being simple and requiring no *immediate* outlay. The problem that arises, however, is that the purchaser does not know precisely when or how much cash will be needed (or who will be the survivor) and thus must always keep a large cash reserve available.

In the case of a cross-purchase agreement, where each surviving shareholder agrees to buy the interest of a deceased shareholder, after the purchase of the decedent/shareholder's interest the survivor's personal savings would be depleted. Corporate surplus, operating capital or current income is often drained where the agreement takes the form of a stock redemption (retirement) plan, because here it is the corporation rather than the individual shareholders that purchases the decedent/shareholder's interest.

Regardless of the identity of the purchaser, after-tax dollars must be used to effect the buyout. This means (depending on the purchaser's federal and state income tax brackets) that more than $1 must be earned to net $1 of purchase money. And monies held in reserve may not be earning as high a return (or any return) as if invested personally or in the corporation.

Unfortunately this drain on the buyer's cash flow occurs at the worst possible time. If the corporation accumulates cash in anticipation of a need, will the liquidity trigger an accumulated earnings tax? If the surviving shareholders are to be the purchasers, will the corporation have the cash to increase their salaries sufficiently so that they can make payments of both principal and interest? Will these increased salaries be considered "reasonable"?

Borrowing

Like cash, borrowing has the advantages of being simple and requiring no outlay until death or disability occurs. The question is: will a bank lend money to a business that has just lost its most important asset, the person who made the corporation what it was? If the bank will make the loan, will the terms or rates be reasonable from the borrower's viewpoint? How will the cash flow demands of repaying the loan impact the operation of the business?

The cost to borrow $100,000 over a given period of time is substantial, as shown in Table 2.1, which assumes the buyer is in a 35 percent combined federal and state income tax bracket and is able to deduct interest payments.

The figures in Table 2.1, of course, do not reflect the effect on current earnings (before income taxes), which is considerable, even after taking into account the severely limited tax deductibility of interest payments. While a C corporation may generally deduct business interest,[3] the deductibility of interest incurred by an S corporation is tested at the stockholder level. In that event, and in the case of a cross-purchase, the deduction for investment interest will be limited to "investment income."[4] Interest incurred in an installment cross-purchase

TABLE 2.1   Cost To Borrow $100,000

Total Combined Cost at	5-Year Loan	10-Year Loan	15-Year Loan
10%	$130,000	$155,000	$180,000
12%	$136,000	$166,000	$196,000
15%	$145,000	$182,500	$220,000
Earnings Required at			
10%	$173,345	$189,600	$205,850
12%	$177,245	$196,750	$216,253
15%	$183,095	$207,475	$231,851

Source: Courtesy Number Cruncher Software, 215-525-6957.

may not, in fact, be classified as investment interest; if it is not, the entire deduction could be lost.

Installment Payouts

An installment payout is often thought to be a feasible means of purchasing the interest of a deceased shareholder.[5] To the buyer an installment sale seems advantageous because it is simple and requires a relatively small outflow each year. Nothing is needed until death occurs, so action apparently can be put off for many years. The decedent/shareholder's heirs appear to profit because they will receive interest on the unpaid balance. Gain can be spread over a number of years.[6] Furthermore, the heirs are creditors of the buyers rather than shareholders of what may be a financially shaky business.

Planners should, however, keep in mind that the installment payout method merely delays the pain: from the buyer's perspective it does not provide the cash to effect the buyout, and from the seller's point of view it does not provide the large sums of cash often needed for estate settlement costs and debts and leaves substantial sums at the risk of the business. So it does not protect the family of the deceased shareholder.

Ironically, from the surviving shareholders' viewpoint an installment payout creates almost as much nuisance as if the surviving spouse still owned the stock—some of the very problems the buy-sell was instituted to avoid. Where will the surviving shareholder, if the purchaser, obtain enough after-tax cash to pay both principal and interest? If payments are strung out too long (say more than 15 years), the IRS may argue that the seller actually has remained a shareholder rather than a creditor, which would mean payments from the corporation are dividends rather than payments for stock. The longer the term of the payments and the greater the obligation, the more adverse the effect on the credit rating of the business.

Can the parties pass the stock from one generation to another using a fair price but using no interest or an ultra-low interest rate and spreading payments out over many years? The answer is no. Interest must be paid on the unpaid balance. In fact, if a buy-sell agreement allows for deferred payments but does not provide for an "adequate" rate of interest on the payments the buyer owes but has not paid, the IRS will impute an interest rate. That is, the IRS will treat the parties as though they had agreed on a payment for the right to defer part of the sales price. That payment (the imputed interest) will be set by reference to the "original issue discount" rules, which reflect current market rates.[7] The rate is based on the time the buyout is effected rather than the date the agreement is entered into. That rate might be much higher than the parties anticipate.

A seller allowing the buyer to defer payments will almost inevitably insist on security for the unpaid amounts. Corporate assets can secure the unpaid balance, but this security may hinder the firm's ability to borrow money to finance expansion or even raise working capital. Corporate assets may not be sufficient to satisfy the seller (now a creditor), and that party may insist on the personal guarantees of the remaining shareholders in addition to the securing of corporate assets. Of course, if the agreement was structured as a cross-purchase, the corporation's assets could not serve as collateral for the unpaid balance (such an agreement would be void for lack of consideration), and therefore the purchasing shareholders would be personally liable.

An installment sale can be incredibly expensive from the buyers' perspective: Table 2.2 illustrates the cost of a ten-year installment[8] payout of $200,000, assuming 13 percent interest is paid on the remaining balance.[9]

The example in Table 2.2 assumes that interest is fully deductible as business or investment interest. Interest paid by shareholders on the deferred portion of the buyout price is "investment interest," which will be nondeductible to the extent that there is not enough investment income.[10] The loss of an interest deduction significantly increases the cost of a deferred-payment buyout.[11]

Because the "debt" takes on the characteristics of equity as its maturity date extends outward, an installment obligation of longer than 15 years may not be possible

TABLE 2.2   Example of High Cost of a 10-Year Installment Payout

Year	Principal Payment	Interest at 13%	Total Payment	Earnings Required before Tax*
1	$ 20,000	$ 26,000	$ 46,000	$ 56,769
2	20,000	23,400	43,400	54,169
3	20,000	20,800	40,800	51,569
4	20,000	18,200	38,200	48,969
5	20,000	15,600	35,600	46,369
6	20,000	13,000	33,000	43,769
7	20,000	10,400	30,400	41,169
8	20,000	7,800	27,800	38,569
9	20,000	5,200	25,200	35,969
10	20,000	2,600	22,600	33,369
TOTALS	$200,000	$143,000	$343,000	$450,692

*35% is the assumed combined rates for federal and state taxes.

with a corporate purchaser. When a debt is reclassified as equity, the redemption will not meet the safe harbor tests discussed in Chapter 5, and the payments to the selling shareholders will be taxed as a dividend at ordinary income rates.[12]

The bottom line is that deferred payments should be used only as an "escape valve" in the event of inadequate insurance rather than as the primary means of financing a buyout at a shareholder's death.

Private Annuity

In exchange for stock a shareholder can agree to receive a private annuity, an agreement that the corporation or the shareholders will pay fixed amounts each year for the remainder of the transferor's life (or the remainder of the transferor's life and his or her spouse's life). This private annuity technique works best when the seller wants to redeem all the stock during his or her lifetime and the successor shareholders will be close relatives or local employees.

A major problem, however, is that as a redemption device a private annuity cannot be "secured." No collateral can be required, and no escrow account can be demanded without loss of the two main advantages of a private annuity:

(1) the removal of the stock's current value and appreciation from the seller's estate and (2) the spread-out of gain over the lifetime of the seller. This means that the private annuity is useful only when the seller has extreme trust in successor management. Because annuity payments probably will be made out of the corporation's profits, the seller may never receive payments if the corporation cannot (or is unwilling to) make them.

The use of a private annuity does not change the rules that must be met for a safe (favorable tax treatment) redemption (see Chapter 5). The seller will have to sell back all of the shares actually owned. If his or her spouse, children, grandchildren, or parents still own any stock after the sale, a successful "waiver" of family attribution rules (see Chapter 5) will be necessary to avoid dividend treatment.

There are yet other potential downside costs and risks. Interest paid by the corporation to the seller (annuitant) is not deductible. As is the case in an installment buyout, the seller in a private annuity may not receive enough immediate cash for estate settlement costs and debts. If payments are not properly calculated or if the valuation of the stock (difficult at best to accomplish either accurately or objectively) is revised by the IRS, unintended but serious gift tax consequences may result.

Mortgaging the Business

Whether business assets can be mortgaged to raise cash for the buyout may depend on when the buyout must be executed. Even when there are assets that can easily be mortgaged, the debt will affect the firm's credit standing, and servicing the debt will drain some of the firm's working capital.

LIFE INSURANCE

For a corporation in a 35 percent total tax bracket to net $343,000 after taxes, more than $450,692 of current earnings is required before income taxes to amortize $200,000 over a ten-year period, assuming a 13 percent interest rate on the unpaid balance (see Table 2.2). Moreover, if the interest expense is not fully deductible, in the case of a cross-purchase for example, the $450,692 cost will be increased by $77,000 to $527,692. Conversely, a net payment of only about $19,805 in premiums need be made over a ten-year period to insure a 40-year-old standard male risk for $100,000, as shown in Table 2.3.[14]

TABLE 2.3   Premium Costs To Provide $100,000 of Liquidity with Discounted Dollars

Age of Insured	Years of Life Expectancy	Death Occurring at the End of:				Life Expectancy
		Year 5	Year 10	Year 15	Year 20	
35	37	$ 9,020	$16,413	$22,050	$26,153	$28,018
40	32	10,855	19,805	26,749	32,001	37,025
45	28	13,133	24,019	32,593	39,199	45,431
50	24	15,821	29,075	39,620	48,025	52,849
55	20	19,488	35,951	49,331	60,201	60,201

Economics, however, are not the only reasons why non–life insurance methods are seldom successful as the sole means of funding a buy-sell agreement. How can a potential purchaser who decides to use cash and establishes a sinking fund to meet obligations under the agreement determine how much to deposit each year? Inevitably sinking funds are inadequate because death or long-term disability of a working shareholder is always "premature."

When business assets are to be used, the predeath development of a sinking fund may strain or even drain the corporation's working capital and may even aggravate or trigger an accumulated earnings tax problem.[15] The same problem, viewed by the heirs of the deceased shareholder, often makes both the predeath sinking fund approach and the postdeath installment payout method unacceptable. The family of the deceased must rely on both the financial ability and the moral responsibility of the purchasers, who must carry on the business without the aid and support of the former employee/shareholder.

Life insurance is the only means of guaranteeing that death, the event creating the need for cash, also creates the cash to satisfy that need. This makes it possible for a stockholder's surviving spouse to receive the full fair market value of the business interest and bail out of the business before it loses value. And it demonstrates to bank loan officers and other creditors that the shareholders are financially responsible.

Premiums can be viewed loosely as advance installment payments that are easily budgeted so the event of the buyout doesn't hurt the cash flow of the business. There are, of course, disadvantages to the use of life insurance. Up-front dollars and the after-tax income they might have earned are required. That money is paid long before the parties feel the urgency of the situation.

Some clients are psychologically offended by an outlay without an apparent immediate economic benefit. Of course peace of mind attained by all parties when the buy-sell is fully and properly funded justifies these costs.

If the buyout occurs during lifetime, the cash values of a life insurance policy can be used to help provide a portion of the purchase price. These cash values can be obtained from the policy on a tax-favored basis through either policy loan, withdrawal or partial surrender of the policy. Unless the policy falls into the classification of a modified endowment contract (MEC), a policy loan, withdrawal or partial surrender can be made income-tax-free up to the policyowner's basis.[16]

How Much Insurance Should Be Purchased?

Ideally buy-sell agreements should be fully funded from inception, because the value of a business interest (and therefore the liability of the purchaser of a withdrawing shareholder's stock) may increase from both real growth and inflationary pressures on price.

If the value of stock grows at only five percent per year, the value of the stock will double every 14.4 years. At a ten percent growth rate, the price that will have to be paid doubles every 7.2 years. (The years it takes for stock to double in value can be found by dividing the growth rate into 72, a formula appropriately called *the rule of 72*.)

As the following figures illustrate, the price the purchaser must pay for stock can quickly become greater than the insurance available to finance the obligation.

Present value of corporation	$ 500,000
With annual growth of 5%	
10 years from now	$ 814,447
20 years from now	$2,326,648
With annual growth of 10%	
10 years from now	$1,296,871
20 years from now	$3,363,749

If for no reason other than to keep up with inflation, full funding at the outset is imperative. Also, after each redemption or purchase upon the death of another shareholder, the value of the surviving shareholders' stock increases. In the case of a cross-purchase plan each surviving shareholder ends up with a larger percentage interest in the same size corporation. Where the corporation is the purchaser, insurance proceeds prevent corporate assets from shrinking proportionately to the stock purchased. This means that insurance coverage must often be increased after every redemption or purchase. Unfortunately a later purchase—if it is possible—is almost always made at a significantly increased cost.

Inflationary and real growth coverage can be provided in a number of ways: Low-outlay yearly renewable term insurance can be purchased to fund future needs. Policy dividends can be applied to purchase one-year term insurance— the so-called *fifth dividend option*. Through the use of dividends to purchase one-year term insurance, inexpensive coverage is purchased automatically (and at no commission or other acquisition costs), with policy dividends in amounts equal to the cash value of the policy.

When the Purchase Price Is Still Prohibitive

When the value of the shares to be purchased is so high that—even with insurance and/or an installment purchase "escape value"—the price seems prohibitive, one solution might be dilution, a reduction in the value of the common stock through a preferred stock dividend or recapitalization. Here is an example:

> Doug Collins and Barbara Edwards are equal (and unrelated) shareholders of the Lankford Bay Marina Corporation. They want to enter into an agreement with Lankford Bay Marina Corporation obligating the business to redeem (buy back) the shares of the first of them to die. But the corporation is presently worth $1 million and probably will increase in value. Doug and Barbara agree that a required payout of one-half of the corporate worth would seriously jeopardize the business. Accordingly they cause the corporation to authorize and issue to them a preferred stock dividend worth a total of $600,000. The redemption agreement calls for a purchase by the corporation of only the common stock, now worth only $400,000. Doug and Barbara and their respective families will retain the preferred stock until the corporation exercises a separate option to redeem it.

There may be other situations where the perpetuation of voting control in a particular shareholder group is important but the proportionate ownership of the underlying equity ownership is not as vital. A recapitalization in which a class of nonvoting common stock was issued may be a viable solution. For example:

> Fred Thum and Walter Simmons each own 30 percent of the outstanding common stock of Sundancer Corporation. They constitute the top management of Sundancer and are responsible for its founding and its growth. The other 40 percent is owned by a number of unrelated individuals, none of whom is employed by the corporation.
>
> It is essential to Fred and Walter and to the economic well-being of the Sundancer Corporation that the survivor retain voting control. However, the value of their common stock is so high that, absent some planning technique, neither Fred nor Walter could conceivably purchase the shares of the first to die. If Sundancer were to redeem the decedent's stock, the survivor's stock interest would be reduced to three-sevenths; thus he would not have absolute control.
>
> To retain control, Fred and Walter cause Sundancer to authorize and issue as a stock dividend a class of nonvoting common stock. Fred, Walter and Sundancer enter into an agreement under which the survivor of Fred and Walter is given an option to purchase the voting common stock of the first decedent. This makes it possible for the surviving shareholder to retain control. Sundancer is obligated to redeem the nonvoting common stock and all unpurchased voting common stock owned by the decedent's estate.

Although complete funding through an installment payout is seldom indicated, partial funding of the purchase obligation through this means is sometimes required or desirable. The survivors can use insurance proceeds to cushion the financial shock of the key individual's death, ease cash flow problems and help find and train a successor. The cash can be placed into the profit stream of the corporation, and the unpaid balance may earn a rate that may be substantially higher than the (tax-deductible) interest that the purchaser would have to pay the seller for the use of the unpaid balance.

An installment payout may prove advantageous to the sellers, the decedent's estate or the heirs. Deferring receipt of payments translates into deferring payment of income taxes on the inherent gain (if any). Rather than bunching income and exposing gain to an abnormally high rate, the seller's family, by spreading it through receipt of installment payments, may lower the total tax by shifting income to lower-tax years.

One note of warning: If an estate sells stock and receives the right to installment payments in return, upon distribution of that right to a beneficiary the installment sale reporting privilege may be lost. In other words, the estate's distribution of the right to receive the balance of installment payments to a beneficiary triggers a taxable event; the distribution of an installment obligation causes an acceleration of gain. It might be best to anticipate this potential tax trap by providing in the agreement that the estate can pass a decedent's stock to his or her heirs and that the redemption (followed by the installment payout) will be made from the heirs; this avoids the disposition-acceleration problem. However, if the beneficiary/seller is in a much higher income tax bracket than the estate, much of the tax advantage of the installment payout may be lost.

The buy-sell agreement should provide, in the case of an installment payout, that the stock to be transferred be held in escrow until payment is received. Periodic releases can be made as payments are made, or the entire block of stock can be held until the final payment. Typically the purchaser will have the right to vote the stock as long as payments are made on a timely basis.[17]

A cross-purchase agreement can add protection by providing that the individual shareholders' obligations are—in the event of default only—guaranteed by the corporation. Likewise, where the corporation is the purchaser, individual shareholders should personally guarantee to pay corporate installment obligations.

Endnotes

1. See Nelson, "What's Missing in Buy-Sell Agreements?", *Best's Review*, August 1991: 27.
2. 1958 Commissioner's Standard Ordinary Mortality Table. Where three business owners are involved, the probability of one dying prior to age 65 increases substantially. For example, the chances are 54.8 out of 100 that one of three men, each age 30, will die prior to age 65. If each of the 30-year-olds were women, the odds drop to 38.3 out of 100.
3. IRC §163(d).
4. IRC §163(d)(1). Note that C corporation stockholders may be able to declare dividends, however, to produce investment income to utilize at least some, if not all, of the deduction. See PLR 9215013.

5. Sale or exchange treatment is available under §302(b) even if an installment method is used to effect the purchase. If an all-cash purchase would have qualified as a sale or exchange, a purchase in return for a bona fide debt instrument should also qualify. See Rev. Rul. 77–467, 1977-2 C.B. 92. This ruling is predicated on the requirement that debt is in fact bona fide and that payments received are not dependent on future earnings or subordinated to general creditors. See also *Estate of Mathis v. Commr.*, 47 T.C. 248 (1966) (Acq. 1967-1 C.B. 2); *Lisle v. Commr.*, 35 T.C.M. 617 (1976).

6. The installment method of recognizing gain requires mainly that at least one payment be made after the close of the taxable year in which the disposition occurs. IRC §453. Gain in a given year is

   Portion of Sales Price Received × (Gross Profit/Total Price)

   Gross profit is the amount that will have been realized when all payments have been made. Interest is ordinary income to the seller.

   For more on installment sales and the estate planning implications, see Leimberg et al., *Tools and Techniques of Estate Planning* (Cincinnati: National Underwriter Co., 1992). Call 800-543-0874).

7. IRC §483(a)(2). See also IRC §1274(b)(2). Under the ambit of these two code sections, where the seller receives the buyer's debt obligation under a buy-sell for all or part of the purchase price,

   a. nine percent interest or, if less, the AFR (applicable federal rate) must be charged where the total purchase price (including the down payment and total interest payments) is $250,000 or less. Interest must be compounded semiannually.

   b. nine percent interest or, if less, the AFR (applicable federal rate) must be charged on the unpaid balance if the seller-financed debt is $2.8 million or less. Interest must be compounded semiannually.

   c. interest at the applicable federal rate must be charged if the seller-financed debt exceeds $2.8 million. Interest must be compounded semiannually.

   If interest is not charged by the parties at these or higher levels, the IRS will treat the seller and the buyer as if these rates had been used. The applicable federal rate (AFR) depends on the term of the debt. If the debt is three years or less, the short-term rate must be used. If the term of the debt is over three years but not over nine years, the mid-term rate applies. Any term over nine years will require the use of the long-term rate. Most commentators feel that it is appropriate to use the AFR rate as of the date of sale rather than when the buy-sell is signed. This creates uncertainty that would make few clients comfortable.

8. The interest rate, amortization schedule and term of the note will depend on the liquidity of the buyer. Planners should keep in mind that the installment method delays the impact but does not create the cash to meet the obligation.

9. This chart is taken from Leimberg, *"Utilizing a System Approach to Buy-Sell Planning,"* *Trusts and Estates*, May 1989: 22.

10. IRC §163(d)(1).

11. A possible solution is for the corporation to pay dividends in amounts equal to the interest portion. This would allow shareholders who don't have enough investment income to fully utilize the investment interest deduction and in essence use tax-free corporate dollars to cover the interest cost. See Jacobowitz, "Structuring and Funding Buy-Sell Agreements," 49th Annual NYU Institute, §3.04.

12. See Rev. Proc. 81-62, 1981-2 C.B. 684 [§5.02(b)(2)] in which no advance private rulings will be granted on a redemption in complete termination of a stockholder's interest if the debt instrument received has a term of over 15 years.

13. See Leimberg et al., *Tools and Techniques of Estate Planning,* (Cincinnati: National Underwriter Co., 1992), call 800-543-0874.

14. The business owner can be insured for $100,000 by a coshareholder (cross-purchase) or corporation (stock redemption) for approximately these costs, assuming dividends were used to reduce premiums. Dividends are illustrative only and are not guaranteed.

15. Where cash is accumulated by a corporation in a sinking fund to purchase a shareholder's interest and payments are to be made for the stock in installments, the accumulated earnings tax should be considered. This tax provides for a levy of a flat rate of 28 percent of accumulated taxable income for the year. IRC §531 et seq.

    Additionally, the buy-sell agreement must specify when payments are to be made, the amounts due and the rate of interest payable on any balance (to avoid the imputed interest rule of IRC §§483 or 1274). Query: On a default by the purchaser, or if the balance due is evidenced by promissory notes more akin to stock than debt, has the seller made a complete [302(b)(3)] or substantially disproportionate [302(b)(2)] termination? See *Lisle v. Comm'r,* 35 T.C.M. 627 (1976), for a case that dealt with the question of whether a 20-year payout, per se, would cause a redemption to fail. The court held that since there was a firm and fixed installment plan, the shareholders could treat the termination of their interests as exchanges rather than as dividends.

16. IRC §7702A.

17. Donald, "Corporate Buy-out Agreements," 106-5th T.M.: A-12.

CHAPTER 3

Funding for the Uninsurable Stockholder

Actuarial statistics indicate that only about 1 out of 20 individuals is not able to obtain personal life insurance.[1] Obviously the inability of a stockholder/ employee to obtain life insurance does not lessen the need for a business purchase agreement; to the contrary, it underscores that need as well as the urgency of placing plans into effect.

THE ALTERNATIVES

Several methods may be used to fund the buyout of an uninsurable stockholder:

1. A lump-sum cash payment
2. A sinking fund
3. Installment payments
4. A lifetime transfer of existing personally owned policies to the potential purchaser
5. "Doubling up" of the insurance on the lives of insurable stockholders
6. A combination Section 303 redemption and cross-purchase buyout
7. Use of notes
8. Mortgage of appreciated property
9. Sale-leaseback
10. Appreciated property "bailout"
11. Some combination of these alternatives

Each of these alternatives has its positive and negative features that must be weighed by both the planners and the client.

Lump-Sum Cash Payment

A lump-sum cash payment at the death of a shareholder obligates purchasers to obtain what often is a large amount of cash in a relatively short period of time. Cash flow problems are inevitable with this type of approach.

Sinking Fund Approach

Setting aside a fixed amount each year beginning when the agreement is signed at least allows some advance preparation.

The uninsurable stockholder may live for a long period of time, over which a well-invested asset reserve can become sizable. Generally, annual deposits made to such a sinking fund should exceed the annual premiums that would have been made had the stockholder been insurable.[2]

The agreement should provide for payment of the difference between the sinking fund assets accumulated and the total amount needed to buy out the deceased stockholder. Often this is accomplished by regarding the amount in the fund as a down payment and then giving the decedent's estate a series of interest-bearing notes that will liquidate the indebtedness within a reasonable period of time.

In lieu of a cash sinking fund, annual-premium deferred annuity contracts are often suggested. In this case the potential purchaser pays annual premiums to an insurance company in return for its promise to pay an annuity for some fixed period of time beginning at a specified event such as death.

This approach has two advantages. Psychologically, because the insurance company holds the assets, funds in the deferred annuity are less likely to be considered available for temporary personal needs (in the case of a cross-purchase buyout) or temporary business needs (where the corporation is to be the purchaser under a stock redemption arangement). Also, the premium notice creates an element of compulsion to meet sinking fund deposit needs not otherwise present.

Naturally, compared to life insurance, the sinking fund approach also has disadvantages. First, because the fund is not self-completing at death, the necessary amount of cash may not be available when needed. Second, life insurance proceeds will be received income-tax-free, but the interest earnings on a sinking fund could be fully taxable.[3]

Installment Payouts

An installment purchase involves spreading payments over a period of years after the death of the uninsurable stockholder. As discussed earlier, this alternative has four major flaws:

1. The deceased's heirs are left without immediate funds to pay death taxes and other final expenses.
2. The heirs are not given a fund—independent of the financial success of the business—to provide for their economic security.
3. As in the lump-sum cash method, a sometimes overwhelming drain is placed on the business at the very time the surviving stockholder/employees are struggling to keep the business going and to replace the talents of the decedent.
4. The burden is especially heavy since principal payments will not be deductible for federal income tax purposes, interest deductions may be partially or entirely unavailable and the source of funds for an installment purchase of an uninsurable individual is taxable earnings. Counsel for the estate of the deceased shareholder would probably insist on as much security as his or her power position would bear. Consider also the effect of a mortgage on corporate assets and its impact on the business's ability to borrow money or deal with trade creditors.

Transfer of Personal Insurance to the Potential Purchaser

In certain situations some of an uninsurable's individually owned life insurance can be transferred to the potential purchaser to fund the agreement. Occasionally, businesspeople own more personal insurance than their families need, because the reason for which they originally purchased the insurance no longer exists. For example, children may be grown and educated, a mortgage may be satisfied or a spouse may have died after the policy was purchased. Sometimes personally owned coverage is not the only existing source of protection. For example, key individual coverage may no longer be needed to indemnify a business.

Most authorities believe that insurance in force for the benefit of an insured's family members should not be diverted from them because that would mean protecting business associates and their families at the expense of the insured's own family. Furthermore, such an assignment may create another problem, the transfer-for-value tax trap.[4]

Although life insurance proceeds received by reason of the insured's death generally are excludable from the beneficiary's gross income,[5] there is an important exception called the *transfer-for-value rule*.[6] In essence, it provides that if a policy or an interest in a policy is transferred for valuable consideration, *only* the amount of the purchaser's consideration (including premiums paid after the transfer) is recovered income-tax-free.[7] The balance is taxable at ordinary income rates.

As an example, assume a costockholder purchased an existing $1 million policy from the insured for use in a cross-purchase plan or a coshareholder purchased a policy owned by the corporation on the life of the insured shareholder. If the purchaser paid $10,000 for the policy and paid an additional $40,000 in premiums, only $50,000 out of $1 million would be income-tax-free; $950,000 would be fully taxable when the insured shareholder died.

Fortunately this harsh rule does not apply to transfers of policies to a corporation in which the insured is an officer or a stockholder.[8] It is safe, therefore, for an uninsurable stockholder to assign existing coverage to his or her corporation to fund a stock redemption plan (although this is not recommended since such a person's family would probably have a high need for the coverage). But the transfer-for-value rule would be invoked if the transfer were to be a coshareholder of the insured or to a third-party purchaser.

Table 3.1 summarizes the transfer-for-value rule and its exceptions.[9]

"Doubling Up" of Insurance on Insurables

Does it make sense to increase the coverage on the insurable shareholder(s) to make up for the lack of coverage on the uninsurable one? For example, is it good planning to purchase a larger face amount (e.g., $200,000 instead of $100,000) or, instead of purchasing an ordinary life policy, to use the extra cash to buy a higher-cash-value policy on the insurable shareholder (e.g., a limited-payment policy instead of an ordinary, or whole, life plan)?

The rationale is that if the uninsurable shareholder dies first, the insured owner will be able to use excess cash values to help purchase the deceased's

TABLE 3.1   Transfer for Value

Policyowner and Transferor	Transferee for Value	Tax Result
Anyone	Insured	OK
Anyone	Partner of insured	OK
Anyone	Partnership in which insured is a partner	OK
Anyone	Corporation in which insured is a shareholder or officer	OK
Anyone	Anyone where basis is determined in whole or in part by reference to transferor's basis	OK
Anyone	Costockholder of insured	Not OK
Anyone	Spouse of insured	Not OK
Anyone	Anyone else	Not OK

business interest. If the insured stockholder dies first, a portion of the death proceeds could be used to purchase the insured shareholder's interest. The remaining ("excess") coverage would be held by the surviving shareholders (cross-purchase) or by the corporation (stock redemption) to buy out the uninsurable shareholder's interest. Some authorities frown on this "hope the insurables predecease the uninsurables" approach and consider it an insurance gamble.

Combination Section 303 Redemption and Cross-Purchase Buyout

Cash flow problems of all parties can be eased by splitting the purchase burden between the corporation and its shareholders. The corporation could purchase part of the uninsurable's stock out of retained earnings—but no more than the amount permitted under the safe harbor rules of Section 303 (see Chapter 31). Here the corporation would purchase an amount equal to the Section 303 protected limits. The balance of the stock could be purchased by the remaining shareholders.

Use of Notes

To ease the strain on the corporation's cash position, the agreement could allow the corporation to pay for its share of stock by giving the deceased shareholder's executor a note. This would give the corporation time to pay for the stock it redeems. The shareholders could provide the estate with liquidity by paying in cash (or the process could be reversed if, in terms of cash flow and taxes, the corporation could better afford the outgo of dollars).

Mortgage of Appreciated Property

A corporation that owns substantially appreciated property could borrow against its equity or increase its mortgage to fund a redemption. This, of course, would create a serious cash flow drain, which the corporation may not be able to afford at the time of the redemption.

Sale-Leaseback

The corporation could sell real property to an irrevocable trust established by the remaining stockholder(s) for the benefit of the surviving family, with the cash proceeds used to finance the purchase of the stock. Continued use of the building by the corporation could be assured through a leaseback agreement. The sale-leaseback technique would also help to shift income (rental payments) and capital appreciation (the building or real estate sold) on a gift-tax-free basis to the possibly lower transfer tax brackets of the family.

The sale-leaseback technique is not without its problems. Planners should consider these issues:

- Where would the irrevocable trust obtain the cash to purchase the stock?
- What assurance does the corporation have that the trust will in fact purchase the asset the business wants to sell?
- What rental charge and what terms will the trust demand for the use of the real estate?

Exchange of Appreciated Property for Stock:
The "Appreciated Property Bailout"

A corporation that distributes appreciated stock, real estate or other appreciated property to its shareholders in return for its stock will have to recognize gain—even if the parties agree and the IRS concedes that the distribution was made to enable the corporation to redeem its own stock. For instance, assume a corporation is obligated to purchase $1 million worth of stock at a decedent's death. Assume also that a building it purchased many years ago for $10,000 is now worth $1 million. Instead of selling the building and paying the tax (currently at ordinary rates) on the gain, it distributes the building in return for the stock held by the deceased shareholder's executor. The corporation must report $990,000 of ordinary income.

A Combination of Approaches

Generally none of these techniques discussed will be wholly adequate or desirable alone. The specific combination of approaches to follow will be dictated by the particular situation.

One possible alternative might be to require the corporation to purchase only the amount of stock for which it has sufficient surplus, with the surviving shareholders required to purchase any remaining stock. Both potential purchasers could be given an option to effect the purchase in installments to avoid a cash flow problem.

Endnotes

1. Note that often a person can obtain relatively high amounts of insurance, regardless of physical condition, occupation or avocation, by joining a group that has "association group" coverage. For example, members of bar, accounting, dental and medical associations can often obtain life insurance coverage without a physical examination or other evidence of insurability. Otherwise uninsurable business owners employing even relatively small groups of employees can often obtain "guaranteed issue" coverage—or normal group life insurance covering them as employees. Creditor life insurance can sometimes be obtained in relatively high amounts as well. Finally, many companies now specialize in writing insurance at increased rates on individuals who were at one time classified as uninsurable. Individuals who have had heart attacks, diabetes and even cancer can obtain either limited coverage or full coverage at an appropriate premium.
2. Parties to the agreement might consider estimating the individual's probable life expectancy, beginning with government ordinary life annuity expected return multiples, and, after adjustments that consider the individual's physical condition and the potential after-tax earnings on the amounts set aside, fund as if that were the period to complete the sinking fund. A better alternative is to use software such as NumberCruncher (215-525-6957), which will instantly compute the life expectancy and probability of survival at any age.
3. IRC §101(a)(1). Corporate-owned annuities also will be currently taxed.
4. IRC §101(a)(2). Tax problems inherent in the use of existing life insurance are discussed more fully in Chapter 14.
5. IRC §101(a)(1).

6. See Leimberg and Doyle, *Tools and Techniques of Life Insurance Planning* (Cincinnati: National Underwriter Co., 1992), call 800-543-0874; and Zaritsky and Leimberg, *Tax Planning for Life Insurance* (New York: Warren, Gorham and Lamont, 1992), call 800-950-1210.

7. IRC §101(a)(2). Note also that if the shareholder sells the policy for an amount greater than his or her net premium cost (total aggregate premiums paid less dividends), the difference will constitute income to the selling shareholder and will be characterized as ordinary income. *Roff v. Comm'r*, 304 F.2d 450 (3d Cir. 1962), *aff'g* 36 T.C. 818 (1961); *Gallun v. Comm'r*, 327 F.2d 809 (7th Cir. 1964); *Comm'r v. Phillips*, 275 F.2d 33 (4th Cir. 1960); *Crocker v. Comm'r*, 37 T.C. 605 (1962); *Cohen v. Comm'r*, 39 T.C. 1055 (1963).

8. IRC §101(a)(2)(B).

9. IRC §101(a)(2).

CHAPTER 4

Basic Income, Estate and Gift Tax Rules

OWNERSHIP

Cross-Purchase Agreements

As introduced earlier, the arrangement whereby shareholders will personally purchase a deceased coshareholder's interest is commonly called a *cross purchase* or *crisscross* arrangement. Each stockholder owns, pays premiums for and is the beneficiary of an appropriate amount of life insurance on the lives of the other shareholders. So, if Charles and Lara were each 50 percent owners of the CL Corporation, the agreement would obligate the survivor to purchase the shares of the decedent.

If the purchase price of each shareholder's interest is estimated to be $500,000, ideally Charles would purchase $500,000 of insurance on Lara's life and Lara would purchase $500,000 of insurance on Charles's life. Should Charles die first, Lara would receive $500,000 of proceeds, which she could then use to purchase Charles's stock.[1]

Stock Redemption Agreements

Also as introduced earlier, under a stock redemption agreement the corporation, rather than the individual shareholders, is obligated to purchase (retire or redeem) the stock of a deceased shareholder. The corporation then purchases, pays premiums on and is beneficiary of an appropriate amount of life insurance on each shareholder's life to fund its future purchase obligation.[2]

For example, the CL Corporation would purchase a $500,000 insurance policy on Charles and a separate $500,000 policy on Lara. It would own both of the policies and pay all the premiums. Upon a shareholder's death the CL Corporation would receive the entire policy proceeds. It would then use that cash to pay all or a portion of the purchase price (depending on the terms of the buy-sell agreement) of the stock to the decedent/shareholder's executor. The executor would in turn pay over the stock to the CL Corporation. The surviving shareholder would then own the entire corporation because he or she held all the outstanding shares.

INCOME TAX

Deductibility of Premiums

Cross-Purchase Agreements. No deduction is allowed where a stockholder, to fund obligations under a cross-purchase buy-sell agreement, purchases insurance on the life of another stockholder.[3] For instance, if Charles buys a policy of Lara's life, Charles will not be allowed an income tax deduction for his outlay.

Stock Redemption Agreements. The Internal Revenue Code (IRC) clearly denies deductions for premiums paid on a life insurance policy covering the life of any officer, employee or other person financially interested in the business when the taxpayer/corporation is either a direct or an indirect beneficiary of the policy. The prohibition applies to premiums paid on insurance purchased to fund stock redemption agreements since the corporation is, in the classic arrangement, both owner and beneficiary of the policy.[4] So if the CL Corporation purchased policies on both Charles's and Lara's lives to fund the stock redemption agreement, its premium outlays would be nondeductible.

In fact the deduction for premiums will be disallowed even when the corporation is not a direct beneficiary. For example, if the proceeds must be used to discharge a corporation's obligation to redeem stock, no deduction will be allowed even if a trust, the insured's spouse or the insured's estate, rather than the corporation, is named beneficiary. In these cases the insurance proceeds indirectly benefit the corporation.[5] For example, if the CL Corporation set up a revocable trust to hold the policies, receive the proceeds, pay over the proceeds to the deceased shareholder's estate and receive the deceased shareholder's stock, premium outlays would not be deductible.

If the IRS is unsuccessful using the provisions of the IRC section just described, it will seek to disallow the deduction on the basis that the premiums were paid to acquire a capital asset (treasury stock) and are thus capital expenditures rather than currently deductible business expenses.[6]

Even though corporate premium payments are nondeductible, shareholders often prefer the stock redemption plan when the corporation is in a lower tax bracket than the shareholders individually. Economically it generally makes sense for the party in the lower combined income tax bracket to pay the premiums since this results in a lower net after-tax cost. Psychologically, even if the corporate and personal brackets are similar, most business owners would rather nondeductible outlays come from a corporate pocket than their own.

Taxation of Premiums to Stockholders

Cross-Purchase Agreements. Premiums paid by a costockholder do not constitute income to the insured.[7] For example, if Lara buys a policy on Charles's life, premiums Lara pays are not taxable to Charles.

Stock Redemption Agreements. As long as the corporation itself is beneficiary (or the beneficiary's right to receive proceeds is conditioned on the transfer of stock to the corporation), premium payments will not be taxable income to the individual stockholders.[8]

Income Taxation of Proceeds

Cross-Purchase Agreements. Generally life insurance proceeds "paid by reason of the death of the insured" are excludable from the beneficiary's gross income.[9] The exclusion extends to individuals in both a personal and a business capacity. So if Lara, as the policyowner and beneficiary, receives the $500,000 life insurance proceeds on Charles's life and the policy was part of a cross-purchase buy-sell, the proceeds will be income-tax-free.

Stock Redemption Agreements. A corporation as a beneficiary receives the same income tax exclusion on the proceeds of life insurance as that afforded to individuals. Thus, in the classic situation where a corporation owns, pays premiums on and is beneficiary of a life insurance policy, the proceeds of which will be used to fund a buyout of a deceased shareholder's stock, the proceeds are received income-tax-free at the insured's death.[10] So if the CL Corporation received the $500,000 proceeds of the life insurance policy on Lara's life, the proceeds would be income-tax-free even if the intention of the corporation was to use those proceeds to buy Lara's stock from her executor.

There is, however, one exception to this general rule that applies to C corporations: the alternative minimum tax (AMT). This tax, which is payable only if it is greater than the corporation's regular tax, is computed by adding certain tax preference items to the corporation's regular taxable income. One of these preference items may be increased by the receipt of life insurance proceeds. If the AMT results, the proceeds that would otherwise have been received income-tax-free and fully available for redemption purposes would be reduced by this tax.[11] This potential tax is covered in detail in Chapter 6.

Effect of Insurance on Cost Basis of Stock Acquired

Cross-Purchase Agreements. Typically, under a cross-purchase agreement the basis of shares purchased by a surviving stockholder is the original basis for the shares owned before the purchase plus the consideration paid for the decedent's shares. In other words, in a cross-purchase arrangement the surviving shareholder(s) can add to present basis (bases) the amount paid for the stock of the deceased shareholder.[12] For instance, if Lara contributed $100,000 for her original interest in the CL Corporation, and she paid an additional $500,000 in cash (from insurance proceeds) to Charles's executor for her stock, she would have a total basis for income tax purposes of $600,000. If she later sold the corporation for $1 million, the $400,000 difference would be includable in income as a capital gain.

The following example may help to illustrate the concept more fully.[13]

Assume a three-person corporation where each shareholder owns a one-third interest, the cost basis of each shareholder's interest is $10,000 and each person's shares are worth $150,000, giving the entire corporation a value of $450,000.

When the first of the three shareholders dies, the surviving shareholders purchase the decedent's interest, each buying one-half of the $150,000 interest;

i.e., each pays the decedent's estate $75,000. After the purchase, corporate ownership is split between the two survivors. Each now has a cost basis of $85,000 ($10,000 original cost plus $75,000 cost for the newly purchased interest). The value of each survivor's interest is $225,000 ($150,000 plus $75,000).

Although the total value of the business remains $450,000, the cost basis of the survivors has increased from $10,000 to $85,000. Contrast this result with the effect of a stock redemption approach.

Stock Redemption Agreements. In a stock redemption plan the surviving shareholders do not personally pay any money for the stock, and the purchasing corporation is considered a separate tax entity. Therefore the cost basis of the stock in the hands of the surviving shareholders is unchanged; they do not receive a new increased basis for the purchased stock. In other words, when the corporation purchases the stock from the estate of a deceased shareholder, since the corporation is considered a tax entity separate from its shareholders, the purchase has no effect on the basis of the surviving shareholders' stock.

Since the surviving shareholders have not personally paid for the stock, their bases remain the same as before the redemption.[14] This results, of course, in a larger potential tax on a subsequent lifetime sale of stock or corporate liquidation than if the stock were held until death and then sold by the deceased shareholder's estate. For example, if the CL Corporation pays $500,000 (from insurance proceeds or some other source) to Charles's executor in return for $500,000 worth of stock, Lara will not receive any increase in basis for the corporation's outlay. Her basis will remain the amount she originally paid for her stock, $100,000.

Stock that is held until a shareholder's death receives a "step-up in basis" to the fair market value of the stock at death (or the alternate valuation date). Built-in gain escapes income tax under the stepped-up basis rules.[15] (In the rare case where the stock has declined in value, the basis would "step down" at death to the fair market value at that time or at the alternate valuation date if elected.)

An increased basis is useful to the estate of a deceased shareholder because it serves to reduce or eliminate the gain that would otherwise be realized when the stock is sold to the corporation. But, as mentioned, the corporation's purchase of the stock does not increase the basis of the surviving shareholders; their bases remain the same.

Where the redemption is not funded by life insurance, the corporation's value is unaffected and the surviving shareholders' bases remain the same. Using the figures for the earlier example of a three-person corporation, corporate assets would be reduced by the amount of the redemption price, $150,000, leaving the corporation with a value of $300,000 ($450,000 minus $150,000). So the two survivors would share equally in a business worth $300,000, but each would have a basis of only $10,000, the amount they originally paid for their interest in the business.

However, if the redemption were fully funded—if there were $150,000 of life insurance on each shareholder's life—upon the decedent/shareholder's death the corporation's value would jump to $600,000 ($450,000 plus $150,000 of tax-free life insurance proceeds, ignoring policy cash values). After payment of the $150,000 to the estate of the deceased, the survivors would own a business with a net worth $450,000, for which they have a basis of only $10,000 each.

Comparing the results of a life insurance stock redemption with a cross-purchase plan shows that a future lifetime sale of each surviving shareholder's stock for $285,000 would generate a taxable gain of $275,000 in the case of a stock redemption ($285,000 realized less adjusted basis of $10,000) but only $200,000 ($285,000 realized less adjusted basis of $85,000) with the cross-purchase approach. This illustrates the relative advantage of a cross-purchase plan with respect to basis.

Effect of Premium Payments on Earnings and Profits

Cross-Purchase Agreements. Because the corporation is in no way a party to the classic cross-purchase buy-sell agreement, the payment of premiums by individual shareholders has no effect on corporate earnings and profits.[16] If, however, the corporation provides additional funds to the shareholders in the form of increased salaries or bonuses and the shareholders use these salaries or bonuses to pay premiums, these payments will reduce earnings and profits.

Stock Redemption Agreements. A part or all of the premium payment reduces corporate retained earnings where a corporation owns and pays for life insurance that will be used to fund a buy-sell agreement. Where the insurance used has no cash value, such as with a typical term policy, the entire premium constitutes an outlay that reduces funds available for the payment of dividends and therefore reduces earnings and profits dollar for dollar.[17] If a policy does develop cash values, the increments in cash values may be added to earnings and profits to the extent that such increments are greater than the premiums each year.[18]

When death proceeds are received later, only the difference between the proceeds received and any policy cash value immediately prior to the insured's death will be added to earnings and profits since this amount represents an economic gain (an income addition that increases the pool of money available to pay dividends) to the corporation.[19]

Effect of Life Insurance Funding on the Accumulated Earnings Tax

The accumulated earnings tax is imposed on both publicly and closely held corporations[20] formed or used for the purpose of avoiding income tax with respect to their shareholders by permitting earnings and profits to be accumulated instead of distributed.[21] The purpose of the accumulated earnings tax is to discourage the use of corporations as accumulation vehicles to shelter individual shareholders' shares of the corporation's earnings and profits (E&P) from tax at personal level rates. Once a corporation accumulates E&P beyond the business's "reasonable needs,"[22] the IRS presumes that the accumulation was intended to avoid the tax unless the corporation can prove otherwise.[23] In other words, the tax is imposed only on those earnings and profits accumulated beyond the corporation's reasonable business needs. If the corporation cannot prove a reasonable business need, the accumulated earnings tax is imposed at a rate of 28 percent on the accumulated taxable income for the year.[24]

Accumulated taxable income (ATI) is defined as taxable income (with certain adjustments) less the sum of

1. a dividends paid deduction and
2. an accumulated earnings credit, which is the greater of
   - $250,000 generally (or $150,000 for certain personal service corporations) minus the accumulated E&P as of the end of the prior year or
   - the amount necessary for the reasonable needs of the business[25] (regardless of how large that amount may be).

Note that since payments for stock redemption insurance do not reduce taxable income, and since such payments do not qualify for the dividends paid deduction, they will be included in ATI unless they fall within the accumulated earnings credit. The accumulated earnings credit is structured so as to permit accumulation of any amount of earnings and profits to meet the reasonable (including reasonably anticipated) needs of the business.[26]

Cross-Purchase Agreements. Since, by definition, the classic cross-purchase agreement does not involve the corporation, the question of an unreasonable accumulation of earnings does not arise.[27]

Stock Redemption Agreements. An unreasonable accumulation of earnings question arises both when funds are being accumulated in anticipation of the proposed redemption (insurance policy cash values) and later, when the proceeds are received at the death of the insured. This issue affects only C corporations, however, not S corporations.

When corporate funds are used to pay life insurance premiums for a stock redemption plan, the focus should be on the purpose of the agreement rather than on the insurance. The IRC allows earnings to be accumulated for the reasonable needs of the business. Reasonable needs as defined by the IRC include both present and reasonably anticipated future needs.[28] Essentially, life insurance cash value accumulations to fund a buy-sell will be considered reasonable only when the redemption has a corporate as opposed to a shareholder (dividend avoidance) purpose.[29]

A number of cases have dealt directly or indirectly with this issue. The IRS will impose the tax if any motive of the corporation for accumulating its earnings was the proscribed one—even though that motive was only secondary to a legitimate business purpose.[30] Most of the cases focus on who is being bought out; i.e., the controlling consideration seems to be the amount of voting stock owned by the stockholder whose stock is being purchased. The question most generally asked by courts is: does the seller own a majority or less than a majority of the corporation's voting stock?[31] Where a shareholder owned 50 percent or less of the corporation's voting stock, the taxpayers have fared better than those owning absolute majority interests.[32]

In the leading case on redemptions of stock from majority shareholders, stockholders owning 80 percent of the common stock wanted to sell during their lifetime.[33] Because they could not find a buyer, they had the corporation redeem their interests. To obtain funds for the redemption, they had the corporation borrow $500,000 to add to $209,000 of retained earnings from the current year (1946). The court stressed that the transaction did not provide a benefit for the business and was obviously intended as a device to avoid tax at the shareholder level.[34]

Accumulations to fund the redemption of a majority interest are not fatal per se.[35] A shareholder who, together with his wife, owned 72 percent of the corporation's voting stock sold stock back to the corporation as part of a plan to increase three key employees' interests to 20 percent, a move designed to retain their management expertise. This "continuity of corporate management" argument is very powerful. But a redemption of the stock of a majority shareholder, wishing to cash out by means of a redemption, is likely to be considered to serve a shareholder (rather than a business) purpose in the typical situation.

Another key case involved two families who each owned half of the corporation's stock.[36] There was a conflict of interest between the families, and a stock redemption was deemed to be an effective means of solving the problem. The court of appeals emphasized that a good corporate purpose was served. It stated:

> Many businessmen now anticipate such problems and provide solutions through agreements, and implementing devices, to take out the estate of a co-venturer who dies, on a basis designed to be fair to the estate, to the enterprise, and to the surviving co-venturers. It has been held that corporate disbursements to buy insurance premiums to provide a fund with which to purchase stock from the estate of a person whose life is insured do serve a corporate, business purpose. . . .[37]

In one case the court, in dictum, enunciated that a showing must be made ". . . that there were dissenting or competing shareholder factions which threatened the corporate health," to justify an accumulation to fund a redemption.[38]

In another case that did not deal directly with the tax on an unreasonable accumulation of earnings but dealt with parallel issues, the court stated:

> What corporate purpose could be considered more essential than key man insurance? . . . Harmony is the essential catalyst for achieving good management; and good management is the sine qua non of long term business success. . . . Petitioner apparently anticipated that, should one of its key stockholder-officers die, those beneficially interested in his estate might enter into active participation in corporation affairs and possibly introduce an element of friction. Or his estate, not being bound by contract to sell the stock to petitioner, might sell it to adverse interests. The fragile bark of a small business can be wrecked on just such uncharted shoals.[39]

These few cases reveal that the imposition of the tax due to policy cash value accumulations will depend on all the facts of the case and not so much on the mere payment of premiums. Premium payments, if reasonable in amount, should not in themselves trigger or even aggravate the accumulated earnings tax problem.[40] The reason for the accumulations is the primary factor. Other factors include the corporation's dividend-paying record and total current and prior earnings and profit accumulations.

The life insurance amount should be consistent with the present and reasonably anticipated needs of the business. Depending on the age and health of the proposed insured, the policy should require the lowest outlay appropriate for the situation; generally this will be a form of whole life insurance.

Most authorities suggest that whether the insured is a minority or majority shareholder, as long as he or she is a key person the insurance can be purchased safely on that basis on the ground that key employee life insurance is clearly a business as opposed to a shareholder need. Therefore, some of these writers suggest that the accumulated earnings tax issue could be avoided by merely designating the insurance as key employee coverage. Such authorities do not make specific reference to the life insurance as the funding vehicle in the buy-sell agreements they draft.

A threat of the accumulated earnings tax occurs not only where funds are accumulated in anticipation of the proposed redemption, but also in the year the redemption occurs. The same factors justifying a predeath accumulation should apply in the case of a postdeath redemption. Absent prior plans, it is even more important for a redemption of stock to occur upon the death of a shareholder, because that course of action may be the only means of assuring a continuation of harmonious management, of avoiding the inherent conflict of interest between the surviving stockholders and the heirs of the deceased and of effecting an orderly transfer of control.[41]

There is a haven for postdeath accumulations that provides (regardless of the current status of the reasonableness test) that reasonable needs of the business include IRC §303 redemption needs.[42] However, the utility of this section to a discussion of life insurance is limited by two factors:

1. The amount of funds that may be sheltered cannot exceed the amount of the redemption that will qualify under Section 303(a), the sum of death (and generation skipping) taxes, funeral and administration expenses.[43]
2. The shelter applies only to accumulations made in the corporate taxable year in which the shareholder died or in later years. Although predeath accumulations are not expressly prohibited, an examination of the rele-

vant sections suggests such accumulations may not be protected except by specific wording in the statutes.[44]

Even so, alarm does not seem to be appropriate in most cases. First, no accumulated earnings tax problem should arise where the proceeds (which will, of course, increase the corporation's earnings and profits) are paid out in redemption of the decedent's stock in the same tax year. Second, where the proceeds are paid out in more than one tax year, no penalty tax problems should arise as long as the corporation is required to pay out the proceeds for the decedent's stock within a reasonably short period of time.[45] But note that even after the corporation has received the proceeds and redeemed the stock there may be a net increase in earnings and profits, especially if the insurance proceeds exceeded the redemption price. Most authorities feel the risk is small and, even at worst, involves only small amounts.[46]

Effect of a Buy-Sell on a Corporation's NOL Carryovers

Cross-Purchase Agreements. A net operating loss (NOL) occurs when a corporation has more allowable deductions than gross income.[47] These NOLs are quite valuable because they can be carried back to a preceding taxable year and used to offset that year's taxable income or carried forward to a future taxable year and used to offset that year's otherwise taxable income. In either event the NOL, by reducing taxes, saves cash.

There is a catch. If there is an ownership change[48] in a corporation that has an NOL (a so-called *loss corporation*), income that can be offset by an NOL carryforward is limited.[49]

Why such a harsh rule? Simple. Say a corporation had incurred losses but due to a drop in business (or for other reasons) the carryback or carryforward of losses would probably be wasted.[50] Assume new owners with a profitable business buy the loss corporation,[51] abandon the line of business the NOL corporation was in and transfer a profitable business to the NOL corporation. Were it not for the limiting rules, losses of the NOL corporation then could be used to offset gain from the profitable venture.[52]

How could a buy-sell precipitate a problem with respect to the NOL limitation rules? The problem is that ownership changes are tested as of triggering "testing dates," which include the following:

- An actual change in the ownership of the stock of a loss corporation that affects the percentage of stock owned by any shareholder owning more than 5 percent of the corporation's stock
- The transfer of an option to or by a shareholder owning more than 5 percent of the corporation's stock (or to or by a person who would own more than 5 percent of the corporation's stock if the option were exercised)
- The issuance of an option by the corporation itself

In other words the IRS could claim that an option to purchase found in a typical buy-sell was tantamount to actual ownership for purposes of determining an ownership shift. It could then limit the loss corporation's utility to offset future income.

Planners should not be overly concerned about these provisions for several reasons:

1. There is a specific exception to the limitation rules for options that can be exercised only upon death, disability or mental incompetence.
2. There is a specific exception to the limitation rules for options exercisable only upon the retirement of a shareholder active in management (if the option was issued prior to the corporation's loss).
3. A right of first refusal (common in many lifetime buy-sell provisions) will probably not be considered an option by the IRS.
4. In the authors' opinion neither Congress nor the IRS intended that any of the common provisions in the typical buy-sell agreement be treated as an option for purposes of limiting the carryforward of net operating losses.[53]

ESTATE TAXATION OF PROCEEDS

Cross-Purchase Agreements. Life insurance policy proceeds are not includable in the estate of an insured under a cross-purchase arrangement if (1) the proceeds are not payable to or for the benefit of the insured's estate and (2) the insured has no incidents of ownership in the policies.[54]

What, if anything, is includable? The value of the decedent/shareholder's corporate stock is includable,[55] as is the value of any policies owned by the decedent/shareholder on the life or lives of surviving shareholders (this is the replacement cost as determined for gift tax purposes). For example, if Charles died, the value of the stock he owned at death would be includable in his estate. His executor would also have to include the interpolated terminal reserve plus any unearned premium at the date of his death on the policy he owned on the life of his coshareholder, Lara.

Stock Redemption Agreements. Where the corporation is both owner and beneficiary of the policy, the proceeds will not be includable separately as insurance in the estate of the deceased insured/stockholder.[56] Only the value of the insured's interest in the corporation will be includable in his or her estate.[57] For example, although the full fair market value of the stock in the CL Corporation would be in Charles's estate if he died, none of the proceeds from the $500,000 policy on Charles's life owned by and payable to the corporation would be in his estate.

The proceeds should have no effect on the valuation of the insured's business interest to the extent the agreement excludes the proceeds from the purchase price and the agreement's formula price is recognized by the IRS and courts as the fair market value of the stock interest for federal estate tax purposes.[58] The result in any given situation, therefore, depends on how the buy-sell agreement has been drafted.

If the corporation gives a shareholder the right to repurchase the policy on his or her life, estate tax inclusion is likely.[59]

GIFT TAX ISSUES

Cross-Purchase Agreements. Can a gift arise under a cross-purchase agreement? Certainly the transfer to a related party of an option to purchase property for less than its fair market value constitutes a completed gift when the option is granted (assuming the option is both binding and enforceable). Assume a cross-purchase agreement required a surviving shareholder to purchase the decedent's shares for $50 a share. Assume at the time the agreement was signed the stock was actually worth $150. In this case no gift occurs until the agreement is carried out; each shareholder retains dominion and control over the stock. But when the agreement is triggered and a sale occurs, the IRS will argue that a gift, equal to the difference between the fair market value and the option price, has been made.[60]

Stock Redemption Agreements. The same reasoning applies to a stock redemption agreement. In the case of related shareholders who provide that the corporation can purchase their stock during lifetime for a price less than the stock's fair market value, the IRS will argue that a gift is being made—indirectly—to the other shareholder(s) at the time the corporation actually purchases the stock.[61]

Unexercised Options. The failure to exercise an option may be treated as a gift.[62] For instance, if a son fails to exercise a purchase option and by not exercising it enriches someone else in his family, the IRS will claim that the nonaction constituted a gift subject to gift taxes. According to the IRS, the mere failure to take advantage of a bargain (the right to buy stock under a buy-sell at less than the stock's fair market value) is a taxable gift.[63]

Endnotes

1. IRC §2033 and Rev. Rul. 56-397, 1956-2 C.B. 599 indicate that insurance on the decedent's life owned by the surviving shareholder will not be includable in the insured stockholder's estate for federal estate tax purposes in spite of the reciprocity arrangement. The value of the decedent's stock, of course, is includable. *Est. of Riecker v. Comm'r*, 3 T.C.M. 1293 (1944).
2. Although the proceeds themselves should not be includable in the insured's estate since they were not payable to the estate and the insured had no incidents of ownership in the policy (IRC §2042), the value of the decedent's business interest is includable. IRC §2033; *Wilson v. Crooks*, 52 F.2d 692 (W.D. Mo. 1935); *Est. of Ealy v. Comm'r*, 10 T.C.M. 431 (1951); *Est. of Riecker v. Comm'r*, 3 T.C.M. 1293 (1944); *Est. of Frank Knipp*, 25 T.C. 153 (1955).

    If an insured is given the right as part of his or her employment agreement to purchase a key executive policy on his or her life should the stock redemption for some reason be terminated, or if for any other reason the corporation decides to discontinue the payment of premiums, will that right be considered an incident of ownership? See Rev. Rul. 79-46, 1979-1 C.B. 303 and *Est. of Smith v. Comm'r*, 73 T.C. 307 (1979), the former of which answers yes and the latter no. It is the authors' opinion that the IRS is likely to claim that a purchase right is an incident of ownership and therefore controlling shareholders should not enter into such an agreement. See PLRs 9128008 and 9127007.
3. See IRC §262, Reg. §1.262-1(b)(1) and IRC §265(a)(1), which disallow deductions because the premiums would be considered personal expenses or expenses incurred in the production of tax-exempt income (the death proceeds). Furthermore, premiums would not be considered ordinary and necessary business expenses under IRC §162(a).

    The IRS might also argue that the premiums (eventually generating the proceeds to be used in the purchase of stock from the decedent's estate) are a capital investment. See *Merrimac Hat Corp. v. Comm'r*, 29 B.T.A. 690 (1934); *Whitaker v. Comm'r*, 34 T.C. 106 (1960); Rev. Rul. 70-117, 1970-1 C.B. 30.

4. IRC §264(a)(1).
5. IRC §162(a); Rev. Rul. 70-117, 1970-1 C.B. 30; IRC §264(a)(1). IRC §264(a)(1) does not provide for apportionment of the premium; therefore, the entire premium will be nondeductible, even though the corporation will receive only part of the proceeds. Rev. Rul. 66-203, 1966-2 C.B. 104; G.C.M. 7997, IX-1 C.B. 210; *Wilcox Investment Company v. Comm'r*, 3 T.C. 458 (1944).
6. Rev. Rul. 70-117, 1970-1 C.B. 30. In the facts of that ruling, insurance was purchased by a corporation on the lives of its two shareholders. The plan was a stock redemption arrangement, but a trustee was named beneficiary.
7. But where the corporation pays premiums on insurance used to fund a cross-purchase agreement between shareholders, the payment may be considered additional compensation or dividends to stockholder/employees who are also policyowners. See Reg. §1.61-2(d)(2); *Atlas Heating and Ventilating Co.*, 18 B.T.A. 389 (1929); *Yuengling v. Comm'r*, 69 F.2d 971 (3d Cir. 1934); *Paramount-Richards Theatres, Inc. v. Comm'r*, 153 F.2d 602 (5th Cir. 1946); *Doran v. Comm'r*, 246 F.2d 934 (9th Cir. 1957); Rev. Rul. 59-184, 1959-1 C.B. 65; see *Schwartz v. Comm'r*, 22 T.C.M. 786 (1963), where premiums were considered constructive dividends to a shareholder/officer.
8. Rev. Rul. 59-184, 1959-1, C.B. 65; *Prunier v. Comm'r*, 248 F.2d 818 (1st Cir. 1967); *Sanders v. Fox*, 253 F.2d 855 (10th Cir. 1958); Rev. Rul. 70-117, 1970-1 C.B. 30. These favorable holdings stem mainly from the nature of a corporation as an entity distinct and apart from its shareholders. So where the corporation is the "equitable" owner of the policy, payment of premiums by the corporation would not be considered a constructive dividend. *Lacey v. Comm'r*, 41 T.C. 329 (1963) *acq.* 1964-2 C.B. 6, follows the equitable ownership rationale. It held that individual shareholders did not receive a constructive dividend when the corporation paid premiums even though the policy designated the shareholder's estate as beneficiary. The insured received no current economic benefit since the policy was assigned to the corporation and the assignment was considered to have vested ownership in the corporation.

   See *Casale v. Comm'r*, 247 F.2d 440 (2d Cir. 1957), which held that a corporation's payment of premiums for a key executive policy that was to be used to finance a deferred compensation agreement payable to a shareholder's beneficiary was not a constructive dividend to the shareholder. However, note that the proceeds were payable to the corporation. But in a situation where a corporation pays premiums for policies owned by individual shareholders on a cross-purchase basis, such payments would be constructive dividends.
9. IRC §101(a); Reg. §1.101-1(a); *U.S. v. Supple-Biddle Hardware Co.*, 265 U.S. 189 (1924). Note that the general exemption will not apply (a) in certain transfer-for-value situations [IRC §101(a)] and (b) where the proceeds are deemed to be taxable as dividends or compensation.
10. IRC §101(a); Reg. §1.101-1(a); *U.S. v. Supple-Biddle Hardware Co.*, 265 U.S. 189 (1924). Note that the proceeds once received tax-free by the corporation become corporate assets and lose their income-tax-free status as life insurance.
11. IRC 56(c)(1). See also Chapter 6 for a more detailed discussion of this problem and possible solutions.
12. IRC §1012. Note that if the policy proceeds are paid directly to the deceased share-

holder's estate or to a designated beneficiary of that shareholder such as a surviving spouse, the IRS might claim that the proceeds do not increase the surviving shareholder's basis. *Legallet v. Comm'r*, 41 B.T.A. 294 (1940); but see *Mushro v. Comm'r*, 50 T.C. 43 (1968), *nonacq.* 1970-2 C.B. xxii, which held that even though the proceeds were made payable directly to the personal beneficiary of the insured, the survivor could include the proceeds in his or her cost basis if there were a legally binding agreement to apply the proceeds to the purchase of the business interest.

13. The estate will not realize gain due to the IRC §1014 step-up in cost basis at the decedent/shareholder's death, because it was presumed that the price set in the agreement equaled that amount; i.e., the price paid equaled the $150,000 stepped-up basis.

14. This drawback is eliminated if the stock is owned until death because of the IRC §1014 step-up basis rules.

15. The essence of a "step-up in basis" rule is this: If an individual owned stock in a corporation that cost him $10,000 and had a fair market value for estate tax purposes of $50,000, his legatee (or estate) would take a $50,000 basis for the stock. The $40,000 appreciation in value would never become subject to income tax. So, if the recipient sold it for $80,000 shortly after receiving it, his or her gain would be only $30,000 ($80,000 amount realized minus stepped-up basis of $50,000). IRC §1014. The same result occurs where the deceased shareholder was a resident of a community property state. Both spouses receive a step-up (or step-down) in basis in their respective interests in the stock.

16. *Earnings and profits* is a corporate tax term used for various purposes: (1) A corporation's E & P serves as the limit or measuring rod for determining the extent to which a distribution by a corporation to its shareholders is considered a dividend [I.R.C. §§301(c)(1); 316(a)]. (2) E & P is important in determining whether an accumulated earnings tax will be imposed (IRC §531). (3) E & P affects characterization of S corporation distributions. (4) E & P is a factor in the determination of AMT, when a corporation receives life insurance proceeds.

17. Earnings and profits would then be increased by the entire amount of proceeds received upon the insured's death. Earnings and profits are defined here as the assets of the corporation available for distribution to shareholders without impairing capital. See Kahn, "Mandatory Buy-Out Agreements for Stock of Closely-Held Corporations," *Mich. L. Rev.* 68 (1969): 1; for the effect of premium payments on a corporation's earnings and profits account, see *Bittker and Eustice, Federal Income Taxation of Corporations and Shareholders*, 5th ed. (New York: Warren, Gorham and Lamont, 1987) ¶7.03 and note 51.

Term insurance can be defined as pure risk insurance—the owner purchases insurance against the risk that the insured will die during the period of coverage. As the insured ages, the risk of his or her death in any period of coverage becomes greater. Where the coverage is yearly renewable term, the insurance premium for a fixed amount of coverage increases year by year or, in the case of level premium term, the premium remains level for a given period of time. Some term policies, especially those that can be renewed for exceptionally long periods of time (e.g., term to age 65 to 70), develop a reserve. That is, there is an overcharge in premium in early years. This overcharge, together with interest earnings, will enable the insurance company to charge a level premium in later years when the premium paid will not equal the cost of protection—until a portion of the reserve is added to it.

In essence whole (ordinary) life insurance is term insurance for life. The insurer charges a level premium high enough in the early years to develop a reserve sufficient—together with interest—to allow the insured to continue paying the same premiums for the rest of his or her life. But if the insured surrenders the policy, the insurance company will not need the reserve to meet its future additional costs. The insured can cash in the policy for its cash value, an amount equivalent in later policy years to the policy reserve. In the initial years of a policy the reserve is likely to exceed the cash (surrender) value, the amount the policyowner could actually receive upon a surrender (or loan).

18. Rev. Rul. 55-257, 1955-1 C.B. 428. See also *Stark v. Comm'r*, 29 T.C. 122 (1957), *nonacq.*, and Katcher, "What Is Meant by Earnings and Profits?," *NYU Institute on Federal Taxation* 18 (1960): 235, 236 n.10.
19. Rev. Rul. 54-230, 1954-1 C.B. 114 states that the excess of proceeds received over aggregate premiums paid constitutes earnings and profits available for later distribution. In other words the proceeds, less any portion of the premiums already included in earnings and profits, will be considered part of the earnings and profits account.
20. S corporations and personal holding companies are exempt from this tax.
21. IRC §532.
22. Reasonable needs of a corporation include bona fide expansion of a business or replacement of its physical plant, acquisition of a business enterprise, retirement of genuine debt, working capital for inventories, investments on loans to suppliers or customers and key employee life insurance.
23. IRC §533.
24. IRC §531 provides for the imposition of a penalty tax in addition to regular corporate income taxes. The rate is 28 percent on the earnings and profits permitted to accumulate beyond the reasonable needs of the business instead of being distributed. IRC §§532 and 533. See also *U.S. v. Donruss Co.*, 393 U.S. 297 (1969).
25. IRC §535(c)(2).
26. IRC §537.
27. Zarky and Biblin, "The Role of Earnings and Profits in the Tax Law," *USC Tax Institute* 18 (1966): 145, 152. The authors rely on *Shellabarger Grain Products v. Comm'r*, 2 T.C. 75, 81 (1943), and on Rev. Rul. 55-257, 1955-1 C.B. 428.
28. However, neither the IRC nor the regulations explain what is meant by "reasonably anticipated" needs in the case of a stock redemption.
29. IRC §531.
30. *U.S. v. Donruss Co.*, 393 U.S. 297 (1969).
31. There are other means for a corporation to raise the necessary funds for a purchase of its stock. For example, see *Murphy Logging Corp. v. U.S.*, 378 F.2d 222 (9th Cir. 1967), where the corporation borrowed the funds from a third party and later repaid the loan from subsequent earnings. See Sexton, "Providing Security for the Outgoing Stockholder and Avoiding Tax Disadvantages to Selling and Remaining Shareholders," *NYU Institute of Federal Taxation* 24 (1966): 555, 584–85. See *Boshwit Brothers, Inc., et al. v. Comm'r*, T.C. Memo 1982-156, where the court rejected the taxpayer's agreement that accumulations were for the business purpose of

redeeming a principal shareholder's interest at death, in absence of a plan or showing of an amount needed to find such a redemption.

32. The courts have concentrated on the amount of stock owned rather than the presence or absence of practical control.

33. Negative control, the power of an equal shareholder to block affirmative corporate action, seems to have been ignored. For example, where the stock of a corporation is owned equally by two individuals and the shares of one are redeemed, surplus set aside to finance the redemption has been held to serve reasonable business needs. See *Mountain State Steel Foundries, Inc. v. Comm'r*, 284 F.2d 737 (4th Cir. 1960), *rev'g* 18 T.C.M. 306 (1959).

34. *Pelton*, 28 T.C. 153 (1957), *aff'd* 251 F.2d 278 (7th Cir. 1958), *cert. den.* 356 U.S. 958 (1958). See also *Lamark Shipping Agency, Inc. v. Comm'r.*, T.C. Memo 1981-284 (redemption of 95 percent shareholder served personal, not business, purposes, despite shareholder disagreements regarding conduct of business).

35. *Ted Bates*, 24 T.C.M. 1346 (1965). The transaction resulted in a detriment to the corporation since, after the redemption, its working capital was 60 percent lower than before the redemption, and it had a $500,000 obligation.

36. *Mountain State Steel Foundries*, 24 T.C.M. 1346 (1965).

37. 284 F.2d 737 (4th Cir. 1960).

38. *Faber Cement Block Company*, 50 T.C. 317 (1968), *acq.*

39. *Emeloid Co. v. Comm'r*, 189 F.2d 230 (3d Cir. 1951). Other cases that (although they do not deal directly with the accumulated earnings tax) are often cited for the proposition that "corporate disbursements to pay insurance premiums to provide a fund with which to purchase stock from the estate of the person whose life is insured do serve a corporate business purpose" are *Mountain State Steel Foundries, Inc. v. Comm'r, supra* note 46, at p. 745; *General Smelting Co. v. Comm'r*, 4 T.C. 313 (1944), *acq.* 1945 C.B. 3; *Prunier v. Comm'r*, 284 F.2d 818 (1958); *Farmers and Merchants Investment Co. v. Comm'r*, 29 T.C.M. 705 (1970).

40. In *C. E. Hooper, Inc. v. U.S.*, 539 F.2d 1276 (Ct. Cl. 1976), earnings were held to be properly accumulated to keep shares in the hands of current shareholders. Shareholders and their estates were bound to offer the corporation a first option on purchase of their shares. The corporation had accumulated more than $64,000 and paid more than $91,000 to the estate of a minority shareholder. The court stated, "It is difficult to surmise that a reserve of at least $64,238 was in excess of what a prudent businessman would retain to enable it to carry out its agreed policy."

41. *Novelart Mfg. Co. v. Comm'r*, 52 T.C. 794 (1969), *aff'd* 434 F.2d 1011 (6th Cir. 1970), *cert. den.* 403 U.S. 918 (1971) has often been misinterpreted as stating that life insurance per se aggravates the accumulated earnings tax. In that case premiums for key executive insurance were included in the taxable base on which the accumulated earnings tax was imposed. (Since premiums are paid with income that has been taxed, such payments do not reduce accumulated taxable income for Section 531 purposes.)

The taxpayer's argument never addressed the issue of the use of life insurance as a means of funding a redemption that itself would serve a corporation purpose. Instead the taxpayer argued that the premiums should not be included in the measure of the tax, an argument the court dismissed as inconsistent with the IRC rules for computing the tax. In fact the court held that the company's reason for the accumulation was vague and indefinite.

42. See the pre–1969 Tax Reform Act case of *Mountain State Steel Foundries*, cited in note 46 *supra* at p. 737. The court reasoned it didn't make sense for Congress to encourage Section 303 stock redemptions on the one hand and to penalize the corporation for acquiring the necessary funds on the other. But final post-1969 regulations specify that only postdeath accumulations should receive favorable treatment under IRC §537(a)(2).

Life insurance proceeds are exempt from tax, and since they are not part of taxable income, they do not become part of IRC §535(a) accumulated taxable income. But death proceeds are considered part of the earnings and profits account and may be considered in determining whether total accumulations are reasonable. Reg. §1.535-3(b)(ii).

43. IRC §537(a)(2).
44. IRC §537(b)(1).
45. *Mountain State Steel Foundries, Inc. v. Comm'r, supra* note 46. In *Oman Construction Company*, 24 T.C.M. 1799 (1965), the court held that the retention of proceeds to redeem the stock of a deceased officer served a reasonable business need. See *Emeloid Co. v. Comm'r, supra* note 52, where the court stated, "If disbursements to create a fund with which to purchase stock serve a corporate purpose, surely the disbursement of the created fund in purchasing the stock serves the same purpose."
46. See Kahn, "Mandatory Buy-Out Agreements for Stock of Closely-Held Corporations," *Mich. L. Rev.* 68 (1969): 27.
47. IRC §172.
48. A change in ownership occurs when a party who owns more than 5 percent of the stock increases his or her or its ownership by more than 50 percentage points as of a "testing date." IRC §382(g)(1). Reg. Sec. 1.382-2T(a)(2)(i).
49. IRC §382. The Section 382 limitation is an amount equal to the value of the loss corporation multiplied by the long-term tax-exempt rate. NOL carryforwards that cannot be deducted because of this limitation can be carried forward until they can be used. Planners should also check the reach of IRC §269, which applies only where the principal purpose of a stock acquisition is tax avoidance. See also *Lisbon Shops, Inc.*, 353 U.S. 382 (S.Ct. 1957).
50. See Scharf, "Buy-Sell Agreement Can Endanger a Corporation's NOL Carryovers," *Estate Planning* (January/February 1991): 22.
51. A loss corporation is technically one entitled to use a net operating loss carryforward or one that has a net operating loss for the taxable year. Reg. Sec. 1.382-2T(f)(1)(i).
52. See *Alprosa Watch Corporation*, 11 T.C. 240 (1948). There the executors of the deceased sole shareholder sold a glove manufacturing corporation's stock to new owners during a loss year (making it a "loss corporation") and used that loss to offset gains from a prearranged purchase and resale of wristwatches.
53. See "Shareholders' Buy-And-Sell Agreements May Precipitate Ownership Change under Section 382," *TMM* 30, no. 2 (Jan. 16, 1990): 28.
54. IRC §2042; Rev. Rul. 56-397, 1956-2 C.B. 599. Note that where proceeds are payable to the estate of the insured or the insured had incidents of ownership in the

policies, the potential for double taxation (inclusion of both the stock and the policy proceeds) exists. However, if the decedent's executor is obligated to apply proceeds toward the purchase price, the stock interest will be includable only to the extent it exceeds the amount of the proceeds, thus avoiding double taxation. *Est. of Mitchell v. Comm'r*, 37 B.T.A. 1 (1938), *acq.; Est. of Tompkins v. Comm'r*, 13 T.C. 1054 (1949), *acq.; Est. of Ealy v. Comm'r, supra* note 16; *Bobrzensky v. Comm'r*, 34 B.T.A. 305 (1936).

Note that Reg. §20.2042-1(a)(3), (c)(2) and (c)(6) provide for the inclusion of insurance proceeds in the estate of a controlling stockholder to the extent the corporation has incidents of ownership in the policy and the proceeds are paid to a third party for reasons other than a valid business purpose. This could create a hardship on the use of split dollar for cross-purchase purposes on the life of a controlling stockholder.

Rev. Rul. 76-274, 1976-2 C.B. 278 appears to clarify the situation and provides examples of how to keep the proceeds out of the estate of the controlling stockholder. Essentially the solution is to give the corporation an interest in the insurance policy that is limited to its outlay. Will this technique work? At least one of the authors feels the IRS will claim, in spite of this ruling, that the corporation's right to any part of the policy will be attributed to the insured and the insured will be held to have an incident of ownership in the policy.

IRC §2033 and Rev. Rul. 56-397, 1956-2 C.B. 599 indicate that insurance on the decedent's life owned by the surviving shareholder will not be includable in the insured stockholder's estate for federal estate tax purposes in spite of the cross-purchase reciprocity arrangement. The value of the decedent's stock, of course, is includable. *Est. of Riecker v. Comm'r*, 3 T.C.M. 1293 (1944).

55. *Est. of Riecker v. Comm'r, supra* note 15.
56. The result is the same if a trustee is the recipient of the corporate-owned insurance assuming the trustee uses the proceeds to purchase the insured's stock on behalf of the corporation. IRC §2042.
57. *Wilson v. Crooks, supra* note 16; *Est. of Ealy v. Comm'r, supra* note 16; *Est. of Knipp v. Comm'r, supra* note 16.
58. See *Newell v. Comm'r*, 62 F.2d 102; *Kennedy v. Comm'r*, 4 B.T.A. 330 (1926); *Est. of Salt v. Comm'r*, 17 T.C. 92 (1951); *Est. of Littick v. Comm'r*, 31 T.C. 181 (1958). It is not clear, as of this writing, whether 1990 tax law changes would alter this conclusion in agreements among family members. See IRC §2703. Also see endnote 2.
59. See endnote 2.
60. See Chapter 14, IRC §2703.
61. See PLR 8140016; Rev. Rul. 55-77, 1954-1 C.B. 187; Rev. Rul. 80-186, 1980-2 C.B. 20.
62. See Kelly, "Waiving Rights Under Buy-Sell Agreement Affects Stock Value", *Estate Planning* (Sept/Oct. 1991): 284.
63. PLR 9117035. See also *Dickman v. Commr.*, 465 U.S. 330 (1984); and *Snyder v. Commr.*, 93 T.C. 529 (1989).

CHAPTER 5

The Taxation of Stock Redemptions

THE IMPORTANCE OF THE DIVIDEND–CAPITAL GAIN DISTINCTION

A stock redemption (also called *stock retirement*) occurs when a corporation distributes cash and/or property to a shareholder in return for its own stock. The shareholder typically receives cash, and the corporation receives stock. Typically the other shareholders in the corporation will not be deemed to have received a constructive dividend as a result of a corporation's redemption of another shareholder's stock.[1]

The major tax issue is the treatment of the distribution from the corporation to the selling shareholder.

The general rule of corporate taxation is simple: Any distribution (no matter what the parties call it) from a corporation to its shareholders with respect to its stock is—to the extent of the corporation's earnings and profits—taxed as a dividend. The entire amount (not merely the gain over the seller's cost) is taxable.

Why such a harsh and arbitrary general rule? Because without such a rule it would be easy for a shareholder to take a corporation's earnings and profits out of the business, obtain sale or exchange treatment (meaning only the gain is taxable and that lesser amount is taxed at capital gains rates) and incur no economic cost.

For example, *X* owns all the stock of the X-On Corporation. He would like cash to pay his son's college tuition, but he is already drawing as much reasonable (and therefore deductible) salary out of the corporation as possible. He would like to avoid dividend treatment. He could sell Yew some of his stock, but that would give Yew—a stranger—some voting power (control), a share in the growth of the company (profits) and a share of the worth of the business upon a future sale or liquidation (assets).

If there were no general rule, X could sell stock back to his own corporation, receive cash and pay tax as though he had made the sale to Yew, a stranger. Yet he would not be giving up any "CPA" (control, profits, assets). In fact, even if he sold every share he owned—except one—back to the corporation, he would still hold 100 percent of the CPA in the corporation.

If the IRS classifies a distribution as a dividend, the entire amount received by the selling shareholder will be taxed at ordinary income tax rates. Ostensibly, ordinary rates reach a maximum of 31 percent subsequent to the Revenue Reconciliation Act of 1990. But after application of adjustments to personal exemptions and itemized deductions, the effective federal income tax rates applied to a dividend could be as high as 34 percent.

On the other hand, if the same stockholder sells his or her stock to a third party, only the gain, the appreciation in value (which will ordinarily be greater to the extent that the corporation has not paid out its earnings as dividends) will be subject to tax. This amount normally will be taxed at the capital gains rate, a maximum rate of 28 percent.[2]

For instance, assume a $1 million distribution to a shareholder in return for stock with a basis (cost) of $300,000. If the distribution is classified by the IRS as a dividend, the entire amount will be taxable, resulting in a tax that could approximate $340,000. But if the transaction is considered a sale or exchange, only the $700,000 gain will be taxable (and that lesser amount is taxable at capital gains rates), so the tax, will be about $196,000 (.28 × $700,000) at most. The $144,000 difference is considerable.

This wide variation between the amount subject to tax (typically the entire amount received in the case of a dividend, but only the gain if the transaction is considered a sale) and even the modest difference in the rate of tax on ordinary income and capital gains makes the IRC provisions dealing with stock redemptions important.

Some corporate distributions made to purchase a deceased or disabled or retiring shareholder's stock are taxed as dividends and are subject to ordinary income tax rates.[3] If a distribution from a corporation to a shareholder is considered a dividend, regardless of what the parties call the transaction or how they characterize it, no recovery of the shareholder's basis is allowed (i.e., the entire distribution, and not only the gain, is taxable).

Other distributions are treated as amounts received "in exchange" for the stock with respect to which they are made.[4] If a corporate distribution is considered "in exchange" for the shareholder's stock interest, with the taxpayer realizing capital gain or loss, that gain or loss is measured by the difference between the amount he or she realizes in the distribution and his or her basis for the stock. In other words, as mentioned above, he or she pays tax only on the gain realized.

Here is another simplified (and perhaps exaggerated) example: Suppose a client contributed $100,000 to form a closely held corporation. In return he received 100,000 shares of stock. Over 20 years the corporation grew to a value of $1 million. When the client dies, the corporation pays his executor $1 million in return for all but 1 share of his 100,000 shares. Thus the entire distribution will be taxed as a dividend, and (assuming the corporation had sufficient earnings and profits) the estate will pay ordinary income tax on the $1 million. The tax will be about $340,000.

But if the client's executor sold the same $1 million worth of stock to an unrelated person and received $1 million in return, only the gain would be taxable. Assuming the gain was $50,000 ($1 million realized on the sale less the newly stepped-up basis of, say, $950,000—the stock's fair market value at death). The federal income tax would approximate $15,000. In this example the difference between dividend treatment (approximately $340,000 tax) and sale or exchange treatment (approximately $15,000 tax) could be well over $250,000!

THE GENERAL RULE GOVERNING CORPORATE DISTRIBUTIONS

As a general rule, any distribution to a shareholder with respect to his or her stock is taxable as a dividend to the extent that the corporation has accumulated or current earnings and profits.[5] Although the IRC does not define the term *earnings and profits*, E & P can be thought of, very generally, as being the same as the earned surplus of a corporation.

Distributions—no matter what they are called—are taxable to shareholders in the following manner:

1. The portion that is considered a dividend is included in the recipient/taxpayer's gross income.
2. The portion of the distribution that is not a dividend reduces the basis of the taxpayer's stock.
3. The portion of the distribution that is not a dividend and exceeds the basis of the taxpayer's stock is treated as a capital gain.

A Simplified Example

The XYZ Corporation has current and accumulated earnings and profits of $20,000. It distributes to X, its sole shareholder, $25,000 of cash. X paid $3,000 for his stock ten years ago.

1. To the extent of XYZ's earnings and profits ($20,000), the distribution is taxable as a dividend to X and subject to ordinary income rates.
2. The portion of the distribution that is not a dividend, $5,000, reduces the basis ($3,000) of the taxpayer's stock (in this case to zero).
3. The third portion, the part of the ($25,000) distribution that is not a dividend and exceeds the basis of the taxpayer's stock, is considered a capital gain.

In this example X would realize ordinary income of $20,000, pay no tax on the recovery of his $3,000 basis and pay capital gains rates on the remaining $2,000.

So that taxpayers are not tempted to indulge in semantic sophistry, IRC provisions make it clear that a distribution is conclusively presumed to be made out of earnings and profits to the extent they exist and out of the most recently accumulated earnings and profits.

The Exceptions to the General Rule

As mentioned earlier, certain distributions in redemption of stock (i.e., where the corporation buys its own stock) are treated as distributions in part or full payment *in exchange* for the stock redeemed.[6] The significance of this exception can be better understood by referring to the previous discussion, which in essence stated the general rule: any distribution from a corporation to its shareholders with respect to its stock—no matter what the form or what the distribution is called—will be taxed to the recipient as a dividend to the extent of corporate earnings and profits.

If the XYZ Corporation has $40,000 of earnings and profits and redeems a portion of shareholder *X*'s stock for $20,000 cash, the entire $20,000 will be considered a dividend to *X*, fully taxable as ordinary income.

Had *X* sold the same stock for $20,000 to an unrelated third party in exchange for money or other property, the transaction would have been viewed as an exchange of stock for cash—i.e., a sale. *X*'s gain would have been measured by the difference between the amount realized, $20,000, and his adjusted basis. If he paid $5,000 for the stock, he would have a capital gain of $15,000 ($20,000 amount realized minus $5,000 basis) rather than ordinary income of $20,000. Thus *X*'s income tax liability would be reduced in the latter case.

"Dividend" treatment, therefore, causes the *entire* distribution to be taxable at ordinary income rates, while "exchange" treatment causes *only the gain*, if any, to be taxed at lower capital gains rates.

In some cases, even though the corporation has earnings and profits, the distribution is not treated as a dividend. If the amount received exceeds the stockholder's basis for the stock, for example, he or she realizes a capital gain as though having sold the stock to a third party.

From the point of view of the stockholder, the circumstances under which a distribution in redemption is considered a dividend and the circumstances in which the distribution will be considered in exchange for the stock redeemed need to be set out. The rules described serve as an arbitrary mechanism to ascertain whether a distribution by the corporation to the shareholder will more closely resemble a sale to an independent third party than a dividend.

The rules discussed in the following section concede that the taxpayer has, in fact or in substance, surrendered physical posssession of the stock. But the real issues to focus on are these:

- What has happened to the shareholder's interest in the corporation?
- What was the effect of the so-called redemption on his or her control of the business?
- Did the sale of stock to the corporation meaningfully diminish his or her stake in the future profits of the business?
- Did the shareholder give up a portion of his or her right to corporate assets if the corporation is liquidated (or sale proceeds if the business is sold)?

So, the crux of the issue is *whether the stockholder's CPA has undergone a meaningful reduction.*

DIVIDEND OR CAPITAL GAIN TRANSACTION— THE SECRET OF SUCCESS

The secret of success in changing what could be ordinary income on the entire distribution into capital gains on only the gain portion is a meaningful change in the seller's CPA. This change can be accomplished in one of two ways: by making the sale to a third party or by meeting one or more of the "safe harbor" rules established by Congress. Fulfilling any one of these criteria will provide shelter from the general rule that distribution from a corporation to its shareholder with respect to its stock is a dividend.[7]

Under the safe harbor rules a distribution made by a corporation to a shareholder in payment for stock is treated as a sale or exchange redemption if:

1. it is "not essentially equivalent to a dividend";[8] or
2. it is "substantially disproportionate" with respect to the stockholder;[9] or
3. it is a "complete redemption" of all the stock owned by the stockholder.[10]

If the distribution is not within one of these categories, it is considered a distribution taxable as a dividend to the extent of the corporation's earnings and profits. Let's examine each of these three exceptions in more detail.

"Not Essentially Equivalent" Redemptions

Where a corporation redeems part of its stock from its sole stockholder or makes a pro rata redemption from all of its stockholders, the redemption is usually treated as essentially equivalent to a dividend. After the redemption each stockholder has the same proportionate interest in the CPA of the corporation as before.

The effect on both the stockholders and the corporation is the same as if a dividend had been declared and paid. For example, assume Charles and Lara are coshareholders in the CL Corporation and each owns 50 of the 100 shares of stock outstanding. No change has occurred in either stockholder's share of the control, profits or asset growth of the business if both sell 20 shares—or even 49 shares apiece—back to the corporation in return for cash or other property. The redemption is essentially the same as if the corporation had made a dividend distribution to each.

Where a corporation redeems all the stock of one particular stockholder, the distribution does not have the effect of a dividend, because the stockholder receiving the distribution ceases to have any further interest in the affairs of the corporation and economically is not in the same position he or she would have been had the corporation paid a dividend. For instance, if the CL Corporation bought all of Charles's shares, his control, share of current and future corporate profits and share of current or future corporate assets are totally changed. This is equivalent to complete termination, discussed in full later in the chapter.

Again, the test is whether the relative economic interest or rights of the stockholder in question have been changed significantly. Whether there is an adequate business purpose for the corporation's redeeming stock, such as curtailment of the corporation's business or the desirability of redeeming a high-dividend preferred stock, is irrelevant.

Although dividend equivalency depends on the facts and circumstances of each case, the regulations state that generally a pro rata redemption will be treated as a dividend if the redeeming corporation has only one class of stock outstanding.[11] So if there are four shareholders in a firm, each owning 25 of the 100 shares outstanding, a redemption of 24 shares from each shareholder will be treated as a dividend distribution. The entire amount received will be taxed as ordinary income.

The use of this general nondividend equivalency test is limited for planning purposes because of its ambivalence and lack of certainty. Typically it will work only if the redemption is an isolated transaction. There also is very little left of the "essentially equivalent to a dividend" test that is not already covered under the substantially disproportinate or complete-termination-of-interest tests. This rule is usually used by counsel as a last resort when a redemption that has already occurred does not qualify under either of the next two tests or under IRC §303.[12]

"Substantially Disproportionate" Redemptions

A substantially disproportionate redemption is one that meets three tests:

1. Immediately after the redemption the shareholder must own (directly or constructively) less than half of the total combined voting power of all classes of outstanding stock entitled to vote.
2. The shareholder's postredemption percentage of the total outstanding voting stock must be less than 80 percent of his or her preredemption

ownership. Stated another way, the redemption must result in a reduction of more than 20 percent in the shareholder's percentage of the total outstanding voting stock (comparing his or her percentage ownership immediately before and immediately after the redemption).

3. The shareholder's percentage ownership of outstanding common stock—voting or nonvoting—after the redemption must be less than 80 percent of that before the redemption. In other words, the redemption must result in a reduction of more than 20 percent in the shareholder's percentage ownership of the common stock outstanding.

The following examples illustrate how this safe harbor rule operates.

Assume that before the redemption A owns 30 out of 100 shares of voting common stock (the only class outstanding) of B Corporation (30/100 or 30 percent) and that the other 70 shares are held 10 shares each by seven other stockholders. If the corporation redeems 10 of A's shares and redeems no shares of any other stockholder, the redemption will qualify as a substantially disproportionate redemption since A's ownership percentage after the redemption, 20/90 or 22.2 percent, is less than 80 percent of A's ownership percentage before the redemption; i.e., it is now less than 24 percent.

Preredemption	*Postredemption*
A owns: 30 shares	A owns: 20 shares
Total shares outstanding: 100 shares	Total shares outstanding: 90 shares
Ratio: 30 percent (30/100)	Ratio: 22.2 percent (20/90)

If, however, the corporation, at the same time or as part of a plan, also redeems a total of ten shares from any one or more of the other stockholders, the redemption of A's ten shares will not be disproportionate. The reason is that A's ownership percentage after the redemption would be at least 20/80, or 25 percent, which is more than 24 percent (80 percent of A's 30 percent ownership percentage before the redemption). Consequently, the redemption would be treated as a dividend.

Similarly, if at the time of the redemption of a part of A's shares one of the other stockholders is a person whose stock is attributed to A (under constructive ownership rules, discussed later in this chapter), the redemption of A's 10 shares will not qualify. (Each shareholder other than A owns 10 shares, so A would be deemed to own the 20 shares he actually owns plus the 10 shares attributed to him—a total of 30 out of the 90 outstanding shares). In that case his percentage after the redemption is 30/90, or 33.3 percent, which is more than 80 percent of his percentage before the redemption, 40/100 or 40 percent.

A redemption solely of nonvoting stock cannot qualify under this test,[13] but a redemption of nonvoting preferred stock can qualify when a simultaneous redemption of voting stock qualifies.

The minimum number of shares that must be redeemed to qualify under the "substantially disproportionate" rule can be calculated through a formula:[14]

$$N = BT/(5T - 4B)$$

B = Number of shares owned by seller before redemption

T = Total number of shares outstanding before redemption

N = Minimum number of shares to be redeemed (add 1 to the number you compute and round up this result to the next-highest whole number)

For example, your clients, Dr. Lew Savar and his friend, Terry Halpern, each own 50 shares of a corporation. Together they hold all the outstanding stock. To solve for N, first multiply BT (50 × 100) to arrive at 5,000. Then compute $5T$ (5 × 100) to arrive at 500. From that, subtract $4B$ (4 × 50), or 200. The result is 300. When 5,000 is divided by 300, the result is 16.67.

$$\frac{50 \times 100}{(5 \times 100) - (4 \times 50)}$$

$$\frac{5,000}{300}$$

Add 1 and round up. N equals 18 shares (16.67 + 1 rounded to the next highest whole number). To test this result, the before-redemption ratio was 50/100 (50 percent). The after-redemption ratio must be less than 40 percent (50 percent of 80 percent). If 18 of Lew's shares are redeemed, he will own 32 out of 82 outstanding, or 39 percent of the outstanding stock, and will therefore meet the test.

Complete Terminations

Two provisions have already been discussed, which, if complied with, will enable a distribution that might otherwise be taxable as a dividend to be treated under much more favorable rules. This third provision is the extreme form of the first two rules: it provides that a redemption of *all* the stock owned by a stockholder is an exchange redemption.[15] To qualify for this favorable treatment a redemption must, in substance as well as in form, completely terminate the stockholder's proprietary interest in the corporation. If *X* and *Y* are costockholders of the XY Corporation, the complete redemption of all of *Y*'s shares of stock in return for cash (and/or other property) will have the same result as if *Y* had sold the stock to *Z*, an unrelated, independent third party. (Favorable tax treatment will also be accorded to *Y* if he sells his entire interest in the business to *X*.) Only the difference between what the stockholder receives and his or her cost for the stock will be taxable—and that gain, if any, will generally be subject to capital gains rather than ordinary income rates.

Because of the "step-up in basis" rules of the tax law, there will rarely be a capital gain on the sale of a deceased shareholder's stock under either a stock redemption plan or a cross-purchase plan. When a stockholder dies, his or her stock automatically receives a new tax basis, which is used in computing gain or loss on a subsequent sale or exchange of the stock. The new basis is the fair market value of the stock for federal estate tax purposes. Because the sale price under a stock redemption (or cross-purchase agreement) may be accepted as the fair market value of the stock, there is usually little or no difference between basis and sale price and consequently little or no taxable gain.[16] For example, assume shareholder *A* dies. Stock he purchased for $10 a share is valued in his estate at $100 a share. Since the price paid under the stock redemption, $100 a share, is the same as the stock's new basis, $100 a share, there is no taxable gain upon an immediate sale.

THE ATTRIBUTION RULES—A FLY IN THE OINTMENT

The safe harbor rules would be fairly simple were it not for the so-called *attribution (constructive ownership) rules*.[17] These rules in effect attribute to one person (or entity) ownership of stock actually owned by another and are used to see if a redemption meets any of the safe harbor rules.

It should be noted, however, that although all three of these rules apply equally to stockholders of C and S corporations, a redemption of stock owned in an S corporation without any earnings and profits from conducting business as a C corporation should result in the transfer being taxed as an exchange. Distributions from such an S corporation are taxed first as a nontaxable return of the stockholder's basis and next as a gain from an exchange. As a result a corporation that has been an S corporation from its inception should not present a problem in this regard.[18]

The rules for determining constructive ownership of stock (see Figures 5.1 and 5.2) are extremely complicated and must be studied carefully.

The attribution rules are based on a presumption of economic solidarity among certain family members and a recognition that in many cases partnerships, estates, trusts and corporations should be treated essentially as conduits so that in a number of circumstances individuals are regarded as owning stock actually owned by these entities. The attribution concept is also often reversed; an entity is treated as if it owned stock in fact owned by an individual.

The seven basic attribution rules are summarized in the following sections.

1. Family Attribution Rules

According to the family attribution rules[19] (See Figure 5.3), an individual is considered to own all of the stock owned by his or her spouse, parents, children and grandchildren. For instance, assume that Mr. and Mrs. Y own all 100 of the outstanding shares of the XYZ Corporation. Y owns 99, and Mrs. Y owns 1 share. XYZ redeems all 99 shares owned by Y. The redemption is not complete, because Mrs. Y's 1 share is attributed to her husband and at that point represents the entire CPA (right to control or receive profits or assets of the corporation). Under the legal fiction of family attribution, Mr. Y is deemed to own 100 percent of the control, profits and assets of the XYZ corporation.

As another example, assume a father and son each own half of the common stock of Douglass Mellor Photography Inc., and the father's stock is sold back to the company. Under the family attribution rules the father is considered to own not only the stock he actually owns but also the stock his son owns. This means that even after the sale of the father's entire interest in the business he is still the constructive owner of all the stock of the corporation.

An individual is deemed to own stock his or her children and grandchildren own. But a grandchild is not considered to own stock his or her grandparents own. Likewise, no direct link is made between siblings. Assume, for example, that two sisters, Hilary and Elizabeth, own all the shares of the HE Corporation. If Hilary sells all her shares back to the HE Corporation, that transaction

FIGURE 5.1   Rules of Attribution

Attributed From	Attributed To	Basis of Attribution	IRC Sections
1. Corporation	Stockholders owning 50% more in the value of corporation's stock	In same proportion the value of the stock owned by such person bears to the value of all stock in such corporation*	318(a)(2)(C); 302; 306(b)(1)(A)
2. Trust	Vested beneficiaries	In proportion to actual interest	318(a)(2)(A)
3. Trust	Contingent beneficiaries	In proportion to actuarially computed interest (if greater than 5%)	318(a)(2)(B)
4. Trust under Subpart E of Part 1 of Subchapter J—relating to grantors and others treated as substantial owners	Person considered owner under Subpart E of Part 1 of Subchapter J	100% interest	318(a)(2)(B)
5. A partnership An estate	Partners Beneficiaries	Proportionately	318(a)(2)(A)
6. Family members Spouse, not legally separated Parents Children Grandchildren Adopted Children	Family member, but not between siblings	100% interest	318(a)(1) 302(c)(1) 304(b)(1) 306(b)(1) 334(b)(3)

*If a person owns 80 percent of a corporation's stock, 80 percent of the stock that corporation owns in any other corporation will be attributed to him or her.

FIGURE 5.1 Rules of Attribution (*continued*)

"Back Attribution"

Attributed From	*Attributed To*	*Basis of Attribution*	*IRC Sections*
1. Stockholders	Corporation	100% interest	304(b)(1)
2. Any persons owning 50% or more in value of a corporation's stock	The corporation that has 50% or more of its stock owned by any person	100% interest	382(a)(3)
3. Beneficiary—unless the beneficiary's interest is a remote contingent interest (less than 5%)	Trust	100% interest	318(a)(2)(B)
4. Person considered owner under Subpart E of Part 1 of Subchapter J	Trust under Subpart E of Part 1 of Subchapter J	100% interest	318(a)(2)(B)
5. Partner Beneficiary	Partnership Estate	100% interest	318(a)(2)(A)

Source: Courtesy of The American College, Advanced Estate Planning Course

completely terminates her interest since she is not deemed to own Elizabeth's stock.

Even where the family attribution rules do apply to connect ownership between the specified family relationships, it may be possible to "break the chain" by waiving family attribution.

For instance, assume a man, *H*, his wife, *W*, his son, *S*, and his grandson (*S*'s son), *GS*, own the 100 outstanding shares of stock of a corporation. Each person owns 25 shares. *H*, *W* and *S* are each considered as owning 100 shares. *GS* is considered as owning only 50 shares—his own and his father's. He is not deemed to own his grandparents' shares.

If *GS* now gives 10 shares to his sister, *GD*, he will own only 40 shares, 15 individually and 25 through his father. He does not own his sister's stock either directly under §318 (the Code section dealing with attribution of ownership) or indirectly since this would require two family attribution steps from *GD* to *S* and from *S* to *GS*.

Exceptions to the Family Attribution Rules. It has been argued—in at least one case successfully—that the rule linking stock actually owned by one family member to another family member is not appropriate if there is hostility between those individuals. Currently there is a conflict between courts in different circuits as to whether such conflicts should block the application of family attribution.[20]

A timely disclaimer may be helpful in breaking the fatal link.[21] Likewise, where a person holds an interest through a trust but can shift that interest in a timely manner to someone else through a special power of appointment and thus divest his or her interest, the link can be severed.[22]

Due to the harshness of the constructive ownership or attribution rules toward shareholders of a family-owned business, there are ways for individuals or entities to avoid or waive the *family* attribution rules.[23] Under these exceptions, if all the stock actually owned by the stockholder is redeemed, the redemption will qualify as an exchange redemption.

The following conditions must be met in the case of the redemption of an individual to waive the family attribution rules:

1. All the stock the seller actually owns must be sold—either to the corporation or to some third party or both—in a simultaneous transaction.
2. The stockholder must terminate all interest in the corporation (except as a creditor), including any interest as officer, director or employee.[24]
3. He or she must not acquire any interest in the corporation (other than by bequest or inheritance) or successor corporation[25] during the ten years following the redemption.[26]
4. He or she must not, during the ten years preceding the redemption, have acquired any of the stock redeemed from any person whose ownership would be attributed to him or her under the constructive ownership

FIGURE 5.2   Stock Redemption Distribution Flowchart

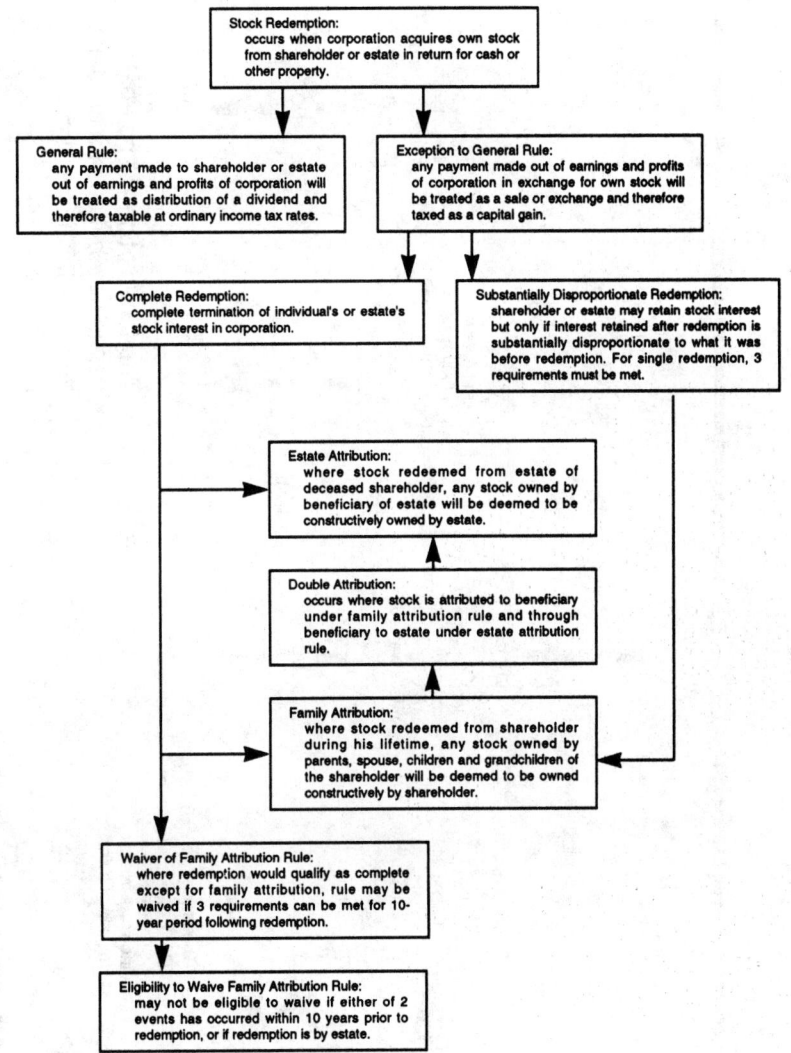

Source: Courtesy of The American College, Advanced Estate Planning Course.
Reprinted with permission.

FIGURE 5.3 Family Attribution

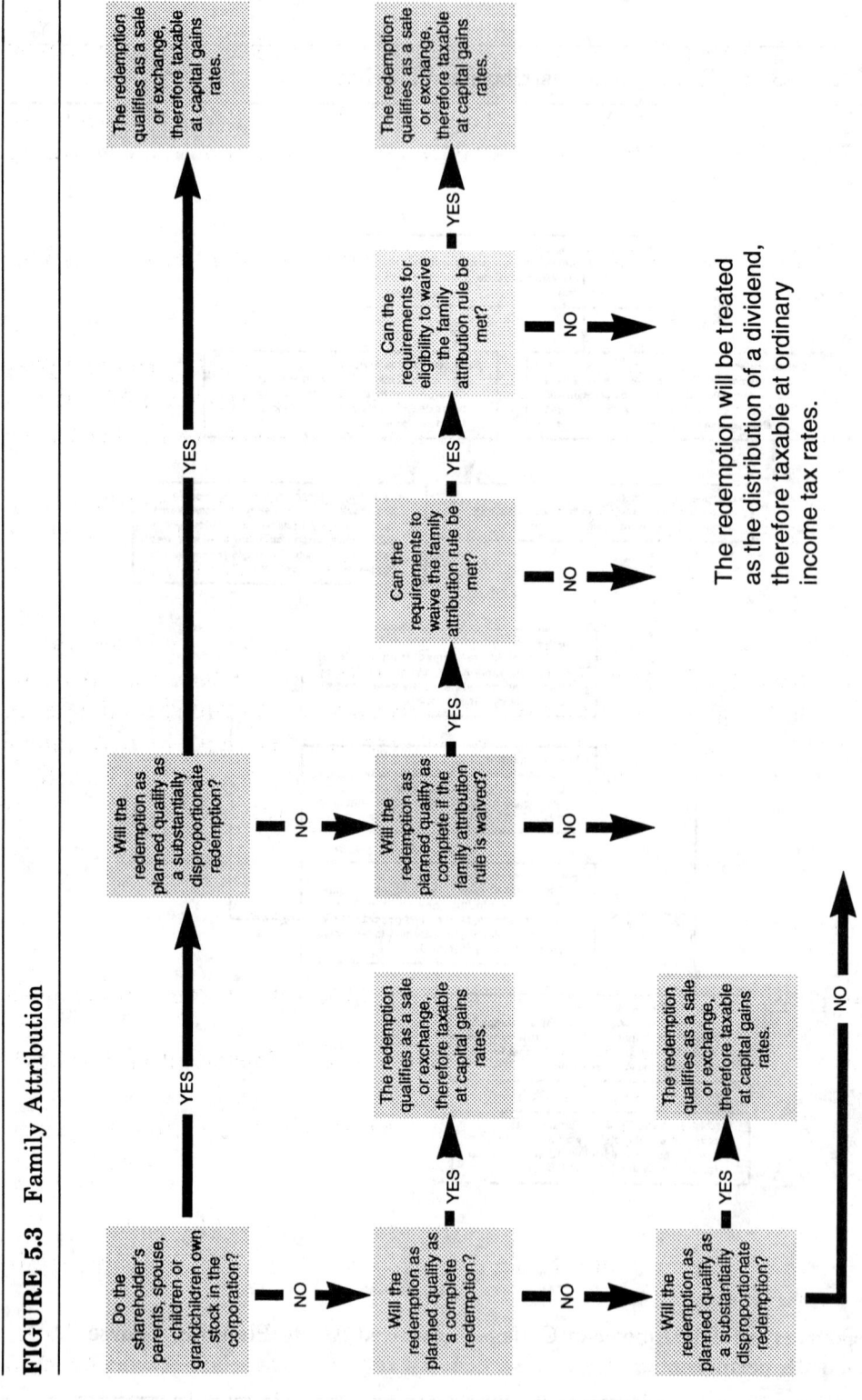

Source: Courtesy of The American College, Advanced Estate Planning Course. Reprinted with permission.

rules of Section 318 or have transferred any stock to any such person who continues to own stock after the redemption.

5. The seller must agree—in writing—to notify the IRS if he or she becomes an officer, director or employee within the ten years following the redemption.[27]

Even if all five of these conditions are met, the family attribution rules cannot be waived if

1. the stock of the selling shareholder was acquired during the ten-year period before the redemption from a person whose stock would—at the date of the redemption—be attributed to the redeemed stockholder under any of the attribution rules[28] or

2. some other person owns stock that—at the date of the redemption—can be attributed to the redeemed shareholder—and had received that stock from the seller within the ten years prior to the redemption.[29]

The requirement that the selling party not own any stock after the redemption has caused problems in a number of situations. One problem is that if he or she receives notes from the corporation the IRS could treat what the seller calls debt as equity.[30] As a result payments on the note would be taxed as nondeductible dividends (not deductible by the corporation and fully taxable to the seller) rather than as tax-deductible interest payments (and tax-free repayments of principal).

The following measures should be taken to avoid this attack:

- The debt should not be subordinated to the claims of the corporation's general creditors.
- Payments of principal and interest should not be dependent on the business's earnings or working capital.
- The noteholder's rights should not be broader in scope than necessary to enforce his or her claims.
- The debt should be evidenced by a note.
- The terms of the note should be acceptable to an outside lender.
- The full principal should become due immediately if the company fails to make timely payments on the notes.[31]
- If the corporation defaults on the debt, no shares of stock can revert to or be received by the redeemed shareholder (nor will the redeemed shareholder be permitted to purchase the stock at public auction).

Be particularly careful of long-term redemption price payouts; if the payout stretches beyond 15 years (as would be the case with a 20-year installment payout or a private annuity on a young seller), the IRS will not issue a ruling on whether or not it will treat the installment sale or private annuity as a disguised form of equity interest.[32]

With respect to the redemption of all of the stock owned by an estate (or other entity), the preceding conditions must be met not only by the entity itself but also by each "related person." For this purpose a "related person" is an individual to whom ownership of the stock is attributable under the family attribution rules if such stock is further attributable to the entity under the entity attribution rules, as discussed earlier.

For example, X, his son, S, and Y, an individual unrelated to either X or S, own equal shares in the SXY Corporation. X turns over to the SXY corporation all the shares he owns in return for $30,000. If X is deemed to own stock actually owned by S, the redemption of X's shares is not a complete termination of X's interest. The $30,000 would in all likelihood be taxable in its entirety as ordinary income (to the extent of the corporation's earnings and profits). If X died owning his stock, which was then redeemed from his estate, the transaction would qualify for exchange treatment under the following circumstances:

1. If S was the sole beneficiary of the estate, his stock would have to be redeemed also, as discussed.
2. If S was not a beneficiary, and his stock was not attributable to a beneficiary, only the estate's interest would have to be redeemed.
3. If S was not a beneficiary, but X's wife, E, was, since S's stock would be attributed to the estate through E, a waiver by E and the entity, both agreeing to comply with these conditions, would sever the attribution from S and allow the redemption to qualify for capital gain treatment.

These exceptions to application of the constructive ownership rules apply *only* in relatively limited situations. The other constructive ownership rules remain in effect, rendering, among other things, estate planning for redemption of stock of a major stockholder in a family corporation difficult.

This difficulty often suggests that when the corporation is family-owned, to be safe a planner must consider the use of a cross-purchase arrangement for effecting a buy-sell agreement (often combined with the use of a Section 303 stock redemption) or through the use of the highly flexible buy-sell agreement known as the *Wait-and-See buy-sell* (discussed in detail in Chapter 29).[33]

The family attribution waiver rules have been expanded to permit entities (such as estates, trusts, corporations and partnerships) to waive any family attribution only if the family members through which the ownership is attributed also agree to the waiver. The link between family members can be cut as long as the beneficiary through whom ownership is attributed joins in the waiver.

For instance, the most common problem is where a father, mother and son each own equal shares of stock in a corporation. Assume the father dies and his stock passes to his executor. The sole beneficiary of the father's estate is his wife. Assume that the corporation is willing and able to purchase both parents' entire stockholding. But the stock owned by the son is deemed to be owned by his mother. The stock she is then deemed to own (representing at that point all the outstanding shares of the corporation) are deemed to be owned by the estate. So absent a successful waiver, neither the shares sold by the estate nor the shares sold by the mother will receive favorable tax treatment. But if both the entity (here the estate) and the related family member (here the mother) waive the family attribution rules, the distribution will terminate both sellers' interest.[34]

An alternative planning technique to avoid the constructive ownership conundrum is to make gifts of stock to persons who aren't considered related under the family attribution rules. In other words, if stockholders include persons who are outside the ambit of these complex and harsh rules (but who are nevertheless part of the family in the social and economic sense, such as a daughter-in-law, son-in-law or brother or sister of a parent), a redemption from the father could qualify for favorable treatment. So in planning gifts of family corporation stock to children, a shareholder should also consider the feasibility of gifts to a spouse as a means of making redemptions possible without attribution problems.[35]

2. Attribution from Partnerships, Estates and Trusts.[36]

Stock owned directly or indirectly by or for a partnership or estate is considered owned proportionately by its partners or beneficiaries (see Figure 5.4). A typical illustration of this rule comes into play whenever stock is redeemed by a corporation from the beneficiary or the estate of a deceased shareholder. If the XYZ

FIGURE 5.4 Estate Attribution

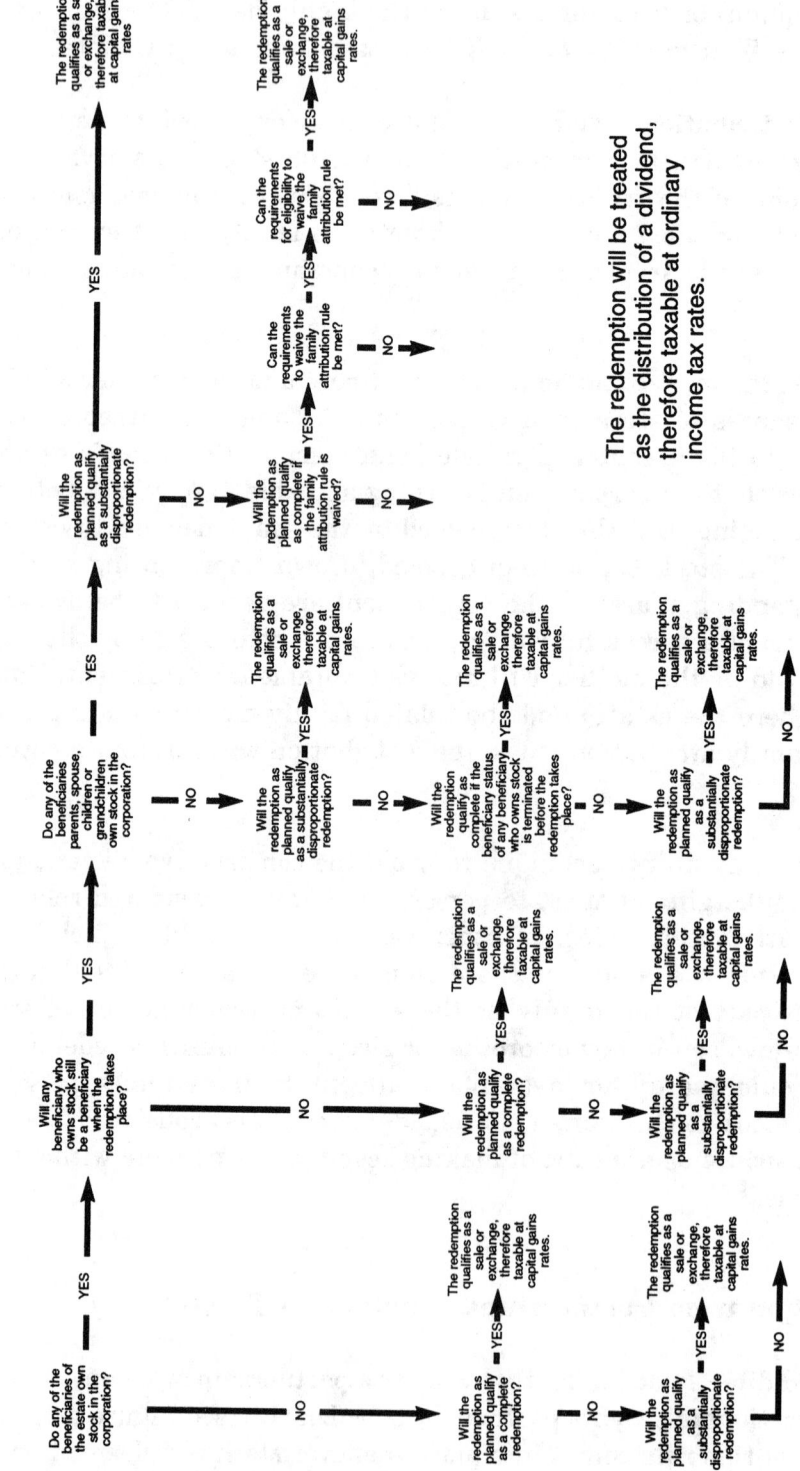

Source: Courtesy of The American College, Advanced Estate Planning Course. Reprinted with permission.

Corporation purchases all 15 shares owned by Aunt Matilda, but she is the beneficiary of three-fourths of Uncle George's estate (including 100 shares of XYZ stock), Aunt Matilda is deemed to own three-fourths of the 100 shares owned by the estate. Therefore a redemption of the 15 shares she owns personally will not be a complete termination of her interest in XYZ. She is deemed as still owning 75 shares because of her beneficial interest in Uncle George's estate.

Likewise, stock owned by or for a trust (other than a qualified pension or profit-sharing trust) is considered owned by its beneficiaries in proportion to the actuarial interest of such beneficiaries in the trust. For example, a trust holds ten shares of RB Inc. stock. Under the terms of the trust Mrs. *B* is to receive income for life, and at her death the principal is to go to the son of *B*. Once Mrs. *B*'s age is found, it is possible to ascertain the actuarial value of her interest and the actuarial value of her son's remainder interest. If the son's interest is equal to 60 percent of the present value of the trust, he is deemed to own 60 percent of the asset in the trust, six shares of RB Inc. stock.

3. Attribution from a Corporation[37]

If 50 percent or more in value of the stock in a corporation is owned directly or indirectly by or for any person (including family and other attributed ownership), that person is considered to own the stock owned directly or indirectly by the corporation, in the proportion of the value of the stock the taxpayer owns in the corporation as compared to the value of all the stock in the corporation.

So an individual who owned 63 percent of the outstanding stock of the XYZ Corporation would be treated as if he or she owned—in addition to stock actually owned—63 percent of the stock (of some other corporation) the XYZ Corporation owned. If the XYZ Corporation owned 100 shares of PBX Inc., the individual, through ownership of XYZ stock, would be deemed to own 63 of its shares of PBX Inc.

4. Attribution to Partnerships and Estates[38]

Stock owned directly or indirectly by or for a partner or beneficiary of an estate is considered owned by the partnership or estate. This is an important rule because quite often a corporation pursuant to a buy-sell agreement will purchase stock of a deceased shareholder from his or her estate. If any beneficiary under the will owns even one share of stock in the redeeming corporation, his or her one share will be deemed to be owned by the estate—so that even if the corporation purchases all the shares actually owned by the estate, the redemption will still not be complete.

For example, Smith and Jones have been coshareholders for many years. Smith dies and leaves his wife, except for a gold pocket watch, his entire estate (consisting mostly of his shares of the Smith-Jones Corporation). In his will Smith leaves his pocket watch to his friend and coshareholder, Jones. This makes Jones a beneficiary of the estate.

Even if the corporation then purchases all the shares of stock actually held by the estate's executor, there has not been a complete termination. This is because stock actually owned by Jones is deemed to be owned by the estate—by virtue of Jones's beneficiary relationship. Because Jones owns all the outstanding stock even after the redemption, the estate is considered to be the owner of all the stock.

The most common form of this estate-beneficiary attribution occurs in the most typical of family-owned business situations. For instance, husband and wife both own stock in a corporation. The husband dies, and the corporation buys back all of his stock (or the wife dies, and the corporation purchases all of her stock). Although it appears that the redemption completely terminates the seller's interest, if the surviving spouse is a beneficiary of the deceased spouse's estate (as is quite often the case), stock owned by the surviving spouse is attributed to the estate. This link makes the redemption incomplete; the estate has not terminated its interest in the corporation because it is deemed to own (through its connection with the beneficiary) all the outstanding stock.

Another common fact pattern is where a father and son each own stock. Assume the father owns 500 shares and his son owns 500 shares, all the stock in the corporation. If the son is a beneficiary in the father's will, when the father dies and the corporation redeems his stock, the seller (the father's estate) is still considered to own the stock its beneficiary (the son) owns. Since at that point the son would own all the outstanding stock, the seller (the father's estate) would be deemed to own all the outstanding stock. This would make a complete or substantially disproportionate redemption impossible.

The solution to the estate-beneficiary attribution problem may be to cut off the relationship between the estate and a stock-owning beneficiary.[39] This can be done only if three conditions are met:

1. The beneficiary has received all the property to which he or she is entitled under the will or through intestacy.
2. The beneficiary no longer has any claim against the estate arising out of the estate-beneficiary relationship.
3. There is only a remote possibility that it will be necessary for the estate to seek a return of property or to seek payment to satisfy claims against the estate for administrative expenses.[40]

The distribution to the beneficiary must therefore be the entire amount due coupled with a tax apportionment agreement executed (and approved by a local court) before the redemption. Beneficiaries are legally able to determine their liability by contract among themselves and with the estate. If that agreement is sanctioned by a state court and irrevocably fixes the beneficiary's share of taxes and other expenses, that beneficiary is no longer a "beneficiary of the estate" for attribution purposes. Unfortunately, this "cutoff" solution is difficult (if not impossible) where the sole beneficiary is also the surviving shareholder.

In the previous example of Smith and Jones where Smith's estate was deemed to own stock actually owned by its beneficiary, if Jones received the watch *before* the redemption, so that Jones was no longer a beneficiary at the time of the redemption, would the result be different? If Jones made a qualified disclaimer (refused his right to the watch), would the result be different? In the authors' opinion, the answer to both questions is "yes." Both techniques should break the link needed for the attribution rules to apply.

5. Attribution to Trusts[41]

Stock owned directly or indirectly by or for a beneficiary of a trust is considered as owned by the trust unless the beneficiary's interest in the trust is a remote contingent interest (5 percent or less of the value of the trust property determined actuarially).

Assume a testamentary trust owned 25 of the outstanding 100 shares of stock of a corporation. *A*, an individual who owns a vested remainder interest in the trust having a value computed actuarially equal to 10 percent of the value of the trust property, owns the remaining 75 shares. Since the interest of *A* in the trust is a vested interest rather than a contingent interest, the trust is considered to own 100 shares. *A* is considered to own 77½ shares (75 actually owned + .10 × 25 shares).

6. Attribution to a Corporation[42]

If 50 percent or more in value of the stock in a corporation is owned directly or indirectly by or for a taxpayer, the corporation is considered to own all the stock owned by or for such taxpayer.

7. Options[43]

A taxpayer is considered to own all stock on which he or she has an option. So if Ted Kurlowicz has an option to purchase ten shares of the MSR Corporation, he is treated as though he owned those ten shares for these purposes.

Combination of the Attribution Rules

In general the rules may be applied in combination. For example, a wife will be considered to own the stock on which her husband has an option or in a trust of which her son is beneficiary. Assume Tex Kurlowicz has an option to purchase ten shares of stock; his wife Alex is then deemed to own the stock that Ted is deemed to own.

However, the family ownership rules cannot be applied two times. Stock attributed to one family member from a second family member will not be reattributed to a third family member. For example, a father is not deemed to own stock that his daughter is deemed to own by virtue of her marriage. That is, a father is not considered the owner of his son-in-law's stock. Similarly, the partnership, estate, trust and corporation values do not apply to create so-called sidewise attribution. That is, partner A is regarded as owning a proportionate share of the XYZ stock held as an investment by the ABC partnership. Partner C, another member of the same partnership, is treated as owning his proportionate share of the ABC partnership stock actually owned by the partnership. But A is not regarded as owning any part of the stock individually owned by C.

Now assume a father and son each own 500 of the 1,000 shares outstanding in a corporation. The father's will sets up both a marital trust and a credit equivalent bypass trust (CEBT) naming the son as beneficiary after the father's wife's death. At the father's death, when the corporation buys back all the stock his estate actually owns, the redemption will be considered incomplete because

- under the trust-beneficiary attribution rules the trust is treated as the owner of stock its beneficiary (the son) in fact owns; and

- under the estate-beneficiary attribution rules the father's estate is considered the owner of stock its beneficiary (the CEBT) owns.

The stock actually owned by the son is first attributed to the trust of which he is a residuary beneficiary and then is attributed from that trust to the estate of which the trust itself is a beneficiary. So even after the executor has sold the corporation all the stock the father actually owns, the estate is the constructive owner of all the outstanding stock of the business.[44]

In summary, in every stock redemption situation the constructive ownership rules must (with one exception) be applied in determining whether all the stock actually or constructively owned by the shareholder is redeemed. Under these attribution rules a shareholder who surrenders physical possession of stock to his or her corporation in return for cash and/or other property may be deemed, for purposes of meeting the three tests, to own stock even though it is actually owned by others. Often, because of this attribution, a redemption that would otherwise seem to be complete (or substantially disproportionate) is not.

Planners should keep in mind the following two rules:

1. Always suspect that there will be an attribution problem when planning a stock redemption in a family-owned business.
2. There can never be an attribution problem if the transaction is totally between the shareholders on a cross-purchase arrangement.

REDEMPTIONS USING APPRECIATED PROPERTY

When a corporation distributes property that has appreciated in return for its stock, the business will recognize gain. For instance, if a shareholder sells stock back to his or her corporation and receives appreciated real estate instead of or in addition to cash for that stock, the built-in gain is taxed to the corporation.[45] The difference between what the corporation paid for the property and its adjusted basis at the time of the redemption is the taxable amount.[46]

REDEMPTIONS PURSUANT TO DIVORCE

A court-ordered transfer to an ex-spouse of the shareholder or the transfer of stock to an ex-spouse pursuant to a settlement agreement is a common occurrence. Many buy-sells require that the corporation and then its shareholders be given the right of first refusal in such cases.

What if a court decree requires a shareholder to transfer stock to an ex-spouse and then the ex-spouse sells the stock back to the corporation under the terms of the decree and the buy-sell? Here, form is everything. If the shareholder sells the stock back to the corporation, a dividend results. But if the transfer is made to the ex-wife and she then sells the stock back, the corporation's distribution to her will not be recharacterized as a redemption of the original shareholder's stock followed by a transfer of proceeds to the ex-wife.[47]

Endnotes

1. Rev. Rul. 69-608, 1969-2 C.B. 42; 58-614, 1958-2 C.B. 920. See also PLR 9028030, where the purchase of a sibling's stock by a corporation owned by other siblings qualified as a substantially disproportionate redemption.
2. The effective rate could in fact be higher if the gain results in adjustments to the personal exemptions and itemized deductions.
3. IRC §§301(c), 316.
4. See, e.g., IRC §302.
5. IRC §316.
6. IRC §§302 to 304.
7. A distribution will also be sheltered if it qualifies under IRC §303, which is discussed in Chapter 31.
8. IRC §302(b)(1).
9. IRC §302(b)(2).
10. IRC §302(b)(3).
11. Reg. §1.302-2(b).
12. But see PLR 8909059 for a situation where a tax-exempt foundation that was the partial owner of a watercooler and dehumidifier company sold stock to the corporation in return for ten-year debentures paying interest semiannually at 9 percent. The IRS ruled that the redemption of stock was not essentially equivalent to a dividend.
13. IRC §302(b)(2).
14. This formula is built into NumberCruncher Software, which is available by calling 215-525-6957.
15. An installment redemption can qualify under IRC §302(b)(3) as a complete termination if the redeemed shareholder does not remain involved in any way in the affairs of the corporation. This means ceasing participation in management, ending access to corporate benefit plans and ceasing to be an officer in reality. But even in the absence of an IRS claim of an attribution (constructive ownership) link making the redemption less than a total termination, the IRS can claim that taking a note or other debt instrument is in reality something less than a termination of ownership interest.

   For cases involving installment payments where the taxpayer won, see *Estate of Mathis*, 47 T.C. 248 (1966), where the stock was held in escrow while the corporation made payments in installments, and *Claude J. Lisle*, T.C. Memo 1976-140, where the payments were stretched over 20 years and the court held that the redemption constituted a complete termination.

16. IRC §2703 provides that for the sale price to be accepted for federal estate tax purposes, the buy-sell agreement must be a bona fide business agreement, must not be a device to transfer assets to the objects of the transferor's bounty for insufficient consideration and must reflect an arm's-length transaction.

   While the first two requirements appear to codify existing law, both tests must be met independently; i.e., the existence of a business purpose does not—prima facie— mean the agreement is not a device to transfer assets to the natural objects of the shareholder's bounty for less than adequate consideration. The Senate report indicates that the statute takes the position discussed in *St. Louis County Bank*, 674 F.2d 1207 (8th Cir. 1982) in this regard. This third requirement is new, involves an analysis of the facts and circumstances of the transaction and places an emphasis on record keeping. Finally, the Senate report notes that the prior judicially established tests for the efficiency of evidencing federal estate tax values by such agreements must continue to be satisfied. See Mezzullo, "New Estate Freeze Rules Replacing 2036(c) Expand Planning Potential," *J. Tax* (Jan. 1991).

17. IRC §318.
18. IRC §1368(b).
19. IRC §318(a)(1).
20. In *Robbin Haft Trust v. Commr.*, 510 F.2d 43 (CA-1 1975), the taxpayer was successful with this family hostility argument. See also *Arthur H. Squier*, 35 T.C. 950 (*nonacq.* 1979), where there was bitter disagreement between an executor who held a minority interest and the family of the majority shareholder. The tax court held that the redemption from the majority shareholder's estate wasn't a dividend despite the attribution rules.

   But the absence of economic solidarity or even the presence of a bitter family feud will not ensure success. In *David Metzger Trust v. Commr.*, 693 F.2d 459 (CA-5 1982), the taxpayer lost. Family hostility was raised in *Cerone*, 43 T.C. 144 (1987), but the court totally ignored the fact that animosity between father and daughter prevented any economic solidarity. Certainly the lack of economic solidarity or the presence of family discord should not be relied on in planning.

21. PLR 9014015. See also PLR 9041005.
22. PLR 9035038.
23. IRC §§302(c)(2)(A), (C). For this purpose, *entity* means a partnership, estate, trust or corporation. IRC §318(c)(2)(C)(ii).
24. The redeemed shareholder cannot even serve as a corporate consultant serving in an independent contractor status. See *Lynch v. Commr.*, 83 T.C. 597 (1984), *revd.*, 801 F.2d 1176 (1986). See also *Chertkof v. Commr.*, 72 T.C. 92, where a complete stock redemption was followed by an agreement that gave the seller broad powers over the company.

   Nonqualified deferred compensation is not considered an interest in the corporation unless it is tied to the earnings and profits of the business. Rev. Rul. 84-135, 1984-1 C.B. 80. Likewise, according to PLR 9019047, the use of office space—for which fair market value rental will be paid—will not be considered a continued interest, nor will continued participation in the firm's group health insurance plan. See "Personal Services after Stock Redemption—the Current Status," *Taxes—The Tax Magazine* (Feb. 1986): 108.

25. If such an interest is acquired within the ten-year period, the statute of limitations is extended. IRC §302(c)(2)(A).

Can the redeemed shareholder safely form or buy a corporation that then purchases the redeeming corporation? In other words, to what extent can a redeemed shareholder engage in the same business as that of the redeeming corporation, and to what extent can the new business of the redeemed shareholder use assets acquired from the redeeming corporation without being considered a "successor" corporation? The answer seems to be that as long as the new corporation acquires the redeeming corporation's assets and not its corporate or tax attributes, the transaction does not concern a successor corporation. In PLR 9018028 the seller, shortly after his shares were redeemed, went into the same line of business on the opposite coast. He later formed a corporation that made an arm's-length purchase of a small (less than 15 percent) portion of the redeeming corporation's assets. The IRS held that this was not a successor corporation.

26. In PLR 9018028, the IRS indicated that if the redeemed shareholder creates a new corporation in the same business, which acquires assets from the redeeming corporation, this rule may not be violated if less than 15 percent of the prior corporation's assets were acquired and the businesses otherwise operated independently.

27. IRC §302(c)(2)(A); Reg. Sec. 1.302-4.

28. This ten-year rule does not apply (so the family attribution rules can be waived) if the acquisition of stock by the redeemed shareholder did not have federal income tax avoidance as one of its principal purposes. See IRC §302(c)(2)(B). See PLR 8907009 for an example of a shift in ownership that was held not to be for a tax avoidance purpose. There the shareholder was terminally ill with a very short life expectancy. To provide for the continuity of the business, he and his wife gave a son (active in the management of the business) stock.

29. This will not be a problem, however, if this person's stock is redeemed at the same time as the seller's stock or if the disposition of stock by the redeemed shareholder did not have federal income tax avoidance as one of its principal purposes. IRC §302(c)(2)(B).

30. See PLR 9023047. An exchange of S corporation stock for a promissory note was held to be a complete termination of interest in PLR 9021052.

31. PLR 9014015.

32. In most private rulings concerning promissory notes the IRS will emphasize, "In no event will the last payment on the Note be made more than 15 years after the date of issuance on the Note." See PLR 8951032, which concerned a 15-year promissory note and a final balloon payment.

33. The *Wait and See Buy-Sell* by Leimberg and Rosenbloom is available with specimen documents for $10 from Financial Data Center, PO Box 1332, Bryn Mawr, PA 19010 or by calling 215-525-6957.

34. See *Crawford v. Commr.*, 59 T.C. 830 (1973), which allowed an entity waiver of family attribution and was codified by TEFRA. See also *Rickey v. U.S.*, 592 F.2d 1251 (CA-5 1979), which held that an estate could waive the estate beneficiary

attribution rules but was overturned by TEFRA, which clearly states that an estate *cannot* waive direct attribution from a beneficiary to an estate.

35. There is, of course, always a cost or trade-off. Planners should be constantly aware of the potential for marital discord and the consequent chaos in business planning that it can cause.

36. IRC §318(a)(2)(A)(B). See LTR 9024076, where the IRS sets forth an attribution method from a sprinkle trust, based on the facts and circumstances of prior distributions to the beneficiaries, and actuarial expectancies. See Kanter and Banoff, "IRS Takes Novel Approach To Trust Attribution," *The Journal of Taxation* (December 1990): 420.

37. IRC §318(a)(2)(C).

38. IRC §318(a)(3)(A).

39. Reg. Sec. 1.318-3(a). See *Estate of Webber, Sr. v. U.S.*, 404 F.2d 411 (CA-6 1968), where the estate retained a claim against the beneficiary (the right to go against the beneficiary for any unpaid estate taxes) and that prevented a severance of the beneficiary's status as such. See Rev. Rul. 60-18, 1960-1 C.B. 145.

40. See PLR 8918056, where the IRS held that all specific legatees will have ceased to be beneficiaries prior to the proposed redemption date, they have no claim against the estate arising out of having been a beneficiary and there is only a remote possibility that the estate would find it necessary to seek the return of property or seek payment from people by contribution or otherwise to satisfy claims against the estate for taxes or administration.

41. IRC §318(a)(3)(B).

42. IRC §318(a)(3)(C).

43. IRC §318(a)(4).

44. See Rev. Ruls. 67-24, 1967-1 C.B. 75 and 71-261, 1971-1 C.B. 108.

45. PLR 9102036 involved a redemption in which the seller received cash, a note and a car. The IRS held that gain would be recognized by the corporation measured by the difference between the market value and the adjusted basis of the car.

46. IRC §311(b).

47. IRC §1041; Reg. Sec. 1.1041-1T(c), Q&A-9; PLR 9046004. If IRC §1041 does not apply, the transaction will be governed by the principles in *Palmer v. Commr.*, 62 T.C. 684 (1974), *acq.* 1978-1 C.B. 2, and Rev. Rul. 78-197, 1978-1 C.B. 83.

CHAPTER 6

The AMT Trap

To prevent a corporation from realizing large profits from a financial accounting viewpoint but reporting a much lower profit for income tax purposes, Congress imposed the alternative minimum tax (AMT).[1] The AMT is generally computed by adding back to the corporation's regular taxable income certain favorable deductions and exclusions, which are ironically known as "preference items."

The recomputed sum, known as the *alternative minimum taxable income* (AMTI) is multiplied by the AMT rate, which is currently 20 percent. If that product is greater than the tax regularly computed, the AMT is payable.

The Tax Reform Act of 1986 added a new preference item that can cause a trap for the unwary. Generally speaking, that preference item equals 75 percent of the corporation's E & P with adjustments (adjusted current earnings or ACE) less its AMTI (computed without regard to this preference).[2]

THE PROBLEM

The receipt of life insurance proceeds and the inside buildup in a life insurance policy are generally free of income tax.[3] In addition, many family-owned businesses have relatively little taxable income after the payment of compensation and other deductible items. When a corporation receives life insurance proceeds or realizes a cash value accumulation within a policy, such otherwise nontaxable sums are included in ACE and exposed to AMT even if these dollars are totally exempt from regular income tax.

Only C corporations are subject to the AMT, because S corporations generally are not subject to tax at the corporate level. The issue arises when the C corporation owns and/or is the beneficiary of life insurance policies or proceeds. This means, among other things, that C corporations with redemption agreements could face the problem illustrated by the following example:

The stock of Itty Bitty Corporation is owned equally by Brooke and Alexander, who have entered an agreement with the corporation to have the shares of a stockholder redeemed at death for $1 million. The corporation purchases insurance to fully fund its obligations. Upon Brooke's death the corporation receives $1 million of proceeds, resulting in the following computation:

Regular Tax

Assumed Taxable Income	$250,000	
Tax Rate	34%	$ 85,000

AMT Adjustment

ACE in excess of Taxable Income	$1,000,000	
Multiplied By:	75%	$ 750,000
Assumed Taxable Income		250,000
AMTI		$1,000,000
AMT	20%	200,000

Tax Result

AMT		$ 200,000
Regular Tax		(85,000)
Additional Tax		$ 115,000

Although the proceeds have been received tax-free, Itty Bitty Corporation will be $115,000 short of its goal to fund the buyout with insurance. Not only will the corporation have to look elsewhere for these funds, but economically it will have received a greatly reduced return on its insurance premium cost.[4]

ESTIMATING THE EXPOSURE

Notwithstanding the potential problem, if a fully funded redemption agreement is desirable for a C corporation, we may estimate the tax exposure and provide sufficient coverage.[5]

Referring to the preceding example:

1. State the Total Death Benefit:	$1,000,000
2. State the Cash Value (assume a term policy):	0
3. Subtract line 2 from line 1 to find the proceeds at risk:	$1,000,000
4. Multiply line 3 by .75:	$ 750,000
5. Multiply line 4 by the AMT rate: .20	$ 150,000

The amount potentially at risk is greater than the amount exposed in the example because of the adjustment for the corporation's taxable income, which, of course, will in all likelihood vary.

To fully fund this agreement in light of the amount at risk, therefore, the corporation must purchase approximately 118 percent of the targeted agreement amount, in this example $1,180,000. After applying the five-step formula, $177,000 would be at risk, leaving the amount necessary to fund the obligation.[6]

OTHER AMT FACTORS

Although application of the AMT may affect the corporation's ability to fully fund its obligation at death, it may in fact be able to recover the additional tax cost in the future. The AMT may be available as a credit against the corporation's regular income tax in future years, but not less than the AMT in any year.

Corporations have a $40,000 exemption from the AMT, which is reduced as taxable income increases. As a result, smaller preference items may be unaffected.

Corporations that pay sufficient regular tax, of course, will not be subject to the AMT.

WHAT TO DO

C corporations with existing redemption agreements should reexamine their insurance coverage and agreement terms. To address this tax trap, the following steps (some of which are discussed in greater detail elsewhere in this book) may be considered:

1. Gross up (increase) coverage (multiply the target amount of insurance by 118 percent).
2. If a redemption agreement remains preferable, a C corporation might consider electing S corporation status. The AMT does not apply to S corporations.[7]
3. If a redemption agreement is not otherwise preferable, the parties may be able to convert the redemption arrangement to a cross-purchase agreement (but beware of a transfer for value).
4. If the corporation pays a sufficient amount of regular tax, the AMT probably will not apply.
5. There is an exemption for up to $40,000 of AMTI, so only large amounts of life insurance are likely to trigger the AMT.
6. If the corporation has a net operating loss carryover, it can use that amount to help offset any AMTI.[8]
7. Any AMT generated by the ACE test is considered a minimum tax credit that can be used to offset future regular (but not AMT) tax.[9] So even if AMT is generated by the receipt of life insurance proceeds, at some point when the corporation paid regular tax rather than AMT the AMT will be recovered by the credit. This means the AMT can be considered not a permanent tax but a "loan" to the IRS.

"The end result may well be that the theoretical imposition of AMT on corporate-owned life insurance will not pose a significant problem as a practical matter."[10]

Endnotes

1. IRC §§55-59. See Jacobowitz, "Structuring and Funding a Buy-Sell Agreement for the Closely-Held Corporation," *49th Annual NYU Institute*: Chapter 3, Sec. 3.02(2).
2. For tax years beginning in 1987–1989, this preference item was generally 50 percent of the corporation's adjusted net book income less AMTI (before this item). The recipient of life insurance proceeds increased adjusted net book income but were not otherwise subject to the regular income tax. The IRS has recently issued final regulations on this book income adjustment. Treasury Decision 8307.
3. IRC §101(a)(1).
4. Computation schedule adapted from Crowell, "Corporate-owned Life Insurance—S Corporations as Solutions to the AMT Problem," *S Corporations Journal* 3 (No. 3, autumn 1990).
5. Planners Michael D. Weinberg and Larry Brody have computed a formula from which they conclude that AMT on insurance death proceeds is eliminated entirely if regular taxable income in the year of death equals or exceeds $1,071,429.
6. Exposure schedule adapted from Leimberg et al., *The Tools and Techniques of Estate Planning*, 8th ed. (Cincinnati: National Underwriter Co., 1990). See also,

Leimberg and Doyle, *The Tools and Techniques of Life Insurance Planning.* (Cincinnati: National Underwriter Co., 1992) and Zaritsky and Leimberg, *Tax Planning For Life Insurance* (New York: Warren, Gorham and Lamont, 1992).

7. IRC §56(f)(4) and (g)(6). See Crowell, "Corporate-Owned Life Insurance—S Corporations as Solutions to the AMT Problem," *S Corporations Journal* 3 (No. 3 autumn 1990): 225; Simmons, "Tax Planning for Stock Redemptions," *Michigan Bar Journal* (March 1989): 274.

8. IRC §56(d).

9. Many tax preferences postpone rather than eliminate taxes. For this reason this minimum tax credit allows corporations to recover an AMT paid in a previous year(s) if the timing differences that generated the preference reverse themselves and create a regular income tax.

10. Weinberg and Brody, "Business Life Insurance Symposium" presented to AALU 1990 annual meeting, March 7, 1990.

Third-Party Ownership of Insurance

No estate planning tool or technique is without its costs or risks. Life insurance used to fund a buy-sell is no exception; no matter what the arrangement, there are potential drawbacks.

Disadvantages of Individual Ownership

Where a cross-purchase arrangement is used and each shareholder owns the policy on the life of the others, four objections are often raised:

1. No one wants to pay premiums with personal (otherwise spendable) dollars.
2. Personal dollars are after-tax (expensive) dollars.
3. Where there are more than three shareholders, many policies are needed every time the corporation's value increases. This could become an administrative burden.
4. Multiple polices are more expensive than one large policy. For instance, one $1 million policy is less expensive than ten $100,000 contracts.

Disadvantages of Corporate Ownership

In the classic arrangement a redemption of stock in a C corporation is funded with life insurance owned by and payable to the corporation. At least two objections to this arrangement can be raised. The first deals with the possible tax at the corporate level. The second potential objection to corporate-owned life insurance to fund a buy-sell pertains to federal estate tax.

Small amounts of life insurance may be received by the corporation income-tax-free, but once a certain point is reached the corporate AMT must be considered. In a worse-case scenario the AMT on life insurance owned by and payable to a corporation could reduce the proceeds by as much as 15 percent.[1]

Life insurance proceeds are considered *tax-free* earnings and profits but then may become locked in. That is, as a general rule a subsequent distribution to a surviving stockholder of the same tax-free death proceeds could be taxed as a dividend (the *entire* amount received for the stock is ordinary income to the stockholder, and no deduction is allowed to the corporation).

As mentioned in Chapter 5, in certain cases when a corporation purchases its own stock the transaction can escape the harsh characterization as a dividend, and the redemption will be treated as a sale or exchange regardless of whether the distribution comes from capital, borrowed funds, taxable or tax-free earnings and profits.

Thus, if the transaction constitutes a complete termination of interest, a substantially disproportionate termination of interest or a redemption not essentially equivalent to a dividend, it is possible to effect a onetime tax-free escape of dollars from the corporation.

But even to the extent the dividend problem is avoided, where proceeds are paid to the corporation to some extent they swell the value of corporate assets for federal estate tax purposes. This, of course, is a moot problem to the extent the marital deduction is available, but in many estates it is not, and many state death tax laws do not provide for a marital deduction.[2]

THE "TRIPLE TAX-FREE ESCAPE OF DOLLARS" TECHNIQUE

Through the "triple tax-free escape of dollars" technique it is possible for

1. surviving stockholders to receive an amount equal to the death proceeds income-tax-free from the corporation; and
2. the deceased stockholder's estate to receive a distribution from the cor-

poration in redemption of his or her stock as a sale or exchange with no taxable gain under the "stepped-up basis at death" rule.

The triple tax-free escape can work like this:

Step 1: Life insurance on each shareholder's life is owned by and payable to a third party (such as an irrevocable trust for the shareholder's spouse or children).

Step 2: Instead of the money being paid to the surviving shareholders or the corporation at a shareholder's death, proceeds are paid to the third-party owner/beneficiary. The burden of premium payment can be relieved through a split-dollar or interest-free loan[3] arrangement between the corporation and the third party, between shareholders or between each shareholder and the trust established for his or her family.

Step 3: Upon receipt of the proceeds the third party lends proceeds to the corporation using arm's-length terms and fully collateralizing the loan.[4]

Step 4: The corporation uses that borrowed money to effect the redemption. The decedent/shareholder's estate receives cash for the stock. Because the price of the stock equals (by design) the federal estate tax value of the stock (which now has a basis stepped up or down to that point), there is no gain. So money paid by the corporation to the estate for the stock is received income-tax-free. That's the *first* tax-free escape of corporate dollars.

Step 5: During the term of the loan the corporation pays tax-deductible interest to the lender; i.e., inexpensive corporate interest payments are made to the trust that owned the life insurance. These interest payments are ordinary income as received. That's the *second* tax-free escape of corporate dollars.

Step 6: At the end of a reasonable period of time (for example, five to ten years) an amount equal to the borrowed insurance proceeds will be distributed from corporate earnings and profits to the surviving stockholder as a tax-free repayment of the loan. That's the *third* tax-free escape.

The triple tax-free escape is also known as *ex post facto thinning*. In this context *thinning* means that more money than otherwise possible is taken out of corporate earnings with minimal taxation. Usually thinning is accomplished by having shareholders contribute minimal amounts of equity and maximum amounts of debt to the capital structure of a corporation. Here the thinning is accomplished—in some cases—years after the formation of the corporation.

This ex post facto thinning technique has a number of added benefits:

- It simulates a redemption, when that type of agreement is appropriate, without concern for the effect of the alternative minimum tax trap.
- The insurance is arranged so that there is no increase in federal estate tax.
- The insurance is removed completely from the claims of the corporation's creditors (and the creditors of the shareholders).
- The proceeds cannot be locked in even if the corporation's payment for stock does not qualify for favorable income tax treatment.

There are, of course, disadvantages of ex post facto thinning:

- Creditors might complain if the corporation must borrow money to make a full stock redemption or even a Section 303 partial stock redemption.
- A corporation is forbidden by state law to purchase its own stock if the purchase would make it insolvent.
- At some point the loan must be repaid by the corporation—with after-tax dollars.
- The surviving shareholders cannot be totally sure that the third-party insurance beneficiary will lend money to the corporation at favorable terms and interest rates.
- If the third-party ownership is financed through split-dollar or group term coverage, an assignment—more than three years prior to death—is required to keep the proceeds out of the insured's estate. This in turn entails a federal estate tax risk and a loss of control over the insurance, and each premium payment will generate both potential income and gift tax costs.

Endnotes

1. See Chapter 6 for more details.
2. See Leimberg et al., *Tools and Techniques of Estate Planning* (Cincinnati: National Underwriter Co., 1992). Call 800-543-0874.
3. For detailed information on interest-free loans by corporations, see Leimberg and McFadden, *Tools and Techniques of Employee Benefit and Retirement Planning*, (Cincinnati: National Underwriter Co., 1991).
4. The loan from the shareholders to the corporation is bona fide and at arm's length: it should be at a rate of interest established in accordance with the applicable federal rate, fully collateralized and with a set date for repayment of principal.

CHAPTER 8

Use of a Trustee

Occasionally shareholders engage an independent trustee to ensure compliance with the terms of the buy-sell agreement. Basically the trustee acts as a disinterested third party on behalf of the shareholders to assure all the parties that the agreement will be carried out fairly, efficiently and objectively, according to the established procedures. The arrangement may also relieve the shareholders of bothersome administrative details. The trustee obtains physical custody of the buy-sell agreement, insurance policies, stock and collateral documents.[1]

The selected trustee is named beneficiary of the policies subject to the agreement. Usually the shareholders (or the corporation as their agent) will pay premiums directly to the insurer. The right to receive dividends and vote the stock is retained by the shareholders.

At the death of an insured the trustee collects the proceeds, applies the agreed-on valuation formulas to ascertain the appropriate price and delivers the proceeds to the decedent/insured's personal representative in an amount sufficient to purchase the appropriate number of shares. The personal representative in turn signs over the stock to the trustee, who then delivers it to the surviving shareholders.

Care should be taken when selecting the trustee, and guidelines similar to those used when choosing other fiduciaries should be applied.[2] In this regard, however, shareholders should think twice before selecting their (or the corporation's) accountant to serve as trustee. The accountant's independence is foremost and may be compromised by this role, thus disqualifying him or her from acting as an "independent" CPA. Similarly, issues of potential conflicts of interest should be addressed prior to naming the firm's attorney as trustee.

ADVANTAGES OF USING A TRUSTEE IN A BUY-SELL PLAN

These are some of the reasons a trustee might prove valuable in a buy-sell plan:

1. The trustee serves as a disinterested party who can help to carry out the terms of the party's agreements without a conflict of interest.
2. The trustee will alleviate a great deal of the paperwork and time-consuming details (such as obtaining and filing documents) that would otherwise drain the time and energy of the surviving shareholders at the very time when the business will need their utmost attention.
3. A trustee may render valuable suggestions to the parties that are more likely to be considered seriously (because of the trustee's objectivity) than if the trustee were one of the parties to the agreement.
4. In a cross-purchase plan where there are three or more shareholders, a trusteed plan that owns one policy per insured reduces the number of policies necessary.[3] Without a trusteed plan, where four shareholders exist, for example, 12 policies must be purchased.[4] The trust approach may reduce the number of required policies to OPPO ("one policy per owner"), which is where the term *OPPO trust* originates. The smaller number of policies saves money as well as reduces confusion and administrative aggravation. Shifting the policy from the corporation to the shareholders avoids the corporate-level AMT and gives the surviving owners the basis step-up advantages associated with a cross-purchase plan.

DISADVANTAGES OF USING A TRUSTEE AS BENEFICIARY

Cross-Purchase

In the opinion of the authors, there is a hidden tax trap in using a trustee to minimize the number of policies necessary. Upon the death of the first shareholder to die, his or her beneficial interest in the policies owned on the survivors' lives shifts to them. The IRS is likely to argue that there has been a transfer of an interest in a policy in return for valuable consideration (each shareholder participating in the arrangement agreed to the buy-sell provisions in return for the other shareholders doing the same).[5]

A good example of the OPPO trust technique is the "modified shareholder purchase approach" (a form of trusteed split-dollar cross-purchase) described in one article on buy-sell agreements. According to proponents of this technique, a master trust is established for all of the shareholders. Additional separate revocable trusts are established for each shareholder. Each deposits his or her shares of stock into the individual revocable trust but retains full voting control over stock placed in the trust and a conditional right to sell shares at any time during his or her life. (The right to sell is conditioned on a first refusal option held by the other shareholders; they have the right to purchase those shares at a set price.)

A split-dollar policy is purchased by the corporation on the life of each shareholder. The corporation pays that part of each annual premium equal to the annual increase in the policy's cash value. The balance of each annual premium is paid by each sharheolder for the policies on the lives of all the other shareholders.

The corporation names itself beneficiary of the insurance but endorses over to the master trustee proceeds it receives over and above the corporation's premium outlay. When a shareholder dies, the master trust purchases the decedent's entire interest at the agreed-on price.

When a shareholder dies, his or her rights as a beneficiary under the master trust "cease." Neither the shareholder, his or her estate, nor the individual trust has an interest in stock held by the master trust.

When the master trust receives the shares it has purchased from the estate of a decedent/shareholder, it distributes those shares to the surviving shareholders in the proportions designated in the agreement. The master trust continues to function until only one shareholder remains. The master trust terminates when it distributes the shares of the penultimate decedent to the last surviving shareholder.

Proponents claim that there is no tax problem with this device, but the authors of this text disagree. There are two potential transfer-for-value tax traps here:

First, when the corporation establishes the split-dollar arrangement that enables each shareholder to obtain insurance on the lives of coshareholders, it is providing insurance coverage (the "benefit") in return for the employee's tacit agreement to remain an employee; i.e., the split-dollar arrangement is an employee fringe benefit provided in return for the employee's continued performance of services. In other words, the employee/shareholders obtain insurance on their coshareholders' lives in return for their "payment" of continued service. When the corporation names the insured's coshareholder as beneficiary of the net amount at risk, there is a transfer. Thus the IRS could argue that there has been a transfer of an interest in a policy in return for valuable consideration.

If this transaction escapes the IRS's notice, it has a second chance: when one shareholder dies, the policies or interests that he or she held a beneficial interest in—through the master trust—are "transferred" to the surviving shareholders (through the master trust) to be used for subsequent purchases. This, the IRS could argue, constitutes a transfer of an interest in a policy. The valuable consideration is that each shareholder took the same risk (losing—at death—the interest held in the policies the trust held for his or her benefit on the lives of coshareholders) in return for the other shareholders doing the same.

The argument that the decedent/shareholder's interest in the insurance on the surviving shareholders "ceases" at the decedent/insured's death conveniently overlooks the reciprocity (consideration) that makes that possible. No shareholder would agree to have a property right (the ownership of an interest in policies on the lives of the other shareholders) vanish with nothing left for his or her heirs—were it not in return for the other shareholders making the same promise.

As discussed previously, if the shareholders are also partners in a partnership that is actually engaged in an enterprise, an exception to the transfer-for-value rules may apply.[6] It is not clear whether the exception would save the day if the partnership were formed at the time of the transfer as opposed to having been already in existence and functioning. The facts and circumstances of each situation, of course, will ultimately be determinative. But the existence of a bona fide partnership involving each of the shareholders as partners (and not the trusteed or escrowed plan) could solve the transfer-for-value problem.

Mention of such a partnership need not be incorporated into the terms of the corporate buy-sell, nor does the partnership have to be involved in the insurance or its transfer. It appears that it is necessary only that each of the shareholders also be partners in the same partnership and that the insurance be transferred either to a partner of the insured or to a partnership in which the insured is a partner.[7]

Such a partnership, however, must stand on its own. In other words it must be a bona fide, legitimate business enterprise carried on by co-owners who have as the impetus for the relationship a desire to make a profit. Absent these conditions, the protective exception to the transfer-for-value rule will not apply, and the policy proceeds will lose their income-tax-free status.

Finally, when insurance proceeds are paid, the corporation's split-dollar interest will be subject to the alternative minimum tax. While the sums attributable to the corporation should be small relative to the policy proceeds received by the shareholders, the corporation may not receive a full after-tax repayment of its participation in the split-dollar agreement.

Often overlooked in the OPPO literature is the shift of the premium burden to the older/majority shareholders. This allocation to the party best able to help pay the premiums is, of course, a positive aspect from a younger/minority shareholder's point of view and may be desirable or even necessary for the buy-sell to work. Yet most owners will not want to buy themselves out—or if they do, they should understand what they are doing.[8]

Stock Redemption

A trustee is sometimes used as an agent of the corporation to hold policies and administer the buy-sell agreement. In this case the trustee should be named beneficiary. Alternative minimum tax consequences, if any, would remain an issue and are not removed by the use of the trustee.

A trusteed stock redemption works this way:

1. A stock redemption plan is adopted requiring the shareholder's estate to sell and the corporation to purchase his or her entire interest upon death.
2. The corporation purchases life insurance on the life of each shareholder to fund the redemption. The corporation pays premiums directly to the insurer although the trust is named owner and beneficiary of the insurance.
3. The trust receives all the stock certificates subject to the agreement from the shareholders and holds them in trust for them.
4. When a shareholder dies, the trust receives the death benefit proceeds from the insurer.

5. The decedent's estate is paid for the stock, and the stock is then turned over to the corporation.

ESTATE TAX IMPLICATIONS

To avoid adverse federal estate tax implications, the trustee (or escrow agent) should be the owner and beneficiary of the policies; the insured should be given no incident of ownership in the policy on his or her own life. The terms of any documents should spell this out explicitly (e.g., "The insured shall possess no incident of ownership in a policy insuring his life"). None of the shareholders involved in the buy-sell should be named as trustee.

THE JOINT OWNERSHIP ALTERNATIVE

Every solution has its advantages and disadvantages, and there are always alternatives. One such alternative is joint ownership of life insurance by the shareholders. If the major reason to use a trusteed or escrowed plan is to reduce the number of policies without giving up the advantages of the cross-purchase approach to the buy-sell, where there are three or more shareholders, planners should consider having each shareholder join with the others in ownership; the result would be one policy per insured life. If there were ten shareholders, there would be only ten policies, but each would be owned jointly by nine individuals.

This alternative does not, of course, sidestep the transfer-for-value rule any better than the trusteed or escrowed cross-purchase plan. An existing bona fide partnership among the shareholders would still be necessary to fall within the safe harbor exception to the transfer-for-value rule. And it lacks some of the advantages of trusteed or escrowed plans mentioned in this chapter. But it is administratively convenient and is almost certainly less expensive if only because no drafting is required and no fees need to be paid to a trustee or escrow agent.

Endnotes

1. Some planners use an escrow agent rather than a trustee to hold the policies and stock and to deliver the proceeds and stock as ordered by the principals when the specified conditions are met.
2. See "How to Select an Executor, Trustee, and Attorney" in Leimberg et al., *Tools*

and Techniques of Estate Planning (Cincinnati: National Underwriter Co., 1992), call 800-543-0874. See also Crumbley, *The Handbook of Estate Planning,* (Homewood, Ill.: Dow Jones–Irwin Inc., 1990); and Plotnick and Leimberg, *How to Settle an Estate* (Yonkers, N.Y.: Consumer Reports Books, 1991), call 800-272-0722.

3. If an escrow agent is used, that "escrowee" will carry out the terms of the cross-purchase buy-sell agreement, which itself will generally include the terms and conditions of the escrow agent's role. However, in some cases a separate agreement will direct the escrowee to perform under the terms of an existing buy-sell that does not contain any reference to the escrow agent.

   The escrow agent would hold one policy per insured. Each shareholder would have a beneficial interest in the insurance on all the other shareholders. Premium payments could be made directly by the insureds or through the escrow agent.

   When a shareholder dies, death proceeds are collected by the escrow agent and delivered to the decedent's estate in return for the shareholder's stock. Each surviving shareholder's account would then be credited by the escrow agent with a pro rata share of the newly purchased stock. The decedent's interest in the policies on the lives of each of the other shareholders is also spread pro rata among the surviving shareholders.

4. The formula for ascertaining the number of policies that must be purchased in a cross-purchase arrangement is $N \times (N - 1)$, where N is the number of shareholders to be covered.

5. See *Monroe v. Patterson,* 197 F. Supp. 146 (N.D. Ala. 1961). See also "Stock Purchase Agreement: Redemption Usually but Not Always Preferable to Cross-Purchase," *Taxation for Accountants* (August 1978): 76. See also Leimberg and Doyle, *Tools and Techniques of Life Insurance Planning* (Cincinnati: National Underwriter Co., 1992), call 800-543-0874.

6. IRC §101(a)(2)(b). PLR 9054004. See the detailed discussion of the transfer-for-value rule in Leimberg and Doyle, *Tools and Techniques of Life Insurance Planning,* (Cincinnati: National Underwriter Co., 1992). See also Brody and Leimberg, "Transfer for Value—The Not So Tender Tax Trap," *Journal of the American Society of CLU* 1984: 32.

7. The point is that there need not be any operating nexus between the corporation and the partnership for the transfer-for-value exceptions to apply.

8. One justification for the senior owner to help a junior owner is that the senior owner is tying the junior worker into the business and enjoying the increase in value produced (perhaps disproportionately to the junior owner's salary).

Problems Caused by Unusual Beneficiary Arrangements

Generally the parties obligated to purchase stock under a buy-sell agreement should be the owners and recipients of the insurance. The surviving shareholders would own and be named beneficiaries in the case of a cross-purchase agreement, while the corporation would be the owner and recipient under a stock redemption plan. There are disadvantages and advantages to variations of these classic approaches.

BENEFICIARIES OTHER THAN THE SURVIVING SHAREHOLDERS IN A CROSS-PURCHASE AGREEMENT

Where the buy-sell obligation takes the form of a cross-purchase agreement, each shareholder should own and be named beneficiary of the policy(ies) owned on the lives of other shareholders. Many potential dangers arise when this classic ownership and beneficiary arrangement is not followed. Planners should be particularly aware of the dangers when the corporation, the shareholder's estate or the shareholder's spouse or surviving children are named beneficiary.

The Corporation

If the corporation is named beneficiary of any insurance proceeds used to fund a buy-sell agreement, the proceeds will probably be treated as a contribution of capital by the shareholders to the corporation. If the corporation then uses the death proceeds to redeem the deceased shareholder's stock, adverse income tax consequences may occur. If the survivors are obligated to pay for the stock personally, the use of corporate funds constitutes taxable dividends to the survivors.[1] It is as if the corporation had made a dividend distribution to each surviving shareholder in the amount of the payments made to the departing shareholder or his or her estate.

The courts have focused on whether or not the corporation relieved the shareholder of an unconditional, primary and currently existing obligation.[2] If a shareholder has the legal duty to pay, but the corporation directly or indirectly makes the payment on his or her behalf, that surviving shareholder will be deemed to have received a dividend in the amount of the corporate payment. There should, however, be no constructive dividend if

- at the time the corporation pays the deceased shareholder's estate for the stock the surviving shareholders had no obligation to purchase the stock but merely had an option to purchase; or
- the agreement among the shareholders allowed a survivor to assign his or her purchase right to the corporation; or
- the assignment of the obligation was made by a surviving shareholder before the shareholder was legally required to perform.

Receipt by the corporation of the life insurance proceeds could also trigger application of the AMT. This potential tax could be avoided if the stockholder/policyowner had also been the beneficiary of the life insurance.

The Deceased Shareholder's Estate or Heirs

Several problems arise when the deceased's estate is named policy beneficiary:

First, if the insurance proceeds are payable directly to the deceased's estate, the executor or administrator must then transfer the stock pursuant to the agreement. Because the purchase price and the stock are both held by the executor, both are subject to the estate's creditors (but both should not be subject to tax since this would amount to double taxation).[3]

Second, in some states, life insurance proceeds payable to an insured's estate will be subject to state estate or inheritance taxes. This needlessly subjects that money to tax since in most states life insurance proceeds payable directly to a named beneficiary other than the estate will be fully or partially exempt.

A third problem in a cross-purchase agreement—where the decedent's estate is named as direct beneficiary of the life insurance—is that the IRS might argue that the surviving shareholders are not entitled to an increase in tax basis. Since the surviving shareholders do not actually receive the proceeds, the IRS could assert that technically the insurance proceeds were not used by the surviving shareholders to purchase the decedent's stock, and thus the stock they acquire has a zero basis for federal income tax purposes.[4] Certainly, upon a later sale of the stock, the surviving shareholders will not be able to show the IRS a check in payment for the decedent/shareholder's stock.

A fourth problem is a very practical issue: If a decedent's surviving spouse or other heirs are named beneficiary of life insurance proceeds used to fund a cross-purchase agreement, the recipient may be tempted (due to misinformation or misunderstanding) to claim ownership of both the proceeds and the stock, despite contrary provisions in the agreement.[5] Since the insurance proceeds are paid directly to the personal beneficiary of the decedent/shareholder, the transfer of stock by the estate to the surviving shareholders might be considered fraudulent if the estate is left without enough funds to pay creditors.

A potential fifth problem exists when an individual owns a policy of insurance on the life of another and names a third party as beneficiary. Upon the death of the insured the policyowner may be treated as having made a taxable gift of the proceeds to the beneficiary, as if the owner actually received the proceeds and then made a transfer to the third party.[6]

A sixth potential problem pertains to basis. If the proceeds are paid directly from the insurer to the executor of the deceased shareholder's estate, the IRS could claim that there is no justification for including that payment in the buying shareholder's basis. Certainly the purchasing stockholder has no proof of the amount or date of payment for the stock.[7]

BENEFICIARIES OTHER THAN THE CORPORATION IN A STOCK REDEMPTION AGREEMENT

Where a corporation purchases policies on its shareholders' lives and the corporation is both owner and beneficiary, the premiums are not considered taxable income to the individual shareholders.[8]

Likewise, when the corporation purchases one shareholder's stock, the remaining shareholder is not considered to have received a constructive dividend when his or her stock is enhanced in value because of the purchase.[9] A mere increase in the survivor's percentage interest similarly will not cause the IRS to treat the corporate purchase of the stock as a dividend to the remaining shareholder.[10]

Where the proceeds of a policy that is owned and paid for by the corporation are paid directly to a surviving stockholder, the IRS could contend that proceeds should be taxable as a dividend.[11] This follows basic tax law: a corporation and its owners are separate tax entities, and insurance proceeds once received (tax-free) by a corporation lose their identity as proceeds of life insurance. Therefore, a later *distribution* of those proceeds to the shareholders is treated as a dividend.[12]

It is likely that the same result will apply when the corporation instructs the insurer to pay proceeds directly to the shareholder/beneficiaries. For example, in one case[13] proceeds were taxable as a dividend when received by shareholders from a trust established by the corporation (corporate-owned life insurance was placed in the trust).[14] If the IRS fails in a claim that the proceeds of corporate-owned insurance payable to a surviving shareholder are dividends, it can claim that the proceeds are taxable as compensation. Alternatively, it could treat premiums for open tax years as dividends or as compensation.

Endnotes

1. Where a cross-purchase method is used and the corporation pays premiums, those outlays may be considered a distribution of dividends to the stockholders if they are the policyowners and beneficiaries. Rev. Rul. 59-184, 1959-1 C.B. 65. Where a shareholder is the actual purchaser, but the stock is paid for by the corporation, the payment will be considered a dividend to the shareholder who made the purchase. Rev. Rul. 58-614, 1958-2 C.B. 920; *Wall v. U.S.*, 164 F.2d 462 (4th Cir. 1947); *Zipp v. Comm'r*, 259 F.2d 119 (6th Cir. 1958), *cert. den.* 359 U.S. 934 (1959); *Holloway v. Comm'r*, 10 T.C.M. 1257; *Shalk Chemical Co. v. Comm'r*, 32 T.C. 879, *aff'd* 304 F.2d 48.

   See also Rev. Rul. 69-608, 1969-2 C.B. 42: "Where the proceeds of a life insurance policy are paid to a corporation as beneficiary, the fund loses its identity after such payment, and dividends paid by the corporation to its shareholders out of such fund are taxable in the same manner and to the same extent as other dividends."
2. *Sullivan v. U.S.*, 363 F.2d 724 (8th Cir. 1966); Rev. Rul. 69-608, 1969-2 C.B. 42. This ruling states a number of alternative situations where a remaining shareholder may or may not be deemed to have received a constructive dividend upon a redemption of shares—tested by the "existing primary and unconditional obligation"

test. See also *Jacobs v. Comm'r*, 698 F.2d 850 (6th Cir., 1983) and *Gerson v. Comm'r*, T.C. Memo 1989-52. See also *Holsey v. Comm'r*, 258 F.2d 865 (3d Cir. 1958), where the remaining shareholder assigned an option to purchase the departing stockholder's interest to the corporation and the court found no constructive dividend.

3. Although the government has contended that the value of both the proceeds and the stock of the decedent should be included, this double tax liability argument has been unsuccessful in the courts. See *Mitchell v. Comm'r*, 37 B.T.A. 1.

4. See *Legallet v. Comm'r*, 41 B.T.A. 294 (1940). But see *Mushro v. Comm'r*, 50 T.C. 43 (1968), *nonacq.* 1970-2 C.B. xxii, which some authorities feel distinguished *Legallet*, while others claim it overruled the case.

5. In one case the widow did collect both due to a lack of clarity of the agreement; *Price v. McFee*, 77 A.2d 11. If the parties agree that the proceeds received by the surviving spouse or estate are to be considered as payment (or partial payment) for the decedent's stock, and then, if for any reason the agreement cannot be specifically enforced, the surviving shareholders are in an unenviable position; the estate has both the proceeds and the stock, while the survivors have only an unenforceable contractual right.

6. *Goodman v. Comm'r*, 156 F.2d 218 (2d Cir. 1946). See also Rev. Rul. 81-166, 1981-1 C.B. 477.

7. See *Legallet v. Commr.*, 41 B.T.A. 294 (1940).

8. *Prunier v. Comm'r*, 248 F.2d 818 (1st Cir. 1957); *Sanders v. Fox*, 253 F.2d 855 (3rd Cir. 1958); and *Casale v. Comm'r*, 247 F.2d 440 (2d Cir. 1957). Premiums are not taxable income to the insured shareholder where a trustee is named beneficiary if the trustee is obligated to use the proceeds to purchase the insured's stock. Rev. Rul. 70-117, 1970-2 C.B. 30.

9. *Holsey v. Comm'r*, 258 F.2d 865 (3d Cir, 1958); *Edenfield v. Comm'r*, 19 T.C. 13 (1952), *acq.*

10. Rev. Rul. 58-614, 1958-2 C.B. 920. *Holsey v. Comm'r*, 258 F.2d 865 (3d Cir. 1958). See also Rev. Rul. 59-286, 1959-2 C.B. 103, and *Priester v. Comm'r*, 38 T.C. 316 (1962).

11. Rev. Rul. 61-134, 1961-2 C.B. 250. Essentially, where the corporation has used its earnings to pay the insurance premiums and had the right to name itself beneficiary, and it names a shareholder as beneficiary, the proceeds become taxable as dividends.

12. *Cummings v. Comm'r*, 73 F.2d 477 (1st Cir. 1934); *May v. Comm'r*, 20 B.T.A. 282 (1936); IT 2131, IV-I C.B. 90 (1925).

13. *Golden v. Comm'r*, 113 F.2d 590 (3d Cir. 1940). In *Doran v. Comm'r*, 246 F.2d 934 (9th Cir. 1957), trustees purchased and were beneficiaries of insurance to be used to purchase stock of the deceased shareholders. The corporation paid the premium; the stockholders were not taxed on the proceeds but probably should have been taxed on the premium payments as either compensation or dividends.

14. But see *Ducros v. Comm'r*, 272 F.2d 49 (6th Cir. 1959), *rev'g* 30 T.C. 1337 (1958). The Sixth Circuit Court of Appeals stated in *Ducros* that proceeds paid directly from the insurer to shareholder/beneficiaries should not be taxed as a dividend. There the court held that the proceeds were not a dividend distribution but retained their identity as insurance proceeds under Section 101(a), while the IRS argued that the proceeds were in effect received by the corporation and then distributed by it to the beneficiaries.

While on its face the conclusion of the court seems patently incorrect, the *Ducros* court noted that *it had not considered whether premiums paid by the corporation were taxable to its stockholders* since that issue was not before it. However, if it were decided that the premiums were taxable to the shareholders, the decision that the proceeds should be received tax-free by the shareholders would be sound.

A number of authorities have questioned the decision in *Ducros*. See Goldstein, "Tax Aspects of Corporate Business Use of Life Insurance," *Tax. L. Rev.* 18 (1963): 133, 179–183. The IRS has refused to follow *Ducros* as a precedent in disposing of similar cases. See Rev. Rul. 61-134, 1961-2 C.B. 250.

Confusion in this area was later compounded by the tax court in *Est. of Horne v. Comm'r*, 64 T.C. 1020 (1975), which stated that where a corporation owned insurance on the life of a controlling shareholder, and where the beneficiary of the policy was that shareholder's wife (herself a shareholder), the death proceeds were not taxable as a dividend and so were excludable from income as life insurance proceeds. It should be noted that the court was concerned with the fact that for federal estate tax purposes the shareholder was deemed to own the policy while for income tax purposes the corporation was to be considered owner.

The *Horne* court felt this dichotomy was unfair. It concluded that since the IRS had already chosen to include the policy in the decedent's estate because he was considered to have incidents of ownership, the proceeds had to be income-tax-free under Section 101. (It would be unfair to claim that the corporation was also the owner for income tax purposes after claiming that the decedent was the owner for estate tax purposes.) In 1980 the IRS announced its acquiescence in this decision. The authors suggest that planners should not rely on such a favorable result in future cases.

Allocation and Economic Impact of Premium Payments

CROSS-PURCHASE AGREEMENT

Under a cross-purchase plan a disproportionate burden is placed on younger shareholders when they are required to purchase insurance on the lives of older shareholders. This factor alone causes the younger stockholder to bear a heavier portion of the premium payments. Moreover, older shareholders often have larger stock interests than do younger ones, meaning younger shareholders must own larger amounts of insurance on the lives of seniors to accomplish the stock purchase. Picture, for example, a 40-year-old who owns 20 percent of a $1 million business and who is trying to pay premiums on the life of the 60-year-old 80 percent shareholder.

When the high outlay required proves prohibitive, the younger shareholder could take one of the following measures to solve the problem:

- Purchase a combination of term and whole life or resort to the use of one-year or decreasing term insurance as a temporary measure
- Cover as much of the purchase price as possible with insurance and provide for the balance to be paid in a series of interest-bearing notes
- Purchase a smaller percentage interest than that to be purchased by those having larger interests[1]
- Have a person holding a larger interest pay part of the premiums on the insurance on his or her life and treat payments as interest-free or interest-bearing loans to be added to the purchase price in the event of his or her death

- Obtain a loan (interest-free or interest-bearing) from another party
- Agree to a split-dollar arrangement with the corporation or with the other shareholders

A few authorities believe that, aside from the cost burden, a second problem relating to the payment of premiums exists: it is possible to purchase a substantial business interest for a minimal premium outlay.

For example, Ed and Herb, both age 35, each own a 50 percent interest in a corporation with a total value of $200,000. Each will own, pay premiums and receive the proceeds of a $100,000 policy on the other's life. If Ed dies first, Herb receives $100,000 income-tax-free. If the policy has been in force for only a few years, Herb will own a business worth $200,000 at a cost of only a few thousand dollars of premiums. Ed's estate receives $100,000 in cash from Herb and also has the policy on Herb's life, which can be surrendered for its cash value or sold to Herb.

Most practitioners feel that rather than creating a problem, however, the use of insurance presents an otherwise impossible opportunity. The younger stockholder, who must pay larger premiums on the life of a coshareholder with a larger ownership interest, is encouraged by the knowledge that actuarially the chances of surviving and obtaining a larger proportionate share of the business are great. The older shareholder benefits by creating a market for his or her business and tying a key person into the business.

Alternatively, Ed and Herb could have purchased insurance on their own lives on a personal basis. At Ed's death his estate would receive $100,000 of insurance and his 50 percent stock interest. If this personal insurance were owned by a third party, it would escape inclusion in Ed's estate. Ed's stock could be redeemed by the corporation through a long-term installment payout.

STOCK REDEMPTION AGREEMENT

When the corporation will redeem the stock, the total premiums are pooled, each shareholder paying in proportion to stock interest rather than in relation to what he or she is buying. For example, under a cross-purchase plan, where Carol owns 30 percent of the stock and Mary owns 70 percent, Carol would have to pay premiums sufficient to buy 70 percent of the value of the corporation.

But in a stock redemption the corporation pays premiums. In essence Mary is indirectly paying 70 percent of the total premiums. She is helping Carol buy her out. Corporate dollars that could have enhanced the value of Mary's interest instead are used to pay premiums on her life (that will eventually benefit Carol).

If this is considered a problem, one solution is for Carol to pay Mary's estate an amount equal to 40 percent of the total premiums (perhaps together with interest) in recognition of the "loan." Mary, then, should have paid premiums necessary to purchase Carol's 30 percent interest. Mary's "actual payment" of 70 percent of the premiums could be considered (to the extent agreed on by the parties) in part (40 percent) a "loan" to be repaid, in addition to the purchase price to Mary's estate. (The same approach could be taken where one shareholder's premium is higher than normal for other reasons such as a "rating" charge for a physical impairment.)

Endnote

1. For example, the 20 percent shareholder really needs only 31 percent more to gain control and could purchase the remaining stock at a later date.

CHAPTER 11

Price and Valuation

PUTTING A PRICE ON A BUSINESS OR PROFESSIONAL INTEREST

Where the triggering event is a shareholder's death or disability, the time to set the price or establish a price-setting formula is when the buy-sell agreement is drawn.[1] Otherwise the agreement guarantees only uncertainty and increases the likelihood of litigation with both the IRS and the other parties to the agreement.[2]

Whatever the price or formula agreed on, it should be

1. reasonable,
2. fair and
3. workable.

While the specific method or combination of methods used will vary depending on the specific facts and circumstances of the case,[3] four particular methods are generally accepted for setting a price in a buy-sell agreement:

1. Book value
2. Agreed value
3. Appraised value
4. Formula value

Book Value

Book value (stated assets less liabilities) is a particularly good place to begin the price-setting process in these eight situations:

1. Where the business in question is primarily an asset-holding company—such as an investment company
2. Where the company is in the real estate development business, and assets, rather than earnings, are the key to valuation
3. Where a one-person corporation is involved—since such a business is often worth only its liquidation value
4. Where the liquidation of the corporation is in process or imminent at the valuation date. The impact of sacrifice sales and capital gains taxation, including the possibility of double taxation as a result of the repeal of the "general utilities" rule,[4] also must often be considered. In other words the true value of a business in many cases is the amount actually available to the stockholders after a sale or liquidation. This can be, and often is, significantly less than the business's value before tax, legal and accounting expenses.
5. Where the business is highly competitive but only marginally profitable. In this case the firm's past earnings record is unreliable as a tool to measure potential future profits
6. Where the assets or the business itself is relatively new
7. Where a merger or consolidation may occur
8. Where the business is experiencing large deficits

Few buy-sell agreements should use raw book value as the formula for determining price. At the least, certain adjustments should be made. This modified method involves adjusting the asset components of a business (which are carried at some figure other than fair market value) to an approximate fair market value for each such component. The balance sheet is then recomputed using these adjusted figures to arrive at adjusted book value. (It is important that the buy-sell agreement define what the parties mean by *book value*[5] since there is no universally accepted definition and also state the accounting method used to compute book value[6]).

Adjustments are necessary to reflect the difference between true market value and book figures under these circumstances:

1. When assets are valued at cost: For example, in the case of a closely held investment company the primary assets of the business are mar-

ketable securities, generally carried on the company's books at cost. Likewise, land is an asset generally carried at cost on a company's balance sheet but in many cases worth considerably more on the open market. The result is a book value that bears little or no relation to the present worth of the business.

2. When assets have been depreciated at a rate in excess of their true decline in value: For example, the typical operating company that produces or sells products or services to the public may have purchased equipment originally costing $500,000 but that on the company's books has been depreciated to $200,000. The equipment may actually be worth a lot more or a lot less than its cost—say $500,000—or the $200,000 figure at which it may be presently carried. This principle also applies to real estate, which is often depreciated much more rapidly for tax purposes than its actual drop in value. In many cases the fair market value of depreciable real estate may be substantially above (or below) its original cost.

3. For items such as probable future lawsuits or unfavorable long-term leases: These may or may not have been disclosed in the footnotes of a firm's financial statements.

4. When assets possessing substantial value have been completely written off: These reflect a total book value far below reality.

5. For assets such as franchises and goodwill: These are carried on the books at a nominal cost.

6. When the business is experiencing difficulty collecting its accounts receivable

7. When inventory includes goods that have become obsolete or are not readily marketable: Inventory may be significantly understated. For example, the LIFO (last-in, first-out) method understates the value of inventory in an inflationary economy.

8. Where insurance proceeds are received by a corporation in a redemption funding situation: As discussed previously, the receipt of proceeds would increase the value of the corporation and must be addressed in determining purchase price.

9. Where the liquidity position of the business is poor

10. When current assets are low in comparison to current liabilities

11. When working capital is inadequate or long-term indebtedness is substantial

12. Where selling expenses and capital gains taxes, corporate and/or individual, are likely to be large should the firm be liquidated.

Where the firm has more than one class of stock outstanding, a second class of stock may have preference over the class of stock in question as to dividends, preference as to assets in the event of a sale or liquidation or in voting powers. For example, the true value of the assets cannot be realized as readily by the owner of common stock if there is a voting, participating, cumulative preferred issue outstanding.

A further factor that often indicates the need for adjusting book value is retained earnings; the book value of a business might in fact be high because earnings have been retained over a long period of time. The value of the company might be lower than it appears if its current earnings are low and the outlook for increased earnings is dim. Obviously the parties should understand that book value does not recognize the importance of intangible factors such as the strategic location of the business or the effect of long-term advertising or hard-earned reputation.

After the necessary adjustments are made, the adjusted book value is divided by the number of shares outstanding to determine the per-share value. A book value agreement should be drafted to state clearly the terms and accounting method used in determining stockholders' equity.

It is extremely important that the agreement also specify the date on which the valuation will be made.[7] Consider the different results of measuring the book value on these dates:

- The date of death
- The end of the month prior to death
- The end of the last accounting period
- The end of the accounting period nearest death

Many authorities feel that the use of the book value as of the end of the regular accounting period nearest the date of death (with appropriate adjustments for the period of time between the date of death and the end of the regular accounting period nearest that date) is the most workable arrangement. But consider again the impact of, say, $1 million of life insurance and the fairness to each of the parties (not to mention the difficulty of paying for a corporation with a value inflated by the insurance) of each of the following approaches. The planning team may want to consider these approaches on the basis of who is to be favored in a stock redemption plan that uses book value in its price setting formula.[8]

To favor the surviving shareholders the planners might suggest:

1. setting the measuring date prior to the insured shareholder's death (e.g., the end of the last accounting period prior to death); or
2. setting the measuring date sometime prior to the insured shareholder's death but providing that book value will be increased by the excess of (a) premiums paid for all key employee life insurance over (b) the cash values of all such policies as of the date of the insured's death.

To favor the insured decedent/shareholder the planners could suggest:

1. setting the measuring date sometime prior to the insured shareholder's death but adding to that value the excess of (a) the death proceeds over (b) the premiums paid on the policy; or
2. setting the measuring date as the date immediately after the insured shareholder's death; or
3. providing in the agreement that in no event will the price paid for the decedent's stock be less than the amount of insurance on his or her life.[9]

Agreed Value

Here the parties specify a per-share value. This method is simple and easily understood. The certainty of price minimizes disputes among the parties, keeps accounting and appraisal fees to a minimum and makes it easier for the parties to plan their estates because they know how much their heirs can expect for their business interests.[10] A stated price is also helpful in funding the agreement—at least initially—because everyone knows how much insurance is needed. But it may be outdated after a number of years, not taking into account changes the parties could not anticipate at the time, and in family businesses a set price will probably not be persuasive as to value for estate or gift tax purposes.

A possible solution to the first problem is to provide a schedule or mechanism for periodic reevaluations and guidelines if a reevaluation is not accomplished. For example, if the parties don't get around to revaluation or if one shareholder refuses, the value may be automatically increased by an inflation mechanism such as the consumer price index.

Appraised Value

This method requires a qualified, independent third party to make an appraisal within a specified time after the valuation date. This is typically accomplished by using either appraisers or the federal estate tax value.

In the independent appraiser approach the estate hires an appraiser, the buyers hire an appraiser and the two appraisers, if they cannot come to terms within a given period of time, hire yet a third appraiser. Alternatively, the price to be paid might be set by the average of the values found by all three appraisers. The cost, aggravation and uncertainty of this method are obvious.

When federal estate tax or state death tax valuation as filed on the estate's return is used, both an ethical and a practical conflict are created for the estate's executor: On the one hand the executor wants to keep the value of the stock down to keep the death tax to a minimum. On the other hand the executor has great incentive to set as high a value as possible for estate tax purposes to "swell" the amount that will be received by the estate under the buy-sell. (If an unlimited marital deduction is available to the decedent/shareholder's estate, the executor will have even greater reason to claim the highest possible value since increasing it will not increase estate taxes but will increase the amount the heirs receive.)

Taken to its extreme, the latter measure could result in the executor's aiding and encouraging the IRS examiner to increase the valuation of the closely held stock. That, of course, would be diametrically opposed to the interests of the surviving shareholders. Think of the conflict of interest it would create if the estate's executor were also the decedent/shareholder's coshareholder and close family friend or relative.

Uncertainty of outcome is another reason that neither the independent appraiser nor the estate tax value of the stock should be used as the price-setting mechanism. From the buyers' viewpoint it is impossible to plan how much money will be needed to fund the agreement. From the family's perspective it is impossible to predict how much liquidity the estate will have or need. In fact with an appraised value price-setting method that depends on a final estate tax value, the buyer will not know the extent of the financial burden, nor will the seller know how much will be received until the estate is finally settled, a process that can take years.

Some planners, however, encourage the outside appraisal approach, fearing an IRS challenge to the agreement price may result in a tax value in excess of the purchase price. They are also concerned about possible unfairness in the apportionment of taxes among estate beneficiaries if, for example, the interest of a beneficiary was related to the sum to be received from the sale of stock.

At first glance it would seem that a simple and inexpensive alternative is to have a financial adviser such as an accountant or financial analyst set the price. But should the firm's regular accountant be used, or should provision be made for an independent outside accounting firm to do the job? The trade-off— at the very least—will be conflict of interest vs. expense. The only highly probable result will be misunderstanding and the conviction of one party that the price paid was not fair. (Before suggesting this technique, obtain estimates of the cost of a business valuation so that the parties have an idea of how very expensive, time consuming and uncertain this price-setting method can be.) In conclusion, the appraised value is used only in rare and limited circumstances.

Formula Value

There are many variations on the formulas used to value a business. Typical of them is the method called *capitalization of earnings*. To understand the concept behind it, picture three "magic money machines." When their cranks are turned, all three spit out $100,000 of U.S. currency in a year. Do they all have the same value?

Assume the first machine was built strongly and has been cranking out money for years. Everyone admired its rugged appearance and fully expected it to continue to crank out $100,000 a year indefinitely. The risk was low, and therefore investors in that machine (spelled business) are willing to accept a modest (say 13 percent) return. At 13 percent, what value does an asset have if it steadily produces $100,000 per year? Figure 11.1 shows a value of $769,231.

Assume the second machine is sturdy but not as well built as the first machine. It breaks down—not often but sometimes—and requires special skill to make it run just right. It too will crank out $100,000 a year for the foreseeable future. The risk, however, that the income stream from the machine will stop or drop is higher. Therefore investors are not willing to accept a mere 13 percent return (perhaps only a few percent more than they could have received on their money had they invested it in very safe government securities for which they would have to do no cranking whatsoever). They want at least a 16 percent return. Yet if the machine produces only $100,000 a year, how much should they invest? Figure 11.1 shows a $625,000 value, almost $150,000 less than the first machine.

The third magic money machine can be cranked only by one person. She alone has the skill and the patience to make it run and keep it going. And she is old—very old. Therefore investors in that machine want to get their investment back much more quickly; they want at least a 19 percent return for their higher risk. Since this third machine produced $100,000 a year—just like the other two—how much should they invest? Figure 11.1 shows that the value of this machine approximates $526,316.

This, of course, is a very simplified example. In real life the valuation of the machines that produce money, whether in the form of business or something else, is much more complex.

Although the principles are the same, the capitalization of adjusted earnings adds one layer of sophistication to the straight capitalization of income concept. Under the capitalization of adjusted earnings method adjusted earnings are multiplied by a factor appropriate for the specific industry at the determined valuation date. The capitalization rate varies inversely with the degree of risk and rate of return required, as is illustrated in Table 11.1. The table—which should be used only as a very general guide to the concept rather than a blindly followed solution—illustrates that the higher the risk, the lower the earnings multiplier (capitalization rate).

FIGURE 11.1   Capitalization of Income

Adjusted Earnings...$100,000

Expected Rate of Return	Value of Asset (Business)	
0.13	$769,231	(Machine 1)
0.14	$714,286	
0.15	$666,667	
0.16	$625,000	(Machine 2)
0.17	$588,235	
0.18	$555,556	
0.19	$526,316	(Machine 3)

Source: Courtesy of NumberCruncher Software, 215-525-6957.

TABLE 11.1 A Risk-Reward Chart

Risk	*Rate of Return Required by Investor*	*Categories*	*Capitalization Rate*
Low to medium	10 to 15%	Old established business with large capital assets and established goodwill. (Few businesses will fit into this category.)	10 to 7
Medium to high	18% range	Established businesses of competitive character needing highly competitive management; e.g., factories manufacturing products under patents and trademarks.	6 to 5
High	Above 20%	Businesses requiring skill in management, but no special or rare type of knowledge; earnings constantly present under highly competitive conditions; large capital not required to enter field.	5
High	Above 20%	Small businesses, highly competitive, requiring small capital.	4
Very high	Above 20%	Businesses depending on special skills of one person or a small group of people; highly competitive; small capital required; mortality high.	2 to 4
Extremely high	Above 20%	Personal business involving minute amount of capital and depending on the skill of one person.	1 to 2

A comparison of two companies, both earning $100,000 a year after taxes, illustrates the concept.

Assume company *A* is older, has a proven record of profits, possesses a strong backup management, has a substantial annual earnings growth rate and has highly favorable prospects for the future. The same investor might be willing to settle for only a 12 percent return given this lower level of risk. In other words an investor might project, say, eight years of $100,000 a year after-tax earnings as the value of the business or a total of $800,000.

Assume company *B* is relatively small and is in a highly competitive industry. It's growing but has not yet established itself. A buyer, to take the risk of purchasing this company, might require a return of 20 percent per year on his or her money. In other words, for this level of risk, the prospective buyer wants to recover his or her capital in five years or less. If the firm earned $100,000 a year after taxes, this buyer would be willing to pay no more than five times $100,000 or $500,000. And this is basically how an investor might value the firm, by multiplying the after-tax earnings by an appropriate capitalization rate. This method is often used in valuing personal service corporations.

Obviously the earnings multiplier (capitalization rate) selected will have a strong effect on the ultimate estimation of value. Remember, Table 11.1 is only a rough guideline—the rate of return demanded by a potential buyer given a specified level of risk will vary from time to time depending on the earnings rates of comparable alternative investments. Likewise, there are no "correct" capitalization rates—even the IRS uses different rates at different times and under different circumstances in its business value computations.

After-tax earnings, to which the selected capitalization rate is applied, need to reflect a realistic appraisal of the earning power of the company. Therefore the following adjustments are made:

1. Add back excessive salaries or reduce earnings if salaries paid were too low.
2. Add back bonuses paid to stockholders or their families.
3. Add back or subtract, respectively, excessive or nominal rents paid to stockholders.
4. Eliminate nonrecurring income or expense items.
5. Adjust for excessive depreciation.
6. Adjust earnings to take into consideration nonrecurring expenses, a major change in accounting procedures, widely fluctuating or cyclical profits, abnormally inflated or deflated earnings or strong upward or downward earnings trends. Earnings are usually averaged over a five-year period, and sometimes the average is "weighted" so that an upward earnings trend is given greater weight.

Per-share value is then determined by dividing the total capitalization result by the number of shares outstanding.

One variation of the adjusted capitalization method is known as the ARM (appeals and review memorandum) 34 method.[11] Although technically this device is outmoded and no longer used by IRS agents officially, in fact it is used quite often to check the reasonableness of the result obtained by a simple capitalization and also sometimes to establish the price or price-setting formula in a buy-sell.

ARM 34 combines the adjusted net asset value and capitalization approaches. Basically a five-step process is used:

Step 1. Figure a reasonable return on tangible assets.

Step 2. Deduct the result of step 1 from the annual earnings figure used. This difference should be the portion of earnings and profits generated by intangibles.

Step 3. Capitalize profits generated by the intangibles to determine what the intangibles are worth.

Step 4. Add the result of step 3 to the net worth of tangibles. This sum will be the total value of the corporation.

Step 5. Divide the step 4 result by the number of shares outstanding to determine the per-share value of the corporation.[12]

Figure 11.2 is an example.

FIGURE 11.2   Going Concern Value Using ARM 34

Average Annual Earnings...$100,000
Estimated Capitalization Rate...0.160
Average Annual Asset Value $500,000

(1) Return on Tangible Assets	*(2)* Earn from Tangible Assets ($500,000 × (1))	*(3)* Earn from Intangible Assets ($100,000 − (2))	*(4)* Total Goodwill Value ((3) ÷ 0.16)	*(5)* Total Value Assets ($500,000 + (4))
0.130	$65,000	$35,000	$218,750	$718,750
0.140	$70,000	$30,000	$187,500	$687,500
0.150	$75,000	$25,000	$156,250	$656,250
0.160	$80,000	$20,000	$125,000	$625,000
0.170	$85,000	$15,000	$ 93,750	$593,750

Source: Courtesy of NumberCruncher Software, 215-525-6957.

CONSIDERATIONS IN SETTING THE PRICE
(OR CREATING THE FORMULA)

The preceding discussion of the various valuation methods illustrates the complexity of the process. Clients must understand, then, the importance of spelling out explicitly all pertinent details in the buy-sell agreement.

The buy-sell agreement should first provide for an adjustment of book value. Then it should provide for an adjustment of earnings. The agreement should then state the rate of return to be used (or an independent standard such as Moody's bond rate or the Section 7520 rate) and the capitalization rate.

Planners also need to be sure clients understand the ramifications of setting the price at a certain level.

A high valuation, for example, means that the heirs receive more cash (and the buyers must pay more for the stock and in return receive a higher income tax basis where a cross-purchase plan is used). This seems to lead to higher federal estate taxes. But planners should keep in mind the unlimited federal estate tax marital deduction.

In contrast, a lower valuation means less cash is payable to the heirs of a deceased shareholder. The corresponding advantage is that the corporation or surviving shareholders are required to make a lower outlay.

Most practitioners tell their clients to assume that both parties (the buyer and the seller) knew everything about the business that the client knows and then ask these questions:

- What would you bid for the stock if I owned it?
- What would you ask for the stock if you owned it and I wanted to purchase it?

This "bid and asked" price technique will help establish an acceptable range or assist the parties in coming to a realistic figure that may be the average of the hypothetical bid and asked prices.

Some commentators have claimed that estate tax returns with unlimited marital deductions will not be audited because the IRS has no incentive to increase or decrease the estate tax valuation; no estate tax is payable in either event. That reasoning sometimes leads—dangerously in the opinion of the authors—

to a suggestion that the stock be intentionally overvalued. Planners should keep in mind that

- estate tax values are not conclusive evidence of the fair market value of property; and
- the IRS can impose a very substantial penalty for either undervaluation or overvaluation.

VALUING A PROFESSIONAL PRACTICE

As the first part of this chapter has shown, valuation of a business is a difficult and uncertain process. Valuation of a professional practice, with its many intangible factors, is still more complex. The rules of thumb applied to valuation of a professional practice for buy-sell purposes may differ widely among appraisers and different groups of professionals.[13]

The characteristics of a professional practice distinguish it from a regular business in many ways:

1. The expertise or, more important, the perceived expertise of the professional involved is a significant determinant of the fees that can be charged and the income earned. The provider's education, training, and experience, along with the service purchaser's dependence on the delivery of those services, are all important factors that must be considered when determining value. A patient who needs brain surgery, for example, does not shop price.
2. Higher education demands, licensing and certification requirements all serve to slow or limit entrants into professional practice. If for any reason licensing or certification is lost, the practitioner can no longer practice. Upon death or permanent disability, the professional's unlicensed or uncertified family members cannot continue the practice.
3. Reputation and recommendations are the lifeblood of the professional practice. Although significant walk-in business may result from location or advertising, many professionals, particularly specialists, depend primarily on referrals from peers and recommendations from clients for new business. Therefore trust, respect, and the likability of the practitioner are crucial to the success of the practice.
4. Substitution of one professional for another may be difficult or impossible. While one computer store or computer store operator may be substituted easily and readily for another, professional skills are, to some extent, not interchangeable. Consider a psychiatrist married to an

attorney: if illness prevents the psychiatrist from working for three weeks, her spouse will not be able to keep her practice running.

5. Another difficulty is that in most professions information constantly becomes outdated, requiring the professional to update information.

6. Goodwill—the expectation of future profits from some source other than capital (dollars) at work—is part of the value of most businesses. In a professional practice there are two types of goodwill—business-oriented goodwill (stemming from the entity) and professional goodwill (originating from the individual). For example, if a firm enjoys $80,000 of earnings on a $60,000 capital investment that can reasonably be expected to return 20 percent given the risk, then $68,000 of income ($80,000 minus $12,000) is attributable to something other than capital. This business-oriented goodwill is an asset of the practice that generates value over and above the entity's net asset value.

Business-oriented goodwill is attributable to those elements of a professional practice that are similar to a regular business: location, operating systems, staff and patient or client base. Business-oriented goodwill can have significant transferable value—value that can be sold to another licensed practitioner.

Professional (personal) goodwill results from the special characteristics of the practice, such as the reputation of the professional. Patients or clients initially visit or return to a professional because of reputation or because they have come to trust, respect, and like him or her. At the professional's death, disability, retirement or other termination, that portion of the practice income attributable to professional goodwill evaporates.

Much of the goodwill value can be transferred in a sale to another practitioner by creating a well-organized transition in which the parting professional lends credibility to the incoming professional. This may be accomplished by bringing in the new owner as a member of the firm, introducing patients or clients to that person and leaving the firm in a manner designed to maximize patient or client retention.

Valuing Transferable Goodwill

Although there are many statistical and informational sources of guidelines for valuing the transferable goodwill of a practice, the most accurate source generally is the firm's own certified public accountant. That person should examine several factors, including the following.

Projected Earnings. Projected earnings are an extension of past earnings. Financial statements and tax returns (specifically income statements and balance sheets) should be examined to determine the answers to the following three questions:

1. What is the level of gross income? Net income may be misleading since principals may be taking profits in the form of perquisites and benefits as well as salaries.
2. Is the earnings trend up or down? At least five years' earnings should be considered, and each year's amount should be measured as a percentage of a base year.
3. Have any unusual or nonrecurring factors inflated or deflated income, hidden the true situation or affected future earnings? Large pension contributions, malpractice claims, fees, court costs and salary structures should be studied particularly carefully. The inability of one or more professionals to work during the period examined will have a strong impact on earnings.

Competition. An increased demand for established practices (which has occurred in some professions because of an increase in the number of new licensees) generally increases prices. An appraiser must consider the number of other practitioners in the area and how thoroughly their practices saturate the market, as well as the price trend for services similar to those being valued.

Size of Patient or Client Base. The greater the number of current patients or clients who are satisfied, the greater the likelihood that a large number of referrals will be made to the practice. More emphasis should be given to this factor when selling the practice than when valuing the practice for purposes of equitable distribution in a divorce settlement.

Payment Vehicles. The means of payment used by the clients influences both the level and the stability of the income. Steps should be taken to measure how likely the practice is to be paid for services rendered and how soon. Government programs typically pay less per procedure than the usual fee, so the source of payment also may be indicative of how much will be paid.

An appraiser should ask the following questions:

1. How many patients or clients are seen each day?
2. Does the practice depend on any particular group of patients or clients for a significant portion of its income?

3. How many new patients or clients have been seen in the last year?
4. What percentage of patients pay bills through private insurance, Medicare, Medicaid or other sources?

Practitioner's Work Load. Income figures alone do not tell how many hours it took to generate a given level of profit. A practice that takes 40 hours of work to generate a given amount of earnings is worth more than one that takes 70 hours to develop the same earnings.

Two factors must be considered:

1. Is the practice a personal type or mass-production type? How much time spent with the patient or client was due merely to the work style of the practitioner?
2. Does the practitioner spend time on administrative matters or other problems that could be handled more efficiently and at lower cost by an office manager or other staff member?

Fee Structure. The fee structure reveals a great deal about the practice. A professional who has been consistently and successfully charging above-average fees probably has developed significant professional goodwill. If fees are average or below average, there may be a problem, but an opportunity to increase revenues may exist nevertheless.

An appraiser should ask the following questions:

1. How do this practitioner's fees compare with fees charged in the community by other practitioners of similar reputation and skill?
2. When was the last time fees were raised?
3. How often have fees been raised in the last five years and for what reasons?
4. Was there measurable resistance to the last increase in fees, such as a drop-off in present or prospective patients or clients? Would there be a sizable loss of patients or clients if a fee increase were instituted?
5. Is billing computerized, and if so, how well does the system work?

Staff Strength. Second only to the principal in importance to the value of a professional practice are the quality and depth of the staff. Staff includes non-owner professionals (who may or may not carry away clientele if they leave), paraprofessionals and clerical workers.

To evaluate this area, the following questions should be asked:

1. How long have the various individuals been with the practice? Would they be likely to stay if the owner/professional were to die, and what patients, clients or essential skills would nonowners take with them if they left? What costs would be involved in recruiting replacements and training them?
2. What duties do the nonowners in the practice perform? What percentage of the total practice can be performed without the owner/professional?
3. How well are nonowners compensated compared with similar employees in similar practices?
4. Are there enforceable employment contracts, covenants not to compete or special fringe benefits that would tie key employees to the practice even after new ownership takes over?

Location of the Practice. In general, practices located in economically vibrant and growing communities are more valuable than those located in unattractive and depressed areas. Obviously most professionals prefer to practice in pleasant and safe surroundings, and the clientele there is more likely to be able to afford to make timely payments. But this is not always true: a dentist may have a higher turnover in an area where preventive tooth care has not been stressed, and a criminal attorney may do more business in a city than in a suburb.

Ironically, a practice producing high income is not especially valuable in a community where there is a shortage of professionals; it would be relatively easy for a new practitioner to take advantage of the demand. Conversely, in a community saturated by and long settled with professionals, the start-up time and expense would be high for a new practitioner. Therefore the value of an established practice with a full appointment book and a well-trained staff is higher.

Physical and Mental Health of the Professional. Particularly in equitable distribution situations, the professional's health is a dominant valuation factor. Significant goodwill may exist if the professional is in good health and can repeat or improve on past earnings. But what if past earnings were generated by years of 80-hour weeks that are no longer feasible? For example, a surgeon who develops an alcohol or other drug dependency problem may not be able to sustain the work load undertaken only a few years earlier.

Age. This is another factor that should be given great weight in a valuation for divorce purposes. Aside from its tangential relationship to health, age can be used to indicate how long a past flow of earnings can be projected into the future. Although the earnings of a young practitioner can be projected for a longer period of time, an appraiser must consider that the earnings of a younger practitioner are lower and less certain than those of a professional close to retirement.

A SHORTCUT APPROACH TO VALUING A PROFESSIONAL PRACTICE

Since nonprofessionals cannot generally hold stock in a professional corporation and most states require the corporation or its surviving shareholders to buy back the stock within a relatively short time, a fully funded buy-sell agreement is essential to protect the interests of all parties. The parties to the agreement may establish a salary continuation plan in which the professional corporation makes deferred salary payments to the heirs of a deceased professional for two to five years.

Frequently the parties to such an agreement are unwilling to hire an independent appraiser to value their stock according to sophisticated methods appropriate in the event of a sale to a third party or an equitable distribution in a divorce. For this reason a quick and relatively inexpensive method of determining value is desirable.

The simplified worksheet in Figure 11.3 provides a quick way to estimate the worth of a physician's practice, and it can be modified for other professionals. The guidelines in the worksheet will vary depending on the circumstances. The value of a solo practice almost always is lower than that of a practice with two or more professionals. This is why many practitioners bring in one or more associates well before they retire and negotiate a buyout.

Prior Transactions Method

Perhaps the most reliable method of valuing a practice is to ascertain its price in a previous transaction when there has been a recent arm's-length sale or exchange. Consideration must, however be given to the magnitude of prior transactions. For example, the purchase of greater than 50 percent of a practice constitutes control and therefore demands a control premium. Conversely, the

FIGURE 11.3   Valuing a Professional Practice

Value of Accounts Receivable

	Age	Percent of Face Value	Example	Your Figures
Input:	0–30 days	80–90	$ 20,000	$
Input:	30–60 days	50–80	$ 50,000	
Input:	60 or more	0 unless insurance	5,000	

Buildings and Land

		Example	Your Figures
Input:	Market value of office building and land	$1,000,000	

Equipment and Furnishings

	Age	Percent of Face Value	Example	Your Figures
Input:	Less than 5 years	40% of cost	$ 30,000	
Input:	5 years or more	20% of cost	4,000	
Input:	Drugs, supplies (last 2 months' bills)		12,000	
Input:	Cash and market value of invested securities		10,000	
Input:	Goodwill (25% of annual gross)		200,000	
	Total estimate of practice assets		$1,331,000	$

Liabilities

		Example	Your Figures
Input:	Balance owed on equipment and furnishings	$ 5,000	
Input:	Salaries, bonuses, severance pay due	60,000	
Input:	Taxes due	40,000	
Input:	Accounts payable	23,000	
Input:	Insurance premiums due	70,000	
Input:	Mortgage balance	80,000	
Input:	Other liabilities	3,000	
	Total estimate of practice liabilities	$ 281,000	
	Total estimate of practice assets	$1,331,000	
	Total estimate of practice liabilities	281,000	
	Estimate of value of practice	$1,050,000	

purchase of less than a 50 percent interest typically results in a minority discount.

Excess Earnings Method

The excess earnings method is a simple, widely used and often court-blessed way of quantifying the value of intangible assets related to excess earnings. Essentially, this is the procedure followed:

1. Earnings (pretax, including the professional/owner's salary and fringe benefits) are adjusted.
2. Then the earnings in excess of those earned by similar professionals in similar practices are computed.
3. The excess is then capitalized (divided by a percentage to arrive at the capital it would take to produce it annually). The result is the estimated value of the goodwill in the practice.
4. The goodwill value is then added to the fair market value of tangible assets to arrive at a total value.

For example, assume that Doctor Know's average annual compensation for the last five years—after appropriate adjustments and weighting for its upward trend—was $180,000. Similar physicians have earned only $120,000 annually during the same time. This indicates that about $60,000 a year was earned due to something other than return on passive investments.

Excess earnings for most professional practices are capitalized at rates between 20 percent (the same as multiplying the excess amount by five) and 100 percent (the same as multiplying the excess amount by one). The median capitalization rate is 33.3 percent (the same as multiplying the excess amount by three). The goodwill values of Doctor Know's practice at various capitalization rates are shown in Table 11.2.

How does the appraiser know what rate to use? There is no fixed and certain answer. A good appraiser will consider such things as

- how many more productive years the professional has;
- where in the income-producing cycle the professional was on the valuation date (the highest income-producing years for most professionals occur between ages 45 and 55); and
- changes in the profession, the economy and government regulation (for

TABLE 11.2 Goodwill Values of Doctor Know's Practice

Rate	Adjusted Excess	Multiplied By	Value
20%	$60,000	5	$300,000
25	$60,000	4	$240,000
33	$60,000	3	$180,000
50	$60,000	2	$120,000
100	$60,000	1	$60,000

instance, skyrocketing malpractice costs are rapidly changing the practicing environment, causing many professionals to change the way they work).

Most appraisers working with professional corporations will be conservative and use a relatively high capitalization rate, such as 50 to 100 percent (meaning a low multiplier), because it is more difficult to maintain excess earnings than earnings produced by passive income investments and because total earnings have been used as a base. If pretax earnings after reduction for owner's compensation and benefits are used, a 20 to 40 percent capitalization rate becomes more appropriate.

As is the case with any valuation method, the excess earnings concept has its drawbacks. First, goodwill can be understated because even a practice without excess earnings may have considerable worth. Second, goodwill can be overstated because it does not consider whether or not the practice is marketable. Third, many subjective judgments are required, such as the appropriate weight to give the trend of earnings, the adjustments to make to earnings and the capitalization rate to use.

Capitalization of Billings Method

A practice can be valued by dividing the cost of capital into net income. For example, if the practice produced an adjusted net income of $100,000 (after owners' salary), and it was assumed that capital should be "costed" at 20 percent (i.e., a buyer taking a similar risk and hoping for a similar opportunity would demand a 20 percent return on his investment), the practice would be worth $500,000.

Some practices have been valued for buy-sell purposes by simply multiplying one, two or three times gross (or net) earnings or a fraction of earnings—such as 50 percent or 75 percent. For instance, if the gross earnings of the firm were $100,000 a year, the parties might agree that the firm was worth a total of three times that, $300,000 or 50 percent of gross earnings, $50,000.

Rough Rules of Thumb

Almost all financial planners use rules of thumb in their practices. Rules of thumb (often called SWAG—scientific wild asset guess) are the by-product of experience. They lie between calculations and pure conjecture and serve as starting places in the valuation process, later to be abandoned or modified. They also can be used where more precise methods are impractical. Some rules of thumb for various professions follow:

- *Medical:* Net asset value plus 20 to 40 percent of annual revenue for goodwill. Referral practices are worth less while continuing client base practices are worth more.
- *Veterinary:* Net asset value plus 60 to 90 percent of annual revenue for goodwill.
- *Legal:* Because a client's files cannot be sold in most states, personal goodwill typically does not enter into the valuation process. Therefore net asset value is the major value determinant.
- *Accounting:* Net asset value plus a goodwill payment of 80 to 130 percent of annual revenue (paid out over time). Another method uses 20 percent of projected fees for, as an example, five years, discounted for both attrition and the time value of money.
- *Dental:* Net asset value plus 30 to 40 percent of annual revenues for goodwill.
- *Engineering:* Net asset value plus 25 to 50 percent of annual revenues for goodwill. Firms with few continuing clients would have little if any goodwill.

Data Needed in the Valuation Process

For a thorough evaluation, valuation experts should review each of the following items:

- The last five years of profit and loss statements and balance sheets (certified financial statements by an independent CPA firm preferred)

- Federal income tax returns for the last five years
- Copies of any business leases
- Copies of fee schedules for the last five years
- Copies of any brochures about the firm
- Articles of incorporation, bylaws and minutes of board and directors' meetings for the last five years
- Appointment books for the last five years
- State employment research data (particularly information from the state professional licensing department)
- Demographic and practice economics information available from state or county professional societies, such as the state or local medical or bar association

This, of course, is merely a summary of only the most important factors to consider. The worksheet in Figure 11.3 is likewise a simplification for introductory analysis.

Definition of Worksheet Terms

Accounts Receivable. This is the amount of money due the practice for services already rendered. Sellers sometimes retain accounts receivable to keep the sale price down. The purchaser may want a practice with accounts receivable to maintain contact with the patients or clients (similar to purchasing a customer list). Bills outstanding for more than one year are considered uncollectible, while those that have been turned over to collection agencies are not considered part of accounts receivable.

The worksheet shows that accounts receivable within 30 days of billing should be worth between 80 and 90 percent of their face value. Between 30 and 60 days, the value drops to between 50 and 80 percent. In most practices accounts receivable are worth little after 60 days unless a government agency or private insurer will pay the claim.

Buildings/Land. The fair market value of the real estate owned by the practice must be used rather than the book value.

Equipment/Furnishings. Equipment depreciates rapidly, partially due to wear and partially due to obsolescence caused by the introduction of more effective, efficient or easier-to-use technology. Some appraisal experts suggest that each item be priced between original cost and present book value. The worksheet suggests that equipment that is less than five years old be listed at 40 percent of its cost. Equipment more than five years old should be valued at about 20 percent of cost.

Drugs/Supplies. Most physicians have at least a two-month supply of drugs and other supplies. Divide the annual supply by six. Unused disposables typically are worth their cost less 10 to 20 percent, although a buyer may not choose to use what is currently in inventory, which would further reduce the value.

Goodwill. In determining goodwill, the worksheet rule of thumb of 25 percent of annual gross can be used. As an alternative, another commonly used guideline is base goodwill on $3 to $5 per record of each patient seen on a regular basis.

Equipment. A potential purchaser views equipment as capital that will have to be replaced.

Pegging the Price for IRS Estate Tax Valuation

Most shareholders of closely held corporations restrict the marketability of coshareholders' stock through purchase options or mandatory buy-sell agreements. Can that argument bind the IRS to accept the value set by the parties?

The answer is clearly no. No matter what the parties say or do, the IRS and the courts are *never* conclusively bound to the price set in the agreement. (Planners should also keep in mind that the Internal Revenue Code imposes stiff penalties for "valuation understatements."[14]) But typically courts will override the IRS and go along with the established price as long as certain tests, described in the following list, are met. If the terms of such agreement definitely fix the values of the shares in question, typically it is not necessary to examine either book value or earnings. The price fixed in the restrictive agreement will serve as the shares' fair market value for purposes of determining the obligations of the parties to the agreement.

To peg the value of such stock for federal estate tax purposes, historically the agreement has had to meet these tests:

1. The agreement as to per-share value must be made at arm's length and must have been reasonable, fair and adequate at the time the agreement was executed.
2. The agreement must be binding during the lifetime of the stockholder; i.e., the stockholder must be obligated to offer the stock to the corporation or other shareholders ("first offer" commitment) at the specified offer price before offering it to an outsider if the stock is to be disposed of during lifetime. The lifetime price cannot exceed the price at death.
3. The agreement must be "binding" at death—the stockholder's executor must be legally obligated to sell the shares to the corporation at the price fixed by the agreement.
4. The price stated in the agreement must either be fixed (e.g., fixed dollar price or book value on the repurchase date) or determinable according to a formula.

As mentioned, under no circumstances will the IRS consider itself absolutely and unequivocally bound to a valuation merely because there is a buy-sell agreement. But when the preceding four criteria have been met, the IRS has generally abided by the price—when those involved were not related by blood or marriage. The Treasury believes that taxpayers in general tend to keep values low, and this suspicion increases when an agreement is solely or mainly between family members. Therefore, restrictions that tend to limit the value of family-owned closely held stock will be scrutinized closely to determine whether or not the agreement is a bona fide arm's-length business arrangement or just a device to pass on the decedent's shares for less than adequate consideration.

Chapter 14 Rules for Family Business

IRS and congressional concern over family members utilizing buy-sell agreements to freeze or otherwise reduce the value of stock for estate tax purposes led to the introduction of legislation in this area. First Congress sought to address this issue (and others) through the best-left-forgotten IRC §2036(c). When all agreed that the provision was unwieldy and ill conceived, Section 2036(c) was repealed retroactively in the Revenue Reconciliation Act of 1990, which in turn introduced the new IRC Chapter 14, dealing exclusively with valuation issues.

IRC §2703 of Chapter 14 discusses under what conditions the price set in an agreement will help to peg the federal estate tax value. If these conditions are not met, the IRS and the courts will be free to disregard entirely the terms of a buy-sell agreement between family members.

The following three tests *each* must be satisfied when family-owned businesses are involved:

1. The buy-sell must be a bona fide business arrangement.[15]
2. The arrangement must not be a device to transfer property to natural objects of the decedent's bounty for less than full and adequate consideration.[16]
3. The terms of the arrangement must be comparable to similar arrangements entered into by persons in an arm's-length transaction.[17]

While the "business purpose" and "device" tests appear to be codification of the law as it has developed historically, Section 2703 requires that each standard be satisfied independently of the other. (Under case law it had been thought that if a "business purpose" were established for the agreement, the transaction would not be viewed as a "device."[18])

The "arm's-length transaction" test is a new requirement and raises the question of what types of records or other documentation taxpayers must maintain to establish that the standard has been met.

In addition to these three tests, the IRS is expected to examine whether the agreement satisfies existing case law (except as it may have been superseded by the new law).[19] In other words the first three of the four general tests applicable to nonfamily businesses must also be met. The new standards are effective for existing agreements that are substantially modified, or new agreements executed, after October 8, 1990.

The types of restrictive agreements that have successfully pegged the value of stock for estate tax purposes are as follows:

- Reciprocal options among stockholders, during life and death; under an option a specified person is given the right to purchase the stock at a designated price for a fixed period of time. Here the buyer controls the event.
- Options granted to one stockholder only (but the price must be fair and arrived at by arm's-length bargaining). Intrafamily arrangements in this category will be suspect.
- Options granted to the corporation.

- Mandatory buy-sell (cross-purchase and stock redemption) agreements under which the estate of a deceased stockholder must sell and the corporation (or other stockholders) must buy at a predetermined price or according to a predetermined formula. The obligation to sell at the agreed-on price, however, must be binding, not only on the decedent's executor at his or her death but also on the stockholder during lifetime. The price at death will not control if a shareholder is free during lifetime to realize a higher price. Restrictions effective only during the decedent's lifetime but not at death are equally ineffective. In a mandatory buy-sell agreement neither party controls the triggering event.

A mere right of first refusal, which requires that any shares offered for sale must first be offered to the corporation (or other shareholders) at the proposed transfer price, does not conclusively peg the value of the stock.

Buy-sell restrictions on the transfer of closely held shares are never conclusive as to value for gift tax purposes but are a factor to be considered in arriving at valuation.

Endnotes

1. When the provision pertains to lifetime sales, instead of a set price the agreement may specify that the potential seller must first offer the stock to the corporation and/or the other shareholders at whatever price desired. If the offer is rejected, the shareholder is free to sell the stock to an outsider—but at a price no lower than that offered to the corporation or other shareholders. Note that if the lifetime price can exceed the price at death, the price will probably not set the shares' federal state or gift tax value.
2. See Hunsberger, "Owners and Estates: a Buy-Sell Primer," *Journal of the American Society of CLU & ChFC* (Sept. 1991): 48.
3. Solk and Grant, "Valuation Techniques for the Closely-Held Enterprise," *Commercial Law Journal*, 92: 255; Janiga and Harrison, "Valuation of Closely Held Stock for Transfer Tax Purposes: The Current Status of Minority Discounts for Intrafamily Transfers in Family-Controlled Corporations," *Taxes* (May 1991): 309; Ellsworth, "Valuing a Closely Held Business: Choosing the Right Approach," *The Journal of Taxation of Estates and Trusts* (Summer 1991): 23; Abbin, "IRS Valuation Process Receives a Billion Dollar Setback," *The Journal of Taxation* (May 1990): 260; Bolten, "Discounts for Stocks of Closely Held Corporations," *Trusts and Estates* (December 1990): 47; Herpe and Howard, "Minority Discounts Revisited: The Estate of Murphy," *Trusts and Estates* (December 1990): 35.
4. General Utilities, 296 U.S. 200 (1935). This case held that upon liquidation a corporation would not recognize gain on the distribution of appreciated assets, but the stockholders would recognize gain on the growth in their investment. But the

Tax Reform Act of 1986 repealed this doctrine. Now a corporation must recognize gain when it distributes property as payment for its stock in a redemption just as if it had sold the property to the selling stockholder. The stockholder then recognizes gain on the distribution (either as a dividend or as a capital gain); hence the so-called double taxation.

5. Where only one class of stock is outstanding, book value is typically found by adding (a) surplus of the corporation to (b) capital paid in for stock and then dividing that result by the number of outstanding shares.

If there is more than one class of stock outstanding:

a. Determine the total book value as above.
b. Determine the per-share value of the preferred.
c. Subtract the value of preferred stock from the total book value to find the value of the common.

6. Donald, 106-5th T.M., Corporate Buy-Out Agreements suggests that if books are kept on a cash basis, book value will not reflect either accounts receivable or accounts payable (although both should be considered in the agreement). Planners should also check the agreement to see if it provides for a reserve for income taxes payable on accumulated earnings. If not, insert a provision reducing book value by the amount of income taxes payable.

7. Two state courts have construed two buy-sell agreements to the detriment of the deceased shareholder's heirs in one case and a retiree in the other.

In *American Bank & Trust Co., of Pa. v. Lied*, 409 A.2d 377 (Pa., 1979), the buy-sell agreement provided that at the death of either Ray or his son Eugene, the sole shareholders, the corporation must buy the stock at book value. Eugene predeceased Ray by nine days. Eugene's estate asserted that the closeness of the two shareholders' deaths frustrated the purpose of the buy-sell agreement, and thus it should not be considered for estate tax valuation purposes. However, the court disagreed; Eugene's stock was valued at book value for an amount of $133,000, and Ray's was valued at $540,000. Thus Ray's estate benefited from the increase in the value of the stock after Eugene's death. Many buy-sell agreements contain a termination clause in the event of death of multiple stockholders within a stated period of time.

In *Lane Gelety Woolsey and Centrone, P.A., Inc., v. Woolsey*, 377 So.2d 743 (Dist. Ct. App. Fla., 1979), the buy-sell agreement stated that upon the retirement of any shareholder his stock would be bought by the corporation at book value, excluding accounts receivable. When Dr. Woolsey retired, he asked for one-quarter of the accounts receivable on a theory of unjust enrichment to the other three shareholders. The court allowed only book value; the court felt "a bargain is a bargain."

8. Donald, 106-5th T.M., Corporate Buy-Out Agreements. Since neither the cash values nor the death proceeds have any effect on the value of stock when a cross purchase arrangement is used, this type of agreement is a potential solution to the inclusion of life insurance problem in price setting.

9. To the extent that the insurance is greater than the value of the stock, this provi-

sion will enrich the deceased shareholder's estate at the expense of the surviving shareholders.

10. To avoid disagreements, misinterpretations and potential disputes, the agreement itself should specify that the agreed-on price takes into account all factors such as goodwill and other intangible assets. The agreement should also provide how value is to be allocated between classes of stock if more than one class is outstanding. If the agreed value is per share, the buy-sell should specify what happens if the number of shares increases (e.g., through stock splits, a recapitalization or stock dividend).

11. A.R.M. 34, 2 C.B. 31 (1921). See Rev. Rul. 68-609, 1968-2 C.B. 327, superseding and restating A.R.M. 34, 2 C.B. 31 (1921), as modified by A.R.M. 68, 3 C.B. 43 (1921).

12. See also Rev. Rul 68-609, 1968-2 C.B. 327, which superseded A.R.M. 34, and Rev. Rul. 59-60, generally outlining valuation of closely held corporate stock.

13. Two highly recommended texts are Pratt, *Valuing Small Businesses and Professional Practices* (Homewood, IL: Dow Jones–Irwin, *n.d.*) and Schnepper, *The Professional Handbook of Business Valuation* (Reading, MA: Addison-Wesley, *n.d.*). NumberCruncher Software provides a quick, simple and cost-effective way to estimate business values. Call 215-525-6957. Biz-Kit, a business valuation, projection and analysis software package from Financial Data Center (215-525-6957) is a sophisticated yet easy-to-use tool in valuing closely held corporations.

    See also the following for useful information: Skoloff, "The Valuation of a Professional Practice and Professional Goodwill," *ALI–ABA Course Materials Journal* 16 (No. 1): 81; Skoloff and Orenstein, *When a Lawyer Divorces: How to Value a Professional Practice* (Chicago: American Bar Association, *n.d.*); Moyse, "The Valuation of Existing Business in a Life Insurance Practice," *Journal of the American Society of CLU & CHFC* (July 1990): 66; Evans, "On the Block," *Financial Planning* (March 1990): 67; Cohrs, "Guidelines for Purchasing an Accounting Practice," *The Practical Accountant* (August 1989): 17; Fairchild and Fairchild, "How to Value Personal Service Practices," *The Practical Accountant* (August 1989): 27; Veres, "Elusive Equity," *Financial Planning* (September 1989): 102; Popell, "Case Study Illustrates a Mediation Approach to Valuing the Small Professional Firm," *Community Property Journal* (winter 1984): 39.

14. IRC §6662. This penalty is equal to 20 (or 40) percent of the estate or gift tax underpayment—depending on the extent of the undervaluation—if the value stated on the estate's (or gift tax) return is one-half or less of the "correct" value.

15. IRC §2703(b)(1).

16. IRC §2703(b)(2).

17. IRS §2703(b)(3). This does not mean the IRS is free to disregard the terms of an agreement merely because its terms differ from those used by a similarly situated company. More than one method of valuation may be appropriate even within the same industry. See Conference Report at 1137.

18. The Senate Finance Committee Report indicates an intention to conform with *St. Louis County Bank*, 674 F.2d 1207 (8th Cir., 1982), which held that preserving control of a business within a family in and of itself does not show that there was no "device." See also Mezzullo, "New Estate Freeze Rules Replacing 2036(c) Expand Planning Potential," *J. Tax.* (Jan. 1991).

19. Senate Finance Committee Report, 101st Congr., 2d Sess. 1990.

CHAPTER 12

The Effect of Death Proceeds on the Purchase Price

One of the first steps in deciding how shareholders should arrange for life insurance in a corporate buy-sell agreement is to determine how the life insurance is to be used or what purpose it is to serve. Only after the appropriate price or formula is determined and agreed on should life insurance enter into the decision-making process.

Life insurance should be viewed as a funding tool rather than as a measuring device. That is, how much a deceased shareholder's estate is to receive should not be based on the existence or nonexistence of insurance policies.[1] (There are, however, situations in which it is proper to make the purchase price the higher of a specified amount or the insurance proceeds received.) The price to be paid should not be tied mechanically to the insurance proceeds for these reasons:

1. If the policy lapses, there will be no proceeds.
2. If the insurer successfully contests a death claim during the one- or two-year contestable period, a return of premiums might be the sole payment from the policy.[2] Conversely, sometimes more cash than expected is received due to accidental death benefits, dividends or a return of unearned premiums.
3. In a redemption agreement, if the corporation is subject to the alternative minimum tax, it may net insufficient proceeds to pay the purchase price.

PROBLEMS UNDER A CROSS-PURCHASE AGREEMENT

Generally speaking, insurance funding does not affect the purchase price in a cross-purchase arrangement. However, it could be argued that where the policies owned by the shareholders are funded through a split-dollar arrangement, the proceeds should be taken into account to some extent because the corporation has provided all or a large portion of the premium outlay.

PROBLEMS UNDER A STOCK REDEMPTION AGREEMENT

When the corporation purchases the decedent's stock, the surviving shareholder could receive a windfall. For example, assume Owen and Barry were equal shareholders in a corporation worth $500,000. Under a stock redemption arrangement the corporation would purchase a $250,000 policy on each man's life. When Owen died, the corporation would receive $250,000 in proceeds, increasing its value to $750,000. If Owen's estate were then paid $250,000, Barry, the surviving shareholder, would own a corporation worth $500,000 (a windfall of $250,000) plus the cash values of the policy on Barry's life. Owen's heirs would receive no benefit from the $250,000 of life insurance.

Receipt of the insurance proceeds should increase the value of the deceased shareholder's stock. If the stock is to be redeemed at fair market value, the corporation will need sufficient liquid assets to cover the added value generated by the insurance.

One solution is to have the formula for determining the purchase price of the stock include a proportionate part of the proceeds of the policy on Owen's life and a proportionate share of the cash value of the policy on Barry's life.[3] This would underfund the buy-sell and entail the purchase of additional insurance to adequately fund the obligation, and unfortunately this measure has a spiraling effect—more insurance would further raise the value of the decedent's stock and spiral the dollar obligation upward.[4] The situation may be further aggravated if additional insurance is to be purchased to cover any shortfall resulting from the AMT.

A potential solution would be to omit insurance proceeds entirely from the valuation formula, but this brings us full cycle. The deceased shareholder receives true value for his or her stock, but the survivors are favored because they receive a windfall in the form of the death proceeds from the life insurance.[5]

There is a middle ground; the purchase price could include the greater of (a) premiums paid to the date of the shareholder's death or (b) the policy's cash value at that time, plus the cash value of the policy on the life of the surviving shareholder.[6]

Endnotes

1. See Horvitz, "Life Insurance as a Planning Tool: Use of Insurance to Fund Partnership Buy-Sell Agreements," *NYU Institute of Taxation* 32 (1974).

   An interesting argument is made in Stern, "A Different Approach to Price Fixing in Stockholder's Stock Purchase Agreement," published in the *CLU Journal* (April 1974): "I have abandoned the quest for the 'true value' of the stock. . . . I now urge clients to consider fixing the highest price for the stock that they can afford to have their corporation fund through insurance, after taking into account pension and profit-sharing plan death benefits and other life insurance the business pays for."
2. Leimberg and Doyle, *Tools and Techniques of Life Insurance Planning*, (Cincinnati: National Underwriter Co., 1992).
3. Strouch, "Buy-Sell Agreements for Close Corporations," *Successful Estate Planning Ideas*, ¶2035 (Englewood Cliffs, N.J.: Prentice-Hall, 1975).
4. See Kahn, "Mandatory Buy-Out Agreements for Stock of Closely-Held Corporations," *Mich. L. Rev.* 68 (1969): 38. If the proceeds of insurance are considered in determining the purchase price, more insurance is necessary since the formula in effect requires "insurance on insurance."

   On the other hand, if the proceeds are not considered in determining the purchase price, the arrangement may be unfair to the decedent/shareholder. Although his or her interest would have been charged with a proportionate share of the premium costs, that outlay would not be reflected in the amount received from the stock surrendered. The harshness is magnified if there is a sizable disparity in premiums because of differences in the shareholders' ages or if other shareholders were insured at substandard rates.
5. Would an agreement that omits the life insurance meet Chapter 14's Section 2703 tests? In the authors' view, this is unlikely.
6. An alternative would be to fund the agreement only partially with insurance, arrange for an installment payout of any cash deficiency and thus make adjustments necessary to eliminate the unfairness without increasing the amount of insurance.

CHAPTER 13

Type of Insurance
To Be Used

TERM VS. PERMANENT

The primary question in most cases is: *how much* insurance is enough? Once that figure is known, the premium costs often will determine what type is right. Only after an adequate amount can be obtained under either term or whole life does the question of type of coverage become meaningful.

The most important rule of planning is: *Match the product to the problem!*[1]

If the insurance is designed to cover a death need only, and the agreement is not likely to continue beyond the shareholders' 65th or 70th birthdays, pure term insurance may suffice. Although term coverage eventually runs out, with renewal potential or with burdensome premium increases, it has two distinct advantages:

1. The initial outlay is low compared to permanent (cash value) protection.
2. If the after-tax earnings of the business are high enough, the time value of money may indicate the use of term, provided the corporation "invests the difference" in the business and does so on a long-term, continuously profitable (after-tax) basis.[2] (Although this may work in theory, the authors have found that it seldom is the best course of action in actual practice.)

Although initial costs are usually higher for permanent (whole life) insurance than for an equivalent amount of term, using whole life to fund a buy-sell plan has several advantages:

1. The policy can be continued regardless of the ages of the shareholders, and the premium remains level indefinitely (if dividends are paid, the premium may decrease or even "disappear," or benefits can increase—depending on the dividend option selected), while term insurance either expires or becomes prohibitively expensive as the shareholders grow older. Conversion from term to permanent coverage, if allowable, is often incredibly expensive at advanced ages.

2. Cash values of whole life contracts (resulting from reserves designed to keep the policy in force through the payment of level premiums until the insured's actuarial death age) can be used to provide a low-cost loan or collateral assets for a business need or to fund a lifetime buyout. There are no cash values in term insurance.

3. Cash values can also be used in the retirement of a shareholder, can serve as security for both the corporation and the individual shareholders and can even be used as a source of funds to make a down payment for the acquisition of the insured's stock during life. Over the long run this type of insurance is often more useful in funding business purchase agreements because of its flexibility.[3]

Alternatively, a universal life policy may offer much needed flexibility, albeit with some increased risk. This product may be purchased with a level death benefit or an increasing death benefit to assist in addressing the future growth in value of the corporation. Moreover, the level of premium payments may be adjusted from year to year, or even not paid in a particular year, without causing a lapse in the policy. Of course reduction in the premium payments may cause a reduction in death benefits, but from a cash flow point of view flexibility is preserved.[4] The added risk in this product arises from whether the insurer's investment performance can approach illustrated interest returns on the basis of which many of these policies are sold.

SPECIAL CONSIDERATIONS FOR CROSS-PURCHASE PLANS

Because premiums will be paid with after-tax personal dollars when the cross-purchase approach is used, term insurance may be indicated in limited situations where cash flow is a major consideration. The term can be converted gradually to whole life insurance. Alternatively, low-cash-value (and correspondingly low-premium) permanent policies are available and are commonly used. These include "modified" contracts that provide for a premium lower than normal during the first three, five or even ten years and "step-rate" policies in which premiums increase gradually in steps on a year-by-year basis.

SPECIAL CONSIDERATIONS FOR STOCK REDEMPTION PLANS

The possible effect of the accumulated earnings tax must be considered in selecting the appropriate type of coverage. Whole life, term policies or some combination of these types is generally used. High-cash-value endowment or retirement income policies are inappropriate in most situations and could have adverse alternative minimum tax implications.

Endnotes

1. Leimberg and Doyle, *Tools and Techniques of Life Insurance Planning*, (Cincinnati: National Underwriter Company, 1992). Call 800-543-0874.
2. The internal rate of return for a whole life policy issued by a high-quality insurer today should be—after tax—7 to 9 percent, assuming death occurs at life expectancy. Of course, if death occurs earlier, this rate of return is likely to be significantly higher.
3. The authors are familiar with a situation where two of three stockholders in a corporation were permanently disabled. Because of a waiver-of-premium feature in the whole life contract, the death benefits under the policies were maintained at the same levels, and cash value and dividend buildup were not interrupted. Cash that previously had been paid as premiums to the insurance company was now available (on a tax-deductible basis) to the shareholder/employees as sick pay.
4. In a comparison with term insurance, the time value of corporate dollars should be considered.

CHAPTER 14

Use of Existing Insurance

PROBLEMS UNDER A CROSS-PURCHASE AGREEMENT

Existing insurance on the lives of the individual shareholders should not be transferred between the shareholders, because the death proceeds will become subject to the transfer-for-value rule.[1] For example, Mark and Dave, two shareholders, each own policies on their own life. Mark transfers a policy on his life to Dave. In consideration of Mark's transfer, Dave reciprocates. There has been a transfer for value.[2]

The entire proceeds received by the survivor (less the value of the contract exchanged plus premiums paid by the survivor after the transfer) will be subject to ordinary income tax. Likewise, if a corporation sells existing key executive policies on a shareholder's life to a coshareholder to fund the buy-sell agreement, there has been a transfer for valuable consideration.

It is important to note that the consideration need not be in monetary form.[3] A term or fully loaned policy, without cash value, is subject to the rule as fully as a permanent or endowment policy when transferred for any kind of valuable consideration.[4]

Perhaps the most insidious example of this tax time bomb occurs where no consideration seems to change hands. In one case the transferee relieved the transferor of certain obligations but paid no purchase price for the policies, and the transaction was seen as having been for a valuable consideration.[5]

A change from a stock redemption arrangement to a cross-purchase plan in which corporate-owned policies on the lives of shareholders are sold to shareholders other than the insured falls squarely within the transfer-for-value trap. The problem cannot be avoided by a double transfer, first to the insured and then to another stockholder in return for a reciprocal transfer. The reciprocity itself forms the valuable consideration. But the transfer-for-value problem may be avoided if the shareholders are also partners, as discussed later in this chapter.

PROBLEMS UNDER A STOCK REDEMPTION AGREEMENT

Policy transfers from a shareholder/insured to a coshareholder and transfers from a corporation to a coshareholder of the insured clearly fall within the transfer-for-value rule. But transfers of an existing policy "to a corporation in which the insured is a shareholder or officer" can occur without loss of the income-tax-free status of the proceeds because of an exception to the transfer-for-value rule.[6]

CONVERSION FROM CROSS-PURCHASE TO STOCK REDEMPTION

If the life insurance ownership arrangement is initially set up on a cross-purchase basis, a subsequent transfer of the policies to the corporation will not invoke the transfer-for-value rule because, by definition, the insured will be a corporate officer or stockholder at the time of the transfer. But, if the corporation originally owned the policy, as mentioned earlier, a subsequent transfer of ownership to a coshareholder of the insured could fall within the transfer-for-value tax trap.

One additional consideration should be made in a conversion of a cross-purchase agreement to a stock redemption arrangement: will the shift in obligations create a taxable dividend? For example, assume Erik and Michael are shareholders of the EM Corporation and have a standard cross-purchase buy-sell agreement. The obligation to purchase becomes mandatory on the death (or retirement or disability) of either. Ten years have elapsed since the agreement was executed, and the corporation's value has increased considerably. The owners decide to shift the increased responsibility of the purchase from each other to the corporation; i.e., they convert the cross-purchase arrangement to a stock redemption plan.

Is there a constructive dividend at the time of the changeover? Probably not, because based on the facts, no legal obligations or binding commitments have attached at the time the obligation is shifted to the corporation. The agreement is executory at the date of the revision. But if the transfer of obligations from the surviving shareholders to the corporation occurred after the commitment to purchase the decedent's stock attached, the corporation's payment to the estate would be considered a dividend to the obligated shareholders.

Life insurance owned by individual shareholders could be safely sold to the corporation, because a sale to a corporation in which the insured is a shareholder is an exception to the transfer-for-value rule. But the sale itself may result in the realization of gain (ordinary income) consisting of the difference between the amount received and the net premiums paid by the selling shareholders. Generally, any loss will not be deductible.

CONVERSION FROM STOCK REDEMPTION TO CROSS-PURCHASE

Conversion from a stock redemption to a cross-purchase agreement has received more consideration since the Tax Reform Act of 1986 expanded the application of the AMT. A recent IRS Private Letter Ruling illustrates the use of an exception to the transfer-for-value rule in achieving this restructuring.

A corporation owned policies on the lives of its two shareholders, who were also partners in a real estate partnership that leased a plant and facilities to the corporation. The corporation transferred the policies to the partnership in partial payment of rent on the premises. Subsequently the partnership made each partner/shareholder the beneficiary of the policy on the life of the other partner/shareholder.

The IRS ruled that while the transfers and reciprocal beneficiary designations were transfers for value, the proceeds would be tax-free upon receipt because the transfer was to a "partnership in which the insured is a partner." Presumably if the corporation distributed the policies on the shareholder's respective life to the other shareholder who was the partner, the proceeds would similarly remain tax-free as a transfer "to a partner of the insured."[7] Note that in this ruling the partnership had been an ongoing enterprise; consider whether the result would be the same if it had been created at the time of or for the purpose of completing this transfer. In the author's opinion, as long as the partnership was in existence, the purpose for which it was established is irrelevant.

Endnotes

1. IRC §101(a)(2) provides that (as an exception to the general rule that the proceeds of life insurance, payable by reason of the death of the insured, are income-tax-free), if a policy or any interest in a policy is transferred for valuable consideration, the death proceeds will be exempt only to the extent of the consideration paid by the transferee and net premiums, if any, paid after the transfer. The remaining proceeds will be taxable as ordinary income. See Chapter 3 for a more detailed explanation. See also, *Tools and Techniques of Life Insurance Planning*, (Cincinnati: National Underwriter Co., 1992). Call 800-543-0874. Also see Zaritsky and Leimberg, *Tax Planning for Life Insurance* (New York: Warren, Gorham and Lamont, 1992); call 800-950-1210.
2. The term *transfer for value* includes not only outright sales but also any transfer for value of a right to receive all or part of the proceeds of a life insurance policy. Reg. §1.101-1(b).
3. For example, where a corporation transfers a policy to a shareholder as a liquidation distribution, the shareholder's surrender of the right to the corporation amounts to consideration. *Lambeth v. Comm'r*, 38 B.T.A. 351 (1938).
4. *Waters, Inc. v. Comm'r*, 3 T.C. 407 (1944).
5. *Monroe v. Patterson*, 197 F. Supp. 146 (N.D. Ala. 1961). In Monroe, an officer/insured purchased a second policy. Later he entered into a buy-sell arrangement with two key employees. They agreed to purchase his stock at his death and make premium payments. In return for their agreement to buy his stock and keep up premium payments, he and the corporation transferred the policies to trustees—partially for use in funding the agreement.

   Even though no purchase price was paid for the policies, the court held that the key employees were transferees for value. The mutuality of obligations represented consideration for the transfer of the policies. The proceeds actually (and constructively) received by the transferees in excess of premiums they paid to the date of the insured's death were taxable as ordinary income.

   Where there is no valuable consideration, there can be no "transfer for value." See *Haverty Realty and Investment Co. v. Comm'r*, 3 T.C. 161 (1944).
6. There are a number of exceptions to the transfer-for-value rule. Here are three for corporate buy-sell purposes:

   1. A sale or other transfer for value to the insured [IRC §101(a)(2)(B)]
   2. A sale or other transfer to a corporation in which the insured is an officer or shareholder [IRC §101(a)(2)(b)]
   3. Where the policy changes hands in the type of transfer that does not result in

changing the tax basis of the transferred assets, e.g., the transfer of a policy between corporations in a tax-free reorganization, statutory merger, consolidation or from an individual or partnership that forms a corporation on a tax-free basis under Section 351 [IRC §101(a)(2)(A)].

See Reg. §101-(b)(3) for the danger where one corporation purchases the assets of another corporation (a non-tax-free reorganization) and those assets include a life insurance policy. The purchase will cause proceeds to be taxable unless the insured is an officer or shareholder of the purchasing corporation. See *Spokane Dry Goods v. Comm'r*, 1 T.C.M. 921 (1943).

The second exception, a transfer to a corporation in which the insured is a shareholder or officer, is especially important since often a policy will become "tainted" by a previous transfer for value. But as long as the last transfer (or last transfer for value) is to such a corporation, all prior taint is removed. The proceeds become tax-exempt again in spite of prior sales or transfers for value. Reg. §1.101-1(b)(3).

Note that for this exception to apply, the insured (not the policyowner) must be an officer or shareholder in the transferee corporation. Furthermore, status as a mere key employee or director is insufficient to qualify under this important exception. Although the regulations don't define *shareholder* or *officer*, the insured must in fact be such. Therefore it is doubtful that a "nominal" shareholder or "token" officer with no real authority or duties would qualify.

See PLR 8951056 for a discussion of exceptions (a) and (c) and the foregoing regulation in the context of a purchase of policies by the insured from an irrevocable trust, followed by the subsequent contribution of the policies to another trust.

A fourth exception to the transfer-for-value rule is a transfer "to a partner of the insured" or a "partnership in which the insured is a partner." IRC §101(a)(2)(B). The transfer-for-value exception under Section 101(a) originally was enacted to prevent speculation on the insured's death while exempting life insurance proceeds paid under contracts transferred for legitimate business reasons. Sen. Rep. No. 1622, 83d Cong., 2d Sess. (1954), p. 14. So to fall within the legitimate business reason theory, the partnership must be a valid, ongoing partnership entitled to recognition as such for federal income tax purposes. *Swanson v. Comm'r*, 518 F.2d 59 (8th Cir. 1975).

7. See Rev. Rul. 69-608, 1969-2 C.B. 43.

Disposition of Policies on Lives of Shareholders

THE PROBLEM IN A CROSS-PURCHASE AGREEMENT

Where the buy-sell agreement has been set up under the typical cross-purchase agreement, each shareholder applies for, pays premiums on and is owner and beneficiary of a policy on the life of each coshareholder. Generally, after one shareholder dies, the policies that shareholder owned on the surviving shareholders must somehow be transferred to them.

For example, if Kit, Kathleen, and Jesse were coshareholders, at Kit's death the policies he owned on Kathleen and Jesse would pass to Kit's estate. There is no way to sell the policy Kit had owned on Kathleen's life to Jesse and the policy on Jesse's life to Kathleen without setting the transfer-for-value tax trap. There are, however, several possible solutions to this problem.

Some Possible Solutions

The first possible solution is for Kit's estate to sell both policies to the corporation. The corporation could then establish a stock redemption plan that meshed with the existing cross-purchase agreement.[1] The result could be a hybrid plan, since Kathleen and Jesse still own policies on each other's lives. Under the hybrid cross-purchase/stock redemption arrangement each shareholder would be given an option to purchase any or all of the other's shares.

In the event (or to the extent) the option was not exercised, the corporation would then be required to purchase the stock. Alternatively, Kathleen and Jesse could transfer the policies they own on each other's life to the corporation and have a full stock redemption agreement.[2]

A second potential solution is for the estate to surrender each policy for cash. Kit's estate would cash-surrender the policies owned on the lives of both Kathleen and Jesse.[3]

Another possible answer is for each surviving shareholder to purchase the policy on his or her own life from the estate of the decedent. The policies could then be continued as personal insurance.[4]

Can the transfer-for-value trap be avoided if a trustee is made owner of all the policies? Probably not. Although upon Kit's death there would be no physical transfer, and legal title to the policies on the lives of Kathleen and Jesse would not change, the beneficial interest in Kit's share of the policies on his coshareholders' lives has shifted to them. Upon each death there would be some transfer of equitable ownership to the surviving coshareholders.[5]

There is also valuable consideration: reciprocity. No policyowner would allow the beneficial interest in a policy he or she owned on another shareholder's life to pass through the legal ownership held by trustee to the other shareholders unless each of the other shareholders did the same. At best the trustee approach on a cross-purchase agreement is clouded with tax uncertainty, and the potential risk seems to outweigh the possible benefits.

Endnotes

1. A transfer to a corporation in which the insureds are also shareholders is excepted from the transfer-for-value rule. IRC §101(a)(2)(B).
2. But note that the decedent/shareholder was paid from the proceeds of policies owned by Kathleen and Jesse individually. They each now own an interest in the corporation worth one-sixth more than before. Stated another way, Jesse now does not have enough coverage to buy out Kathleen completely and vice versa. The difference could be made up with the purchase of additional coverage and/or provision for an installment payout for any balance.
3. This alternative would result in an even more serious underfunding of a future buyout between Kit and Jesse.
4. As in two prior methods, the problem of an underfunded buy-sell exists even though IRC §101(a)(2)(B) protects the proceeds from taxability under the transfer-for-value rule.

5. IRC §101(a)(2) refers to a transfer not only of a policy but also of an interest in a policy. The IRS probably would claim that the phrase encompasses a beneficial as well as a legal interest. On the other hand, it could be argued that to some extent the "transfer" or shift in equitable ownership has been not only to the coshareholder of the insured but also to the insured. To that extent at least, the transfer may fall within an exception to the rule.

CHAPTER 16

Overcoming
Inadequate Funding

Life insurance may provide insufficient funds to effect a complete purchase for a number of reasons:

1. A shareholder was uninsurable prior to the execution of the agreement—or became uninsurable subsequent to that event—and no new coverage could be obtained to compensate for the increasing value of the corporation.[1]
2. The parties have failed to keep insurance coverage commensurate with the formula buyout price under the agreement—often merely through neglect or because of inflationary increases.
3. In a redemption agreement the AMT could reduce the net proceeds available for the purchase.

Whatever the reason for the inadequacy, a grossly underfunded arrangement may render the buyout a practical nullity.[2]

An option held by the corporation to purchase an amount of stock equal to the insurance proceeds available to it would seem to satisfy the corporation's problem and may achieve the important buy-sell objective of corporate continuity. But it will not help convert a decedent/shareholder's stock into a liquid asset for the benefit of his or her estate and beneficiaries. Such an option might cause dividend treatment if the sale resulted in other than a complete or substantially disproportionate redemption. An option exercisable "only as to all of the decedent's shares" is likewise deficient if the option becomes mandatory only in the event insurance proceeds are adequate to accomplish a complete buyout.

156

THE HYBRID PLAN IS A SOLUTION

Can the combination of a corporate stock redemption and a shareholders' cross-purchase plan ensure continuity in the hands of the surviving shareholders and also turn the decedent/shareholder's stock into cash? A number of alternatives—with varying tax implications—are possible:

First, a cross-purchase arrangement could be set up, with the agreement providing for a mandatory corporate purchase as a backstop if the shareholders for any reason cannot or do not effect a complete purchase. But, as mentioned, if the surviving shareholders are under a primary unconditional obligation to purchase the decedent's stock, a redemption by the corporation will be considered a constructive dividend to the survivors.[3]

One possible answer is to place the primary obligation on the corporation and give the shareholders only secondary responsibility. But what if the corporation, due to inadequate insurance coverage, is able to purchase only a small portion of the stock, and the balance is bought by the individuals? Focusing solely on the corporation's purchase, the redemption would clearly not be a complete termination and possibly would not meet the "substantially disproportionate" tests.[4] Although it should not be relied on for planning purposes, in one case a partial stock redemption followed by a cross-purchase of the remaining stock by the surviving shareholders was held to qualify—because the two transactions were in reality part of a single plan or event.[5]

Perhaps the best approach would be an initial purchase option in favor of the corporation with a secondary option held by the surviving shareholders, coupled with a provision that if for any reason they do not exercise all or a part of the option the corporation is bound by a mandatory redemption requirement to purchase any and all remaining shares. This would clearly satisfy the "complete termination" requirements of the IRC, when and if the corporation redeemed stock of the decedent. Since none of the survivors would be under a primary and unconditional obligation to consummate the purchase, the constructive dividend tax trap should be sidestepped.

Another advantage of this method is that when the event creating the need for cash occurs (the very time the surviving shareholders are best able to measure their ability vis-à-vis the corporation to purchase the stock), the survivors can judge just how much they should purchase individually and how much the corporation will redeem. At this time the surviving stockholders should have a better idea of their expectancies—for themselves and the corporation. This wait-and-see approach to the buy-sell agreement is described in more detail in Chapter 29.

Endnotes

1. See Sherman, "Problems of Inadequate Funding of a Buy-Sell Agreement," *Trusts and Estates* (December 1971).
2. An escape valve in the form of a deferred-payment arrangement should be included in most agreements to cover such a contingency. However, note the high cost where the imputed interest provisions of IRC §1274 are considered.

   Security devices may be dangerous. For example, if a deferred-payment plan is considered not to result in a complete termination—i.e., if the "terminated" shareholder is deemed to have retained any equity interest in the corporation—payments to him or her may be taxed as dividends. For example, if the deferred payment takes the form of a corporate note secured by the stock to be redeemed, and the note matures in more than 15 years and/or the payment depends on corporate earnings and profits, the potential characterization as a dividend is evident.

   Likewise, if the note is subordinated to the claims of the corporation's general creditors or the "ex-owner" had a right to reassert ownership rights in the event of a default, the security arrangement will give the "seller" something more like an equity position than a creditor. See Reg. §1.302-4(d). See also *Lisle V. Commr.*, 35 T.C.M. 627 (1976), where the court stated that a 20-year payout would not, per se, cause a redemption to fail the complete termination test. There the court found a firm and fixed installment plan for the purchase of all of the shareholder's stock.
3. Rev. Rul. 58-614, 1958-2 C.B. 920; Rev. Rul. 59-286, 1959-2 C.B. 103; *Sullivan v. U.S.*, 363 F.2d 724 (8th Cir. 1966), *cert. denied* 387 U.S. 905 (1967); *U.S. v. Wall*, 164 F.2d 462 (4th Cir. 1947); see *Apschnikat v. U.S.*, 421 F.2d 910 (6th Cir. 1970); *Holsey v. Comm'r*, 258 F.2d 865 (3d Cir. 1959); *Zipp v. Comm'r*, 259 F.2d 119 (6th Cir. 1958).

   In substance the corporation, when it purchases stock the shareholders are already obligated to purchase, is satisfying and discharging their personal debt (but "it is not until that duty to perform becomes unconditional that it can be said a primary and unconditional obligation arises"). Rev. Rul. 69-608, 1969-2 C.B. 42. See also *Jacobs v. Comm'r*, 698 F.2d 850 (6th Cir. 1983), and *Gerson v. Comm'r*, T.C.M. 1989-52.
4. IRC §302(b)(2), (3).
5. *U.S. v. Carey*, 298 F.2d 531 (8th Cir. 1961). See also *Zenz v. Quinlivan*, 213 F.2d 914 (6th Cir. 1954), and *McDonald v. Comm'r*, 52 T.C. 82 (1969).

CHAPTER 17

Salary or Bonus Funding

One of the most convenient methods of arranging the funding of a cross-purchase buy-sell is by the salary or bonus method. Under this arrangement the shareholders authorize the corporation to pay insurance premiums and charge them (as employees) with additional compensation income.[1]

It works like this: each shareholder purchases, owns and is beneficiary of a policy on the life of each coshareholder. With a C corporation this makes corporate payments deductible as compensation, assuming:

- the employee is the policyowner;
- the employee can designate the beneficiary (or the proceeds are payable to the employee's beneficiary or estate);
- the employer has no ownership rights or beneficial interest in the policy; and
- any additional salary or bonus so paid is reasonable compensation.[2] This arrangement works especially well when the corporation's income tax brackets (federal and state) exceed the shareholders', which is often the case.

Care must be taken to avoid dividend classification. In several cases the courts have held that premium payments by the corporation could be considered disguised dividends where total compensation was unreasonable or there was no evidence that premiums were intended to be additional compensation.[3]

This issue can be avoided if the corporation simply pays increased compensation to the shareholders, as long as it is reasonably certain that the individuals will, in fact, use this money to pay premiums. Of course with a C corporation reasonable compensation remains a prime consideration.

The situation may be simplified somewhat for an S corporation. Reasonable compensation is no longer an issue since the shareholders are generally taxed on all corporate earnings, and there is no corporate deduction to be preserved. As long as the corporation has not distributed all of its earnings and profits in a year, further distributions for that year should not result in additional taxes, since the shareholders have already paid tax on the income.[4] Thus the corporation is being availed of as a source of funds, not to generate a corporate deduction.

One disadvantage of an S corporation, however, is that distributions to shareholders in excess of their compensation,—i.e., dividends—must be in proportion to their share of ownership. Thus unequal premiums will leave the shareholder paying less with excess cash after the payment. When a minority shareholder must buy a larger policy to fund the buyout of a majority shareholder, the problem is increased: the majority shareholder not only will receive a bonus of excess cash due to smaller premium payments but also must receive a proportionately higher sum from the corporation.

Endnotes

1. Reg. §1.61-2(d)(2); *Canaday v. Guitteau*, 86 F.2d 303 (6th Cir. 1939); *Yuengling v. Comm'r*, 69 F.2d 971 (3rd Cir. 1934); *Lee vs. U.S.*, 219 F. Supp. 225 (D.C. S.C., 1963); *Pettit v. Comm'r*, 19 T.C.M. 679 (1960). Only the net premium is taxable income to the employee if dividends are used to reduce premiums.
2. IRC §162(a); Reg. §1.162-7; *Brown Agency, Inc. v. Comm'r*, 21 B.T.A. 1111 (1931), *acq.* XI-1 C.B. 9; *Berizzi Bros. Co. v. Comm'r*, 16 B.T.A. 1307 (1929), *acq.* XI-1 C.B. 6. Note that Reg. §1.264-1(b) provided the deduction will not be denied merely because the employer will derive an indirect benefit from an employee's increased efficiency.

   If the total amount paid to or on behalf of a stockholder/employee is unreasonable, the IRS may treat premium payments as constructive dividends rather than compensation. Thus the minutes of the corporation should reflect the fact that such premium payments are to be considered additional compensation. See *Semon Bache & Co. v. Comm'r*, 22 B.T.A. 200 *aff'd* 53 F.2d 1084 (2nd Cir. 1931); *C.F. Smith Co. v. Comm'r*, 13 T.C.M. 607 (1954); *Champion Trophy Mfg. Corp. v. Comm'r*, 31 T.C.M. 1236 (1972).
3. *Champion Trophy Mgf. Corp. v. Comm'r*, *supra* note 102; *Paramount-Richards Theatres v. Comm'r*, 153 F.2d 602 (5th Cir. 1946).
4. Generally, with an S corporation with no earnings and profits from C corporation

years, or a corporation with S status from its inception, distributions to the extent of a shareholder's basis (which includes earnings) are taxed first as a nontaxable return of capital and thereafter as gain from a sale or exchange. IRC §1368(b). For other S corporations distributions are taxed in the following manner:

- As nontaxable return of basis to the extent of the AAA account (the accumulated adjustments account, which generally speaking represents an S corporation's undistributed income that has been taxed to the shareholders)
- As dividends to the extent of the earnings and profits
- As nontaxable return of remaining basis
- As gain from a sale or exchange [IRC §1368(c)]

CHAPTER 18

Group Term Life Insurance as a Funding Vehicle

Group term life insurance might seem to be the ideal means for funding a buy-sell agreement. Generally the outlay for group term is low, premiums are tax-deductible, the insured pays no tax on coverage of up to $50,000[1] and even uninsurable shareholders can be covered. But a price must be paid to receive these tax benefits. Group term insurance plans must be nondiscriminatory with respect to eligible participants and the benefits they will receive. Otherwise the employees in whose favor the plan is maintained will be taxed on the cost of their entire policy (not only the excess over $50,000). The cost is determined by the so-called Table I rates contained in the Treasury regulations or the actual cost to the corporation, whichever is higher.[2]

Shareholder contributions to the cost of group term life insurance will reduce tax liability. (In the case of an S corporation, however, the tax benefits to the corporation and the shareholders are available only to shareholders owning less than 2 percent of the stock.[3]) Finally, the corporation will lose the deduction for premium payments if the compensation paid to the shareholder/insured, taken as a whole, is unreasonable.[4] Other substantial tax problems, for cross-purchase and stock redemption plans, also exist.

DISADVANTAGES IN A CROSS-PURCHASE AGREEMENT

In a 1962 private ruling[5] a deduction was denied to a corporation for the payment of premiums on group insurance on the lives of stockholders under a cross-purchase plan. In that situation each stockholder/employee designated the other as beneficiary of the group insurance. The ruling stated:

> This is in response to your request for rulings concerning various federal tax aspects of group term life insurance.
>
> You propose to issue an equal number of shares of your stock to each of your two stockholders for a consideration. Immediately thereafter the stockholders will enter into an agreement under the terms of which each of them will bind his personal representatives, heirs and assigns to sell his stock, upon his demise, to the surviving stockholder for $125,000. In order to provide the surviving stockholder with sufficient funds to make the purchase of the stock from the estate of the deceased, life insurance protection will be obtained on the life of each stockholder.
>
> You state that such an arrangement is often used in closely held corporations to insure that the control of the corporation will remain in the hands of the surviving stockholder-employees and to insure that the heirs of a deceased stockholder will receive an equitable price for their stock interest. You also state that it has been a common practice for stockholders to insure one another with individual policy contracts in order to make the purchase upon death.
>
> You propose to accomplish the objectives described above by the use of group term life insurance instead of individual policies. In order that the cost of group coverage can be kept to a minimum, the maximum amount of coverage that the insurer will issue is to be placed upon the lives of the stockholders, and only modest amounts of coverage are to be placed upon the lives of the other eight employees covered by the group plan. This will be accomplished by scaling the amounts of coverage so as to give only $2,000 of coverage to employees with salaries of $6,000 per year or less, and $100,000 of coverage to employees with salaries above $6,000 (the stockholder only).
>
> The IRS recognizes that group term life insurance premiums do not constitute additional compensation to the employees whose lives are insured. Nevertheless, where the payment of these premiums constitutes "an investment in increased efficiency" by reason of creating in the covered employees the feeling of contentment which knowledge that provision has been made for dependents brings, such premiums constitute proper deductions under the head of "ordinary and necessary" expenses. (L.O. 1014 C.B. 2, 88).

The payment by you of premiums on group life term life insurance, insofar as the premiums are for insurance on the lives of your two stockholders, cannot be said to be likely to bring about a feeling of contentment to your employees who own none of your stock. Nor can it be claimed that such a feeling is brought to a stockholder in his capacity as an employee; for it is not his heirs or dependents who will be most benefitted in case of his death, but the other stockholder.

Thus the objective sought to be accomplished is one that is personal to the stockholders and is not one directly related or pertaining to your trade or business.

Under the facts, as you have described them, we do not consider the payment of premiums on group term life insurance on the lives of your stockholder-employees as being directly related or pertaining to your trade or business. Accordingly it is held that such premiums are not deductible for federal income tax purposes.

Section 3.02 of Revenue Procedure 60-6, C.B. 1960-1, 880, expressly prohibits the issuance of advance rulings on matters involving the prospective application of the estate tax law to the property or the estate of a living person. Accordingly, it is regretted that no action can be taken on your request for rulings as to the estate tax consequences of the proposed transaction.

We have carefully considered your request concerning whether there will be a transfer for a valuable consideration of life insurance policies or any interest therein, for the purpose of Section 101(a)(2) of the Code, in the event Messrs ... and ... execute the proposed agreements. However, in the interest of sound tax administration it is deemed inadvisable to issue an advanced ruling on this question.

Beyond the problem described in this ruling it is possible that the premiums would be considered constructive dividends, taxed as ordinary income to the shareholders.

Another serious problem involves the potential use of the transfer-for-value rule by the IRS. For example, if the shareholders purchase group term life insurance through the corporation, name each other as beneficiaries and use the proceeds to fund a buy-sell agreement, each shareholder is naming the others in consideration of the others' reciprocal actions; i.e., a promise for a promise or a performance for a performance.[6] For example, if Fred Kirkland names Bob Best as beneficiary of the insurance on his life, and Bob names Fred as beneficiary of the group term policy on his life, there has been a transfer of an interest in a policy for valuable consideration.

The regulations state that the "creation for value of an enforceable right to receive all or part of the proceeds of a policy may constitute a transfer for a valuable consideration of a policy or an interest therein."[7] If the transferee is unable to place a dollar value on the promise or action of the cotransferees, the IRS might attempt to include all of the proceeds in the transferee's gross income.

A subsequent private letter ruling was even more to the point. In this situation each of the two shareholders of a corporation purchased a life insurance policy on his own life, naming himself as owner. Sometime later each shareholder assigned the policy on his life to the other shareholder. The purpose of the assignments was to provide each shareholder with funds to enable him to purchase the other's stock interest at the insured's death.

The IRS held that the assignments constituted a transfer for value. The ruling noted that the transfer-for-value rule, IRC §101(a)(2), extends beyond an outright sale. The ruling states that the naming of a beneficiary in exchange for valuable consideration would constitute a transfer for value.[8]

Can the rule be avoided by designating the respective spouses of the shareholders as beneficiaries and then providing in the buy-sell agreement that upon receipt the proceeds will be regarded as the consideration paid for the deceased spouse's stock? Perhaps, but only at the cost of a new problem. The proceeds are never received by the surviving shareholders, so how can they be considered part of the purchase price for the stock? In other words the cost basis of the surviving shareholders may—or may not—be increased by the price "paid" for the stock.[9]

DISADVANTAGES IN A STOCK REDEMPTION AGREEMENT

Group term life insurance is designed as an employee rather than an employer benefit. For this reason many state insurance laws require such coverage to benefit persons other than the employer. This type of state law precludes the designation of the employer as beneficiary of the stockholder/employee's interest in the group contract. Some states also frown on "jumbo group" policies that give too much coverage to shareholders. New York, California and other states provide that such contracts are not "group insurance" as defined by state law. The IRS might then claim that company-paid premiums are nondeductible by the corporation and taxable to the employees.

No deduction is allowed for income tax purposes where group term life is payable to the employer. The IRC specifically states:

> No deduction shall be allowed for premiums paid on any life insurance policy covering the life of any officer or employee or any person financially interested in any trade or business carried on by the taxpayer, when the taxpayer is directly or indirectly a beneficiary under such policy.[10]

Since the corporation would be a direct beneficiary, the income tax deduction would be forfeited for that portion of the premium attributable to the stockholder/employee's interest in the master group contract. Moreover, the corporation's receipt of the proceeds could have AMT consequences—thus a double tax whammy.

There are practical disadvantages as well. First, as a shareholder grows older, premiums increase. Second, some authorities define the effect of using group term as that of each party buying himself or herself out. (Instead of receiving both the maximum amount of group term life insurance possible and the proceeds of a properly valued business interest, the deceased's heirs receive only the group term life.)

In the case of a two-stockholder corporation, when the first stockholder dies, the surviving shareholder could change the beneficiary designation from the corporation to his or her spouse. The spouse would then receive both the insurance proceeds and all the stock.

Third, a group term policy typically provides coverage for an employee only while serving on an active full-time basis. If the stockholder retires but retains stock interest, the availability of funds to execute the buyout is no longer ensured. An employee who wants to continue coverage beyond this point would have to convert the policy at his or her attained age, which may entail prohibitive premiums.

Not only is the cost to the retiring employee extremely high—$65 to $70 per thousand for a standard-risk male aged 65—but the employer also incurs a cost: a charge of $65 to $80 per thousand of insurance converted. Furthermore, the retired employee would be paying premiums for whole life while costockholders would be paying for premiums on group term coverage. Group coverage does not contain a disability waiver-of-premium feature. If a policyowner covered by a whole life policy with waiver of premium becomes disabled, cash values and dividends will continue uninterrupted and can be used at least partially to fund a buyout.

Endnotes

1. IRC §79.
2. Treas. Reg. §1.79-3.
3. IRC §1372
4. IRC §162(a). Treas Reg. §1.264-1.
5. The 1962 ruling was given to Century Planning Corp. of New York City and signed by Arthur Singer, acting director of the tax ruling division of the IRS.
6. See *Monroe v. Patterson, supra* note 197 F.Supp. 196 (1961).
7. Reg. Sec. 1.101-1(b)(4). Exceptions include transfers to the insured, to a partner of the insured, to a partnership in which the insured is a partner and to a corporation in which the insured is a shareholder or an officer. See Leimberg and Doyle, *Tools and Techniques of Life Insurance Planning* (Cincinnati: National Underwriters Co., 1992), Call 800-543-0874.
8. PLR 7734048.
9. *Legallet v. Comm'r*, 41 B.T.A. 294 (1940); but see *Mushro v. Commr.*, 50 T.C. 43 (1968); *nonacq.* 1970-2 C.B. xxii.
10. IRC §264(a)(1).

CHAPTER 19

Using a Pension or Profit-Sharing Plan To Fund a Buy-Sell

THE ADVANTAGES

Planners occasionally suggest that the trustee of a qualified pension or profit-sharing plan purchase life insurance to fund a buy-sell agreement. The advantages of this arrangement seem impressive. First, the employer deducts contributions to the plan. Second, except to the extent of the current economic benefit (P.S. 58 cost) provided by the pure protection element of any insurance purchased, contributions made by the employer are not currently taxable to the employee.[1] There are, however, disadvantages as well.

THE DISADVANTAGES

Pension Plans

A provision in a pension plan allowing a participant to direct the pension trustee to buy life insurance on *another* person's life may cause disqualification of the plan.[2] But what if participants are currently covered with insurance on their own lives by the plan, and each shareholder names his or her coshareholder as beneficiary? This seems to reopen the transfer-for-value tax trap discussed earlier. The net amount at risk, instead of being income-tax-free, would become subject to ordinary income taxes.[3] Furthermore, the cash value portion of the insurance death benefit would be taxable income.

Profit-Sharing Plans

A profit-sharing plan may provide for a plan participant's self-direction of investments, sometimes referred to as *earmarking investments*.[4] A plan participant can direct the trustee to purchase a particular investment and credit it to his or her account. Under one theory shareholder *A* could direct the trustee to purchase insurance on shareholder *B*'s life (and vice versa) using funds invested in shareholder *A*'s account. Should *B* predecease *A*, the proceeds could then be used to purchase *B*'s interest in the business. The stock would take the place of the insurance proceeds in *A*'s account. This technique would eliminate the need for each shareholder to name the coshareholder as beneficiary of the insurance on his or her own life (the same transfer-for-value trap that would occur in the case of a pension plan).

There are two potential flaws in this earmarked or self-directed approach. One is the threat that premium outlays by the profit-sharing plan trustee might be considered current distributions. This would make the funds used to pay premiums fully taxable to the "buyer."[5] The second potential problem is that a profit-sharing plan may not be considered qualified if it provides death benefits over and above "incidental" amounts.

One further problem may occur in the case of certain professional corporations. If only professionals are permitted to hold stock under state law, stock purchased by the plan must be beneficially owned by such professionals. Stated conversely, nonprofessionals can have no interest in the stock under state law, and so none may be credited to the accounts of such individuals. It is the authors' opinion that the IRS could seek to disqualify the plan because of the discrimination in favor of shareholder/employees.

THE "END RUN" PENSION PLAN BUY-SELL SOLUTION

Assume your clients are brothers, Gene and Gary, who operate a closely held corporation worth a total of $1 million. Neither shareholder desires to be in business with the other's family. Their advisers have recommended a stock redemption buy-sell. Both Gene and Gary suffer from high blood pressure and are highly rated. Both shareholders draw high salaries. The corporation is in a high federal and state income tax bracket, has only six other employees (most of whom receive low salaries) and is about to install a pension (and/or profit-sharing) plan.

Gene and Gary have told you that paying extremely high premiums with after-tax dollars is difficult for their company and almost impossible to do with their own personal after-tax incomes. If either Gene or Gary dies, his survivors will need substantial dollars for estate settlement costs, payment of debts and living expenses.

One possible solution may be to purchase a substantial amount of life insurance ($500,000) on each brother through the retirement plan. Each shareholder establishes an irrevocable trust that provides (among other things) "income to my wife for life. After her death, the remainder is to go to my children."

Each shareholder authorizes the trustee to make loans to the company if the trust is given adequate interest and security and the interest rate is at least equal to or in excess of the average rate for loans from four specified banks in their city.

At the death of either Gary or Gene the insurance proceeds ($500,000) would be payable to the decedent's irrevocable trust, and the decedent's executors would elect to treat this disposition as a qualified terminable interest property (QTIP), thus qualifying as an estate-tax-free transfer under the marital deduction. Assume the trust lends $500,000 to the corporation for ten years at 10 percent interest. The corporation then uses the $500,000 it has borrowed from the irrevocable trust to complete the redemption. So it pays the decedent's executor $500,000 in cash and in return receives the decedent's stock. Over the term of the loan (ten years in this example) the corporation pays $50,000 per year interest (deductible) to the trust for ten years (on which the decedent's surviving spouse is taxed). At the end of ten years the corporation repays to the trust the principal of the loan out of earnings and profits.

This "end run" approach has a number of advantages:

1. The estate has received payment for the stock from the corporation: $500,000.
2. The trust has received $500,000 as taxable interest from the corporation.
3. The trust has received a return of capital, tax-free, of $500,000.
4. Thus $500,000 insurance has generated $1,500,000.
5. None of the insurance is taxed at the death of the deceased shareholder, provided he is survived by his spouse.
6. None of the life insurance increased the value of the deceased shareholder's stock, nor did it trigger a corporate AMT, since the insurance was neither owned by nor payable to the corporation.

7. None of the life insurance was subject to the claims of creditors of the corporation or creditors of the deceased shareholder.
8. The entire outlay (including any extra premium because of the shareholders' health condition) was tax-deductible by the corporation. Of course the insured shareholders must pay P.S. 58 costs, and the trust must pay income tax on the cash value portion of any life insurance it receives at death. But the P.S. 58 costs are for a standard-rate insured and do not reflect the extra-mortality-risk rating.
9. A client can control the beneficiary designation and change it anytime without loss of ownership or gift tax cost. This "up to the last minute" control and freedom from gift taxes is not possible with assigned split-dollar or assigned group term or group permanent policies.
10. This technique poses no problem if death occurs within three years. Even if death occurs one day after the plan purchases insurance on a shareholder/employee's life, the marital deduction remains available, so the proceeds are not taxed. Since there is no gratuitous lifetime transfer from the shareholder/employee to his beneficiary, the "transfers within three years of death" section will be inapplicable.
11. If there were no life insurance in the plan, the entire distribution would have been subject to ordinary income tax. With life insurance in the plan, a substantial amount (at least everything in excess of the policy's cash value) will be income-tax-free.

There are, of course, disadvantages to this approach. The major drawback is that within a reasonable period of time the corporation must pay back the loan with after-tax dollars.

THE "SPIN-OFF END RUN" TECHNIQUE

At the time the buy-sell agreement is being formulated and the amount that each owner desires to receive is being determined, the parties should consider whether a portion of the purchase price should come from insurance purchased by a qualified retirement plan. The parties may be able to use Prohibited Transaction Class Exemptions 77-7 and 77-8 to their advantage in the following manner.

If a defined-benefit pension plan purchases ordinary life insurance contracts on Gary and Gene, the cost of the new death benefit will be deductible (as a contribution to the pension) by the corporation.

Assume that after approximately seven years the annual increases in the cash surrender value of the policies purchased by the pension plan equal or exceed the amount of the annual premium. Alternatively, each policy could be purchased for its cash surrender value by the insured participant. Gary would own the policy on his life, and Gene would own the policy on his life.

Prohibited Transaction Class Exemption 77-8 allows an insured participant, a relative of such a participant, the employer of such a participant or another employee benefit plan to purchase the contract for the amount necessary to put the plan in the same cash position as it would have been had it retained the contract, surrendered it and made any distribution owed to the participant under the plan. The insured could obtain the money necessary to purchase the policy from a policy loan.

The insured could then assign the policy to a beneficiary or to a trust for that person's benefit. The new owner—at the insured's death—could lend the corporation (at a fair interest rate and with appropriate collateral) an amount sufficient to effect either a Section 303 redemption or a Section 302 complete redemption. The corporation could then redeem the decedent/shareholder's stock.

The advantages of the "spin-off end run" technique are several:

1. The estate receives cash in payment for its surrender of stock and is not dependent on the future success of the business.
2. The decedent's family receives income from the corporation—paid by the corporation, perhaps, as tax-deductible interest.
3. None of the insurance is in the estate of the shareholder (and might also be kept out of the estate of his spouse), provided that the shareholder survives for three years from the date of the assignment.
4. The insurance does not increase the value of the shareholder's stock, nor does the receipt of proceeds result in AMT.
5. No creditor of the corporation can claim the proceeds.
6. The entire outlay is tax-deductible by the corporation (the insured must pay P.S. 58 costs, and the recipient must pay some income tax on the cash value portion of the insurance proceeds if the policy is held by the plan until the insured's death).

The plan need not purchase new policies. Prohibited Transaction Class Exemption 77-7 permits an employee benefit plan to purchase a life insurance contract from a plan participant if the policy insures that person's life. A policy may also be purchased from an employer if employees of that employer are covered by the plan.

In other words a pension plan can purchase an insurance policy covering the life of a key individual, thus not only relieving the corporation of a cash flow burden but also actually increasing its positive cash flow through the purchase proceeds and the additional contribution deduction. From the viewpoint of an individual, the participant who sells the policy to the trust, personal dollars—previously taxed—are freed up.

Endnotes

1. Note that IRC §2042(2) provides that life insurance proceeds (which generally comprise the death benefits payable under a qualified retirement plan) are not included in the employee's estate if the employee possesses no "incidents of ownership" in the insurance policy, including but not limited to the right to designate a beneficiary. Unless the "subtrust" concept works, pension proceeds are estate-tax-includable. See Leimberg and McFadden, *The Tools and Techniques of Employee Benefit and Retirement Planning* (Cincinnati: National Underwriters Co., 1992), call 800-543-0874; and Zaritsky and Leimberg, *Tax Planning for Life Insurance* (New York: Warren, Gorham and Lamont, 1992), call 800-950-1210.

   In addition, at retirement the employee, or his or her designated beneficiary should such employee die prior to retirement, realizes taxable income to the extent of the cash surrender value of the life insurance policy owned by the qualified retirement plan.

2. Rev. Rul. 69-523, 1969-2 C.B. 90, deals with a pension plan containing a provision that permits any participant to invest a specified portion of contributions made on his or her behalf in life insurance contracts on the life on anyone in whom the participant has an insurable interest. The plan provided that in the event of death of the insured the proceeds of the contract would be allocated to the participant's account and paid to him or her when the other plan benefits become payable.

   The ruling held that the provision for investments in life insurance contracts does not provide incidental death benefits through means of insurance on the life of the employee as contemplated by Reg. §1.404-1(b)(1), but rather provides insurance on the life of anyone in whom the participant may have an insurable interest, such as a debtor. If the debtor or other person dies, the employee will collect on the insurance contract. Hence he or she will be provided a benefit in addition to the definitely determinable benefits.

3. IRC §101(a)(2). A transfer to a coshareholder of the insured is not within the exceptions to the transfer-for-value rules.

4. Rev. Rul. 70-611; 1970-2 C.B. 89, modified by Rev. Rul. 85-15; 1985-1 C.B. 132 and Rev. Rul, 66-174; 1966-1 C.B. 81. Death benefits provided by a qualified retirement

plan must be incidental to the plan's primary purpose of providing benefits after retirement or deferring compensation. Reg. §1.04-1-1(b)(1).

The IRS has ruled that death benefits may be considered incidental in any type of money purchase pension or profit-sharing plan if, for any individual, the cost of such benefits does not exceed 25 percent of the total cost of providing the plan's benefits. If less than 50 percent is used to pay premiums on ordinary life insurance policies, the 25 percent test will be satisfied because approximately one-half of the premiums paid for such policy are for pure insurance protection.

Revenue Ruling 74-307 provides that death benefits under a pension plan of any type, including a defined-benefit pension plan, will be considered incidental if either

  a. less than 50 percent of the employer contribution credited to each participant's account is used to purchase ordinary life insurance policies on the participant's life, even though the total death benefits consist of both the face amount of the policies and the amount credited to the participant's account at the time of death, or
  b. such death benefits would be considered incidental under Revenue Ruling 68-453, and the total death benefit before normal retirement date is equal to the greater of

  • the proceeds of ordinary life insurance policies providing a death benefit of 100 times the anticipated monthly normal retirement benefit or
  • the sum of (i) the reserve in ordinary life insurance policies plus (ii) the participant's account in an auxiliary fund.

Revenue Ruling 68-453, 1968-2 C.B. 163, states that if a split-funded pension plan providing that the total death benefit before normal retirement date is equal to the greater of (a) the proceeds of ordinary life insurance policies providing a death benefit of 100 times the anticipated monthly normal retirement benefit or (b) the sum of (i) the reserve under the ordinary life insurance policies plus (ii) the participant's account in the auxiliary fund, then such total death benefit is incidental within the meaning of Section 1.401-(b) of the regulations. However, if the total death benefit is equal to the sum of the proceeds of such ordinary life insurance policies plus the participant's auxiliary fund account, such total death benefit would not be incidental.

Revenue Rulings 57-213 and 54-51 provide that a profit-sharing plan will not fail to qualify under IRC §401(a) if the amount of trust funds used to purchase ordinary life insurance for a participant is less than one-half of the total contributions and forfeitures previously allocated to the account of the employee. Earnings and capital gains and losses of the trust fund are not taken into account in determining the amount of trust funds, which may be used to pay premiums on the ordinary life insurance contracts.

It is anticipated that the Department of Labor will issue revised regulations concerning participant self-direction of plan investments within the first quarter of 1991.

These regulations may limit or affect the use of life insurance as an earmarked investment. The Department of Labor's proposed regulations on participant-directed individual account plans, which were issued on September 3, 1987, do not specifically mention the use of life insurance as a self-directed investment.

5. Comments by Isidore Goodman to the Association for Advanced Life Underwriting, March 39, 1970. At least one authority feels that Rev. Rul. 69-523, 1969-2 C.B. 90, also applies and would cause a disqualification to the plan itself.

Note also that funds used to pay premiums must have been accumulated prior to use for at least two years, according to Rev. Rul. 71-295, 1971-2 C.B. 1984.

Also, the "exclusive benefit" rules may prevent the investment of profit-sharing funds in the stock of a closely held corporation. Under these rules

    a. the cost of the investment must not exceed its fair market value;
    b. a fair return must be provided;
    c. sufficient liquidity must be maintained to permit distributions according to the plan; and
    d. safeguards including diversity of investment (to which a prudent investor would adhere) must be maintained.

See Morrison, "Funding Stock Purchase Agreements with Insurance in Qualified Plans," *CLU Journal* (January 1978): 40.

CHAPTER 20

Funding a Buy-Sell Through an Employee Stock Ownership Plan

Employee stock ownership plans (ESOPs) have been proposed as a means of directly or indirectly making life insurance deductible and at the same time usable to purchase a decedent's stock.[1] For instance, a corporation could establish an ESOP and use it to purchase key executive insurance on the lives of the two major shareholders. Upon the death of a shareholder the trust would receive the insurance proceeds and then negotiate with the representative of the deceased shareholder for the purchase of his or her shares at the current fair market value.[2] Because employer contributions of cash or stock to the ESOP are deductible, the shareholders have effectively converted what would have been nondeductible key executive insurance premiums into a tax-deductible item.

Can an ESOP carry insurance on the life of a shareholder/employee? Some currently do. The death proceeds are considered plan assets and are allocated to the accounts of participants in the same ratio that other plan earnings are credited to those accounts. Contributions by the corporation to the plan are deductible, and therefore the cost of the life insurance is, in essence, deductible. When the proceeds are received, those funds can be used to buy company stock, which in turn may be allocated to the accounts of participants.

POSSIBLE PROBLEMS

There are at least four potential problems with this approach:

1. An ESOP may not enter into a binding agreement that obligates it to purchase employer stock at the death of a shareholder. The IRS position

176

is that an ESOP must not otherwise obligate itself to acquire securities from a particular security holder at an indefinite time determined upon the happening of an event such as the death of the holder.[3] This clearly and categorically means that an ESOP cannot be used as the buyer in a traditional mandatory buy-sell agreement.

2. The IRS will probably not approve an ESOP where a binding buy-sell agreement exists between the ESOP and a stockholder to purchase stock at death, because of the "exclusive benefit" rule, which requires that a qualified plan must be mainly for the exclusive benefit of employees. In other words, the plan might be for the benefit of the stockholders more than the employees.

3. When a corporation purchases the stock of its shareholder, the proceeds from the sale may be subject to dividend treatment. A shareholder who would like to sell stock to an ESOP may be able to obtain a private letter ruling that such a transaction is a sale, subject to capital gains treatment. Otherwise the full amount of the distribution could be taxable as ordinary income.

4. The amount of insurance that can be purchased by the ESOP to facilitate the stock purchase is limited.[4] The term *employee stock ownership plan* means a plan designed to invest primarily in qualifying employer securities. The word *primarily* has not been defined by the IRS. The Department of Labor has stated that no fixed minimum or maximum of plan assets must be invested in employer securities for the "primarily" requirement to be satisfied. However, the Department of Labor has indicated that a facts and circumstances type of analysis must be made over the life of the ESOP to determine whether the requirement has been satisfied.

ESOP RULES

Generally distributions from an ESOP to participants or their beneficiaries may be in cash or employer stock or a combination, but the participant has the right to demand employer stock. In addition, when the stock is not traded on an established market, the participant holds a put option and can force the employer to purchase the securities following the distribution.

The investments of the trust itself, however, need not be solely in stock of the employer company. In addition, regardless of whether the employer's stock is publicly traded, in certain instances voting rights associated with the employer's securities must pass through to ESOP participants. This may be more than the owner of a closely held corporation will be willing to provide.

INDIRECT FUNDING OF A STOCK REDEMPTION AGREEMENT

It is highly feasible to use an ESOP to fund a stock redemption agreement indirectly as follows:

Step 1. The corporation contributes treasury stock in an amount equal to or greater than the premium payments directly into the ESOP. The fair market value of such stock is deductible, resulting in income tax savings without a corporate expenditure of cash.

Step 2. The corporation can then use the newly available cash to fund the purchase of key executive insurance—outside of the ESOP—for the purchase of stock redemption.

Step 3. At the death of the insured the corporation receives the insurance proceeds income-tax-free and can then redeem all of the stock owned after the distribution of the deceased/insured's share of ESOP-owned stock. Likewise, the increased cash flow can be used to help the stockholder/employees fund a cross-purchase agreement by using corporate dollars for split-dollar insurance.

Alternatively, if the corporation owns the policy, it can receive the proceeds tax-free, use all or a portion of those proceeds to make additional contributions to the ESOP (thereby generating tax deductions) or lend the ESOP the proceeds and then have the ESOP purchase the stock. This way the proceeds rather than the premiums are deductible.

If an ESOP acquires employer securities by purchasing them directly from an employee or his or her estate, subject to certain substantial requirements and restrictions, no gain need be recognized by the employee or estate.[5] To receive tax-free rollover treatment for sales of employer securities to ESOPs, the employee or estate must obtain "qualified replacement property"[6] within a fixed time period using the proceeds of the sale.

Endnotes

1. In this text *ESOP* means any type of stock bonus plan that is a qualified plan under the IRC that is designed to invest primarily in company stock. An ESOP that satisfies certain requirements set forth in IRC §4975 is commonly called a "leveraged" ESOP.

   IRC §1.401-1(b)(1)(iii) provides that a stock bonus plan is a plan established and maintained by an employer to provide benefits similar to those of a profit-sharing plan, except that the contributions by the employer do not necessarily depend on profits and the benefits are distributable in stock of the employer company. For the purpose of allocating and distributing the stock of the employer that is to be shared among its employees or their beneficiaries, such a plan is subject to the same requirements as a profit-sharing plan.

2. If the insurance does not cover the entire purchase price of the stock, the balance can be paid for by the trust in installments.

3. Reg. §§54.4975-7 and 54.4975-11.

4. Department of Labor Advisory Opinion No. 83-6 (January 24, 1983).

   Additionally, premiums for life insurance protection in a qualified plan generally must not exceed 25 percent of contributions and forfeitures that have been accumulated for less than two years (so in the case of a term policy the premiums may be as much as fifty percent of the contributions and forfeitures). But some commentators, such as attorney John D. Menke, in "The ESOP as Defined by Final IRS Regulations," *CLU Journal* (October 1979), feel that despite the preamble to the final regulations, the purchase of life insurance by an ESOP may be subject to different considerations than in the case of a purchase of life insurance by other qualified plans. For example, an ESOP must be invested "primarily" in employer stock. Thus, from a purely technical standpoint, nothing prohibits an ESOP from investing up to fifty percent of its plan assets in insurance premiums. Problems can arise upon the distribution of the benefits.

   In the case of the incidental life insurance policy, no particular problem is presented since the policy itself can be distributed to the employee upon retirement. In the case of death the proceeds are, of course, paid directly to the beneficiary. In this regard it should be noted that incidental life insurance policies are an exception to the general rule that benefits from an ESOP must be distributed in the form of employer securities.

   In the case of key executive insurance, however, various problems can arise. For example, a participant who retires before the death of the insured may claim that the investment was not prudent, even though it is allowed by the regulations. Presumably this argument would not succeed, because the participant had the benefit of insurance protection. In the case of a whole life policy, he or she will also have had a guaranteed return on the investment. Accordingly, this objection would probably not succeed unless it can be shown that the key executive was not in fact a key executive, or that the insurance protection far exceeded the possible worth of the individual to the company. Another avenue of attack might be that the purchase of key executive insurance violates the exclusive benefit rule and/or the requirements of diversification.

A more serious problem may be the practical one of distributing benefits in the case where the policy has matured. For example, if the key executive dies, the ESOP will receive the life insurance proceeds. If the key executive's estate is the principal shareholder of the corporation, and if the estate refuses to sell additional employer stock to the ESOP, then the ESOP will have a large portion of the fund invested in cash, which somehow must be converted to company stock prior to distribution. One solution to this problem might be for the ESOP to purchase preferred stock from the company for purposes of making the required distributions.

An argument can also be made that the purchase of life insurance on the life of the shareholder constitutes a prohibited transaction in that it represents the use of plan assets for the benefit of a party in interest. However, the purchase of employer securities by an ESOP from a party interest is specifically exempt from the prohibited transaction rules. Since the life insurance policy is purchased to facilitate the stock purchase, the purchase of the life insurance should also be exempt from the prohibited transaction rules.

5. IRC §1042.
6. Generally this means securities issued by a corporation different from the employer.

CHAPTER 21

Funding a Buy-Sell Through a Split-Dollar Arrangement

Split-dollar insurance in its most classic form is an arrangement whereby employer and employee split or share premium outlay, cash values and death benefits.[1] Where a cross-purchase buy-sell agreement is indicated but stockholders cannot afford or do not want to provide the entire premium outlay, or where the corporation is in a lower income tax bracket than the shareholders, a splitting of premium dollars may be advisable. In addition, where there is a notable difference in the ages or health of the shareholders, a split-dollar agreement may assist the younger or healthier shareholder by shifting a portion of the responsibility for paying a larger premium to the employer.

An "employer pay all" collateral assignment type of plan is often used. This means the employee/shareholder applies for, owns and is the beneficiary of the policy. But to provide the employer (which will pay the entire premium) with security for its premium outlay, the employee/shareholder collaterally assigns the policy to the employer. Each shareholder purchases a policy on the life of each coshareholder. At a death the survivor(s) receive the insurance (less the amount paid to the corporation equal to its entire outlay (sometimes with interest). If the surviving shareholder(s) still do not have enough cash from the insurance proceeds to buy the deceased's interest from his or her estate, the corporation can loan its share of the proceeds to the survivor(s).

For example, the SJ Corporation, which is worth $200,000, has two equal shareholders, Stan and Joe, both of whom are employees. Stan and Joe sign a cross-purchase agreement requiring the survivor to purchase the stock of the first to die. Assume that the purchase price of $100,000 is to be funded by life insurance, with the premiums paid through a classic split-dollar arrangement with the corporation.

The corporation will pay the premiums for each policy up to the policy's annual increase in cash value. Each shareholder will pay the balance of the premium for the policy owned on his coshareholder's life. So Stan will pay any premiums in excess of the corporation's share for the policy on Joe's life. If Joe dies, the proceeds of the policy, less the cash value portion paid to the corporation, will be paid to Stan. Stan will then use those proceeds to buy Joe's stock from his estate.

TAX CONSEQUENCES

Taxation of this arrangement is governed generally by various revenue rules.[2] In a nutshell Stan will be charged with a current economic benefit measured by the pure insurance element provided in the contract he owned on Joe's life to the extent paid for by the corporation. Stated in another way, each year Stan recognizes gross income to the extent that the value of the term insurance element exceeds the amount of premiums Stan pays.[3]

If one of the stockholders is a "controlling" (more than 51 percent) stockholder, the portion of the split-dollar policy paid to the other stockholder will be included in the estate of the deceased stockholder under Section 2042 unless the corporation holds no incidents of ownership in the policy.[4] That means the corporation must have no rights other than as a secured lender and must not be able to recover anything more than its premium outlay.

The split-dollar technique may be especially useful when a redemption agreement would result in alternative minimum tax consequences. The proceeds received by the shareholders from policies owned by them would not be subject to the AMT. It is true that the sums paid to the corporation would be subject to the AMT, but the consequences are likely to be insignificant since the annual cash value increase would have already been taken into account for that purpose at smaller (relatively speaking) annual increments.

Illustrative Ledger Statements

Assuming that Joe is 33, Stan could look forward to the following results under a classic split-dollar plan using an increasing term rider to maintain his share

FIGURE 21.1   Ledger Statement for Classic Split-Dollar Plan
Increasing Term Rider[5]

Age: 33 Male   Amount of Insurance: $1,000,000
Date: Nov. 1, 199—   Annual Premium: $9,750

Year	Premiums Advanced by Owner	Reportable Income of Owner	Tax Cost	Death Benefit to Owner	Death Benefit to Beneficiary
1	$9,750	$ 510	$ 179	$ 9,750	$1,000,000
5	9,750	480	168	48,751	1,000,000
10	0	600	210	78,002	1,000,000
15	0	830	290	78,002	1,000,000
20	0	1,180	413	78,002	1,000,000
Age 65	0	3,630	1,270	78,002	1,000,000

of the proceeds. The illustrations are based on current assumptions. Eight premiums are necessary to cause the policy to endow when Joe is 95. If the entire premium is paid by the corporation, Joe would have reportable income each year equal to the P.S. 58 costs. Joe's reportable income and P.S. 58 costs are illustrated in Figures 21.1 and 21.2 and assume a 35 percent individual tax bracket.

Another alternative might be to use a so-called P.S. 58 split-dollar plan, where the employee's contribution in each of the years before the premium vanishes is measured by the amount of P.S. 58 cost incurred (see Figure 21.2). After the

FIGURE 21.2   Ledger Statement for P.S. 58 Split-Dollar Plan

Age: 33 Male   Amount of Insurance: $1,000,000
Date: Nov. 1, 199—   Annual Premium: $2,008

Years	Advanced by Owner or Assignee	Premium Paid by Insured	Insured's Tax Cost	Death Benefit to Owner	Death Benefit to Beneficiary
1	$8,771	$506	$ 0	$ 8,771	$991,229
5	8,616	461	0	43,992	956,008
10	0	0	196	70,379	929,621
20	0	0	385	70,379	929,621
Age 65	0	0	1,182	70,379	929,621

vanish the employee would pay tax on the reportable income incurred for the economic benefit. This makes the employee's contribution each year most efficient, because the net P.S. 58 cost is offset by the annual contribution. Under this alternative the net coverage in the net split-dollar benefit is reduced. Stan's share would be $929,621 when Joe retires and Stan's equity in the cash value would be over $225,000.

Transfer for Value

Will a transfer-for-value problem arise? At least one author believes that, to the extent each shareholder recognizes income, the shareholder "purchased" that portion of the insurance coverage from the corporation.[6] But if each shareholder is the initial purchaser, owner and beneficiary of the policy on the other's life, a transfer-for-value problem is unlikely. A collateral assignment of the policy to the corporation as security for its portion of the premium payments should not invoke the transfer-for-value rule.[7]

However, if the corporation is the original policyowner and subsequently names Stan as beneficiary of the policy on Joe's life (or vice versa), the danger of a transfer-for-value attack is a real threat. The remedy is for Stan to apply for the policy on Joe's life and request that the corporation be named as policyowner and beneficiary to the extent of the cash value. Stan will name himself as beneficiary for the balance of the proceeds. In this case the corporation has not transferred any interest in the policy to Stan.

The endorsement method generally should be avoided because it can cause transfer-for-value problems. The transfer by a corporation, as owner, of a right to the coshareholder in consideration for his services as an employee may be deemed a transfer for value. Recall that a co-shareholder of the insured is not in the exempt group of transferees. The endorsement method can also cause estate problems for a sole or controlling shareholder, as we have seen.

Endnotes

1. Split-dollar insurance is not a type of insurance but rather a technique by which an employer can provide life insurance benefits for employees at minimal tax cost and outlay. Under a split-dollar arrangement an ordinary life insurance policy is issued on the life of an employee. Under the classic split-dollar arrangement the

employer provides the funds for that part of the premium that is equal to the increase in the policy's cash surrender value for the year of the payment, and the employee provides the funds for the balance of the premium.

Upon the death of the employee or surrender of the insurance policy, the amount of the policy's proceeds that is equal to the total outlay provided by the employer will be returned to the employer. The remainder of the proceeds is payable to the beneficiary named by the employee.

Thus, in the initial years of the policy, when there is little or no cash surrender value, virtually all of the premiums are paid by the employee. As the policy's cash value builds, the amount of the annual premium payable by the employee is reduced, and after a number of years the employee may not be required to make any payment at all.

Since the amount provided by the employer is a charge against the proceeds of the policy, each additional contribution of the employer diminishes the amount of proceeds payable to the employee's beneficiary; consequently the effect of the plan on the employee is essentially the same as providing him or her with decreasing term life insurance—the employee has no equity in the policy, and the insurance coverage is reduced each year.

However, this deficiency can be minimized by the use of the so-called fifth dividend option. Annual dividends are applied to purchase one-year term insurance equal to the policy's cash value. This tends to keep the total death benefit to the employee's beneficiary fairly even. Alternatively, the use of paid-up additions as the dividend option will tend to maintain a more-or-less level, or even increasing, death benefit to the employee's beneficiary in the long run.

Although there are many combinations of benefits and contributions for employer and employee, the plan may be one of two basic patterns: (1) the endorsement method or (2) the collateral assignment method. The endorsement method refers to an arrangement in which the employer purchases the policy and has a direct ownership right in the policy; the collateral assignment method refers to an arrangement in which the employer's only interest is that of a secured creditor holding a collateral assignment in a policy owned by an employee (or a third party).

See Thomas, "Special Uses of Split Dollars," *CLU Journal* 22 (July 1968: 40; Nolan, "Split-Dollar Applications," *CLU Journal* 18 (July 1964).

2. Rev. Rul. 64-328, 1964-2 C.B. 11, provides the basic income tax rules for split-dollar plans. Essentially it provides that an employee is to be taxed on the value of the economic benefit received from his or her employer's participation in the split-dollar arrangement. Rev. Rul. 66-110, 1966-1 C.B. 12 provides that:

> The value of the insurance provided the employee is usually ascertained by determining the cost per $1,000 of term insurance, as established in tables promulgated in the Service's rulings (generally known as the 'P.S. 58' tables).

Where the split-dollar technique is used to finance a survivor's obligation in a cross-purchase buy-sell agreement, the economic benefit is based on the insurance on the life of the insured even though the owner is another shareholder.

If the employee's insurer has published rates for term insurance which are lower than the rates set forth in the Service's rulings, and if the insurer's lower published rates are available to all standard risk applicants, then the insurance cost may be determined by using the insurer's rates. (Rev. Rul. 66-110, 1966-1 C.B. 12; Rev. Rul, 67-154, 1967-1 C.B. 11.)

3. Rev. Rul. 55-747, 1955-2 C.B. 288. See also Rev. Rul, 66-110, 1966-1 C.B. 12, for a discussion of the taxation of policy dividends in a split-dollar plan.
4. Some authorities believe that, rather than increase the purchase price in a buy-sell agreement and create greater exposure to federal and state death taxes, a better solution is to provide the extra dollars through split-dollar life insurance. The insurance is unrelated to the existing buy-sell agreement.

   Split-dollar insurance paid to a shareholder's personal beneficiary should be out of his or her gross estate if the insured possessed no incidents of ownership, direct or indirect, through the corporation (if majority shareholder). IRC §2042; Reg. §20.2042-1(c)(6). Originally the IRS ruled there should be no attribution from the corporation to the majority shareholder/employee if the employer's incidents of ownership are limited to its interest in policy proceeds. Rev. Rul. 76-274, 1976-2 C.B. 278.

   Under Rev. Rul. 76-274 the corporation could safely be given the right to an amount equal to the policy's cash value (as a loan, upon surrender or as part of the death benefit) as long as the right was limited to its outlay. A corporation in which the majority shareholder is the insured should not be given the right to surrender the policy or elect a settlement option for all the proceeds even if that power is limited to exercise only with the consent of the employer's personal beneficiary. See *Est. of Dimen v. Comm'r*, 72 T.C. 198 (1979). In Rev. Rul. 82-145, 1982-2 C.B. 213, the IRS reversed course and modified Rev. Rul. 76-274, ruling that the corporation's right to borrow, even if limited to premiums paid, constituted an incident of ownership that would be attributed to the majority shareholder. The entire policy, as a result, would be pulled back into the estate.
5. Based on a composite of three companies.
6. Kahn, "Mandatory Buy-Out Agreements for Stock of Closely Held Corporations," *Mich. L. Rev.* 68: 59.
7. See Jacobowitz, "Structuring and Funding a Buy-Sell Agreement for the Closely Held Corporation," *NYU Institute on Federal Taxation* 49.

CHAPTER 22

Special Policies To Fund Buy-Sell Agreements

JOINT LIFE FIRST-TO-DIE POLICIES

A joint life first-to-die policy provides insurance protection on two (and typically limited to three) shareholders' lives. Death benefits are paid when the first of two (or more) persons dies.[1]

Premiums for such policies are often lower than if each party was insured separately, and cash values are proportionately lower. Since the problem anticipated in the buy-sell agreement and faced by a two-owner business exists only at the first death, this type of policy is an appropriate funding solution.

First-to-die policies generally are sold with an option to continue coverage for surviving insureds. Because only one policy is issued regardless of the number of insureds, from a mechanical standpoint no unilateral action can be taken on policy loans, beneficiary changes or assignment of the policy as collateral.

Joint life policies are sometimes used to provide an equitable solution to a problem inherent in the classic cross-purchase insurance-funded arrangement. Assume George and Grace each own 50 percent of the stock of Headhunters Inc., a company worth $500,000. Each shareholder has purchased a $250,000 policy on the other's life. Should Grace die, George will obtain a business worth $500,000 at a cost of only $250,000. Grace's estate receives only $250,000 in cash plus the cash values in the policy on George's life.[2] Many stockholders object to this apparent inequality. Where it is considered a significant obstacle, a joint life policy may be useful.

A potential solution would be for George and Grace to purchase a single joint life policy with a face amount of $500,000. Death proceeds would be paid regardless of which shareholder died first. If Grace died first, half of the $500,000 would go to George, to be used to purchase Grace's stock pursuant to the buy-sell obligations. The other $250,000 in proceeds would be paid directly to Grace's personal beneficiary. George would have a business worth $500,000, while Grace's estate and personal beneficiary would receive a total of $500,000.[3]

One potential problem with joint life first-to-die coverage under one contract is that the insured (as a joint owner of the insurance) always has an incident of ownership in the policy on his or her life. Even though a coshareholder may receive the entire proceeds, the IRS will probably attempt to include them in the insured/decedent's gross estate. If one irrevocable trust owned the joint policy and the coshareholders were the beneficiaries of that trust, each insured (as a beneficiary of the trust) has an incident of ownership in the policy on his or her life.

The course of action most likely to succeed is this: When setting up a joint life policy to fund a cross-purchase plan, the insureds should set up irrevocable trusts for their families and make the trustees parties to the buy-sell. The trustees should jointly apply for, own and be the beneficiaries of the joint life first-to-die insurance policy. No incident of ownership should be given to the insured. At the death of an insured the trustee will collect the proceeds and pay them to the insured's estate in exchange for the decedent's stock. The problem here is that estate tax exclusion is obtained at the cost of loss of control of the corporation, a price more than most shareholders are willing to pay even if the new owner is a family member.

Another problem posed by a joint life first-to-die contract is that each shareholder has less control. With individual policies, upon the dissolution of the business or replacement of a co-owner separate contracts are easily assigned to each insured.[4]

Are first-to-die policies less costly? "You pay less because you are buying less coverage. Sometimes it makes sense to pay less for less insurance. . . ."[5] One article on the subject compared a separate $1 million life policy with a joint $1 million life policy for a 55-year-old male and a 50-year-old female and concluded that separately the premiums would come to $29,000 per year and jointly the cost would be only $24,000 per year. What the article failed to point out, however, was that in the former case $29,000 purchased $2 million of coverage (each dollar of premium purchased $68.96 of insurance), where in the latter case $24 million purchased $1 million of coverage (each dollar of premium purchased only $41.66 of insurance).

Yet if only $1 million of coverage is needed, some authorities would suggest that first-to-die coverage makes sense. This might be the case if two individuals owned a business worth $2 million and the survivor needed only $1 million to buy out the other's interest.

How are premiums to be paid? If a split-dollar plan is used, which life determines which owner's P.S. 58 cost? What happens to affordability when the insureds reach their late 60s or 70s? If no split dollar is used, how do you divide the premium responsibility? Currently there are no clear and certain answers to these important questions.

Many authorities recommend that, if a joint life policy is to be used, the plan should be set up on a stock redemption basis with the corporation as applicant and owner. This, of course, poses its own potential problems and drawbacks, such as the corporate AMT.

NEXT-DEATH WHOLE LIFE POLICIES

A next-death policy provides insurance protection on two (or as many as ten) stockholders' lives through the issuance of a separate and distinct permanent cash value policy on the life of each shareholder. At the death of a shareholder the death benefits will be paid according to the following virtually simultaneous steps:

Step 1. All policies terminate.
Step 2. The cash value of each policy is paid to the owner of that policy.
Step 3. New next-death policies are automatically issued on the survivors.
Step 4. The quarterly premiums for the survivor policies, to the end of the quarter following payment of proceeds, are paid from proceeds. This avoids the disruption in coverage that might result from the trauma and confusion of death. Premiums so withheld are returnable within 30 days should any individual elect within 30 days not to continue coverage.

It is this deduction feature that guarantees the automatically continued coverage of the plan, including the guaranteed renewal and payment for simultaneous deaths. Surviving members of next-death plans could literally be lying comatose in a distant hospital or vacationing in the Himalayas, and their continued coverage would be guaranteed.

Step 5. The balance of the proceeds (face amount minus the cash values for all policies and the quarterly premiums for the survivor policies) is paid to the beneficiary.

The automatic-issue feature covers simultaneous or consecutive deaths. If only one survivor remains, the coverage will be automatically issued as ordinary life.

ADJUSTABLE LIFE POLICIES

Insurance Marketing magazine contained a statement of the utility of adjustable life in buy-sell agreements:[6]

Adjustable life policies are specifically designed to provide flexibility, making it unnecessary to project how much future coverage will be needed and how much the coverage will cost.

The policy enables the holder to determine the amount of necessary coverage, and affordable premiums within limits. The smaller the premium, the shorter the term of protection and the smaller the cash values and accumulated dividends on the policy. The larger the premium, the longer the term of the protection and the larger the cash value and accumulated dividends.

At any time, coverage can be increased or reduced by either adjusting the premium, the term of protection, or both, to accommodate the holder's changing needs and income.

With it, a person can buy a relatively inexpensive term life policy when just starting out, increase the premium and face amount, switch it to whole life and pay higher premiums when a career is established, cut back the amount of coverage and monthly cost in case of a cash flow problem and increase it when possible.

The minimum term of an adjustable life policy is 10 years. Offered at the lowest premium, an adjustable life policy with a 10-year term is technically term, rather than permanent. But it does build a cash value. To prevent the premium from increasing in later years, it must be set higher in early years than a premium based on the buyer's actual mortality expectation. The "excess" premium, less one-time costs and charges, goes to create cash value.

To increase his coverage, an adjustable life policyholder usually will have to undergo a medical examination, although there are exceptions. The policy permits the holder to increase his insurance by as much as 20% every three years, without a medical examination to help keep up with inflation. Also, for an extra premium, the policyholder can obtain a guarantee of certain increases before he reaches the age of 40, when he marries or becomes a parent.

Adjustable life fills the need for flexibility in buy-sell agreements. In one case, for example, two business partners each needed $100,000 in coverage on the life of the other. This would provide the cash needed by the surviving partner to buy the dead partner's interest in the business from his estate.

In such a case, the conventional insurance solution calls for each partner to pay for $100,000 in life insurance covering the other partner. However, the difference in the partners' ages would prove a stumbling block, one being 35 years old and the other 45. The younger partner would have had to pay a yearly premium of $2,489 for insurance on the older partner. The latter would have had to pay a yearly premium of only $1,653 to cover the younger man.

By purchasing an adjustable life policy, the premium for each partner would be $1,750, thus providing $100,000 insurance on each of them. The difference between the policies is in the term of protection; the policy on the 35-year-old covers him to the age of 81, on the 45-year-old to the age of 68.

EXCHANGE PRIVILEGE RIDERS

An opportunity for flexibility in funding buy-sell agreements is presented by an exchange privilege rider, which allows the owner to exchange the policy on one insured for a new and actuarially equivalent policy on the life of a new insured. This rider makes it possible to save administrative and acquisition (commission and underwriting) costs by reissuing a policy in force on the life of one executive/shareholder who terminates employment, as of the original issue date, on the life of another. So, if a shareholder who was insured for five years sold his or her stock to another employee, who was 40 years old, a policy with premiums, dividends and cash values issued five years earlier to a 35-year-old would be issued on the life of the 40-year-old.

The exchange privilege rider is important because it guarantees the continuity of the policy without a loss in values. This, in turn, could justify the use of the favorable ratable charge method of accounting since it permits the policyowner/corporation to match costs and revenues as far as the acquisition of life insurance is concerned.

The new policy can be for the same or a lesser amount than the original policy, and the new insured must be insurable. Suicide and incontestability periods begin to run again at the issuance of the new policy.

The exchange may have negative income tax implications. This transaction apparently will not qualify for tax-free-exchange treatment under IRC §1035. If the IRS is successful with its argument, the new policy's issue in return for the old policy could be a taxable event. Gain would be reportable by the policyowner at ordinary income rates.[7]

SURVIVORSHIP (LAST-TO-DIE) POLICIES

A survivorship policy provides insurance protection on two or more persons' lives. Death benefits are paid only at the *last* death in the insured group. Last-to-die policies are used most often in estate planning cases, where liquidity is essentially a "second death" problem. For example, second-to-die coverage is often written on the lives of a husband and wife whose estate plan utilizes the maximum marital deduction, deferring federal estate taxation until the death of the survivor. Last-to-die policies can be used advantageously in some stock redemption or cross-purchase situations, particularly those that involve two families that each own one-half of a business. At the death of one member of a family the surviving member may wish to continue as a co-owner, but at the death of the second member the whole family should be bought out.

A last-to-die policy will be less expensive than separate policies on each insured because the policy will not mature until *more* than one of the risks insured occurs. Its applicability to buy-sell agreements is limited to situations that call for a buyout only at the death of the second to die, without regard to the first.

Endnotes

1. Joint life insurance is issued on a whole life, limited payment life, endowment and sometimes term insurance basis. Some plans provide that the surviving insured may convert the coverage, but other plans terminate all coverage when the first death occurs. The premium per $1,000 of joint life on two lives is less than the sum of the premiums per $1,000 of insurance on each individual life but greater than the premium per $1,000 on either single life. See Gatewood, "Shifting Shareholder Control—Why? When? How?", *Life Association News* (August 1991): 140.
2. This does not take into account premiums George has paid for the policy on Grace's life.
3. Grace's estate, for federal estate tax purposes, would include both the value of her stock ($250,000) and the value of the insurance paid to the beneficiary she selected. See Hoffman and Smith, "The 'Next Death' Approach to Funding the Business Buy-Out," *CLU Journal* (January 1978): 21.
4. Some insurers eliminate this objection by providing an option that allows either conversion into a single life policy on one of the insureds or splitting of the joint life policy into two separate contracts, one for each insured (limited to the amount of the joint life coverage).
5. See Korn, "When Two Can Insure Cheaper Than One," *Financial Planning* (October 1991): 80.
6. July 1968.
7. See Leimberg and Doyle, *Tools and Techniques of Life Insurance Planning* (Cincinnati: National Underwriter Co., 1992), call 800-543-0874; and Zaritsky and Leimberg, *Tax Planning for Life Insurance* (New York: Warren, Gorham and Lamont, 1992), call 800-950-1210.

CHAPTER 23

Use of Salary Continuation Plans

Postdeath salary continuation arrangements are sometimes considered as a supplement to "minimum value" price fixing and funding of buy-sell agreements. Postdeath salary continuation plans may also be used to complement a buy-sell that has a reasonable set price or formula.[1] Such plans, known as *survivor's income benefit (SIB)* or *death benefit only (DBO)*, are relatively simple to create.[2]

The classic plan works like this: The shareholder/employees and the corporation enter into a contract stipulating that a stated sum (often a multiple of the shareholder/employee's salary up to a certain limit) will be paid by the corporation to a specified class of beneficiaries (such as "the surviving spouse" of the covered employee or "the surviving children of the employee"). Benefits are payable if and only if the employee dies while employed by the firm and before the employee reaches a specified retirement age.

If the payments to the covered employee's heirs are to be excluded from his or her estate, the following prohibitions must be observed:

- The stockholder must not have the right to change the beneficiary, either directly (e.g., through a life insurance beneficiary designation or by contract with the employer) or indirectly (e.g., "if the beneficiary predeceases the stockholder, the benefit is paid to the stockholder's estate").
- Generally, except for qualified retirement plans, the stockholder/employee must not be entitled to any postemployment lifetime benefits, such as disability or retirement income, under this or any other employer-sponsored plan.

Compared to conventional "maximum value" buy-sell agreement funding, a "low but reasonable value" buy-sell coupled with a salary continuation arrangement may be highly advantageous for the following reasons:

1. Benefits under a bona fide properly arranged salary continuation plan may escape federal estate taxation.[3]
2. The salary continuation arrangement can be provided for a shareholder/ employee with no current income tax cost. A corporation can purchase key executive life insurance coverage on the life of each shareholder, and the premiums will not be constructive dividends even if the policies are purchased specifically to fund the corporation's postdeath salary obligation.[4] Although premiums are not deductible, the proceeds of such policies would be received by the corporation income-tax-free.[5]
3. The beneficiary of a deceased stockholder can exclude the first $5,000 of the death benefit from income.[6] Any remaining payments are taxed as received.
4. The employer can deduct payments to the shareholder/employee's beneficiary as they are paid, assuming such compensation is not considered either a constructive dividend or unreasonable.[7]

Endnotes

1. Stern, "A Different Approach to Price Fixing in Stockholder's Stock Purchase Agreements," *CLU Journal* (April 1975).
2. See discussion in Leimberg et al., *The Tools and Techniques of Estate Planning*, 9th ed. (Cincinnati: National Underwriter Co., 1992); Leimberg and McFadden, *The Tools and Techniques of Employee Benefit and Retirement Planning* (Cincinnati: National Underwriter Co., 1990); Leimberg and Doyle, *The Tools and Techniques of Life Insurance Planning* (Cincinnati: National Underwriter Co., 1992), call 800-543-0874; and Zaritsky and Leimberg, *Tax Planning for Life Insurance* (New York: Warren, Gorham and Lamont, 1992), call 800-950-1210.
3. Cases considering estate tax inclusion of DBO payments under IRC §2039 include these:

   Est. of Schelberg v. Comm'r, 70 T.C. 690 (1978), *rev'd* 79-2 USTC ¶13, 321 (2d Cir. 1979), which held that the existence of a long-term disability plan is not, per se, a lifetime postemployment benefit and could not therefore be coupled with a DBO plan to cause inclusion under §2039.

   Fusz v. Comm'r, 46 T.C. 214 (1966) in which the court held that Section 2039, in referring to "lifetime payments," was considering retirement or disability payments and not salary. So the mere payment of wages to an employee will not cause an inclusion of death benefits where no lifetime rights were possessed by the employee. See Ltr. Rul. 7851010 for a situation where a noncontractual company plan was held includible under Section 2039 under the rationale that "since the company has consistently paid benefits to widows of eligible employees who have retired, the plan is deemed to be a contract."

Planners must also consider potential inclusion under IRC §§2036 and 2038:

Kramer v. U.S., 406 F.2d 1363 (Ct. Cl. 1969), considered both Section 2036 and Section 2038 problems. No retained interest in property paid to a beneficiary pursuant to the terms of a post-death-only salary continuation plan was held by the decedent. See also Ltr. Rul. 7827010 for a Section 2038 situation in which no inclusion was required where the decedent's power to change the beneficiary was exercisable only in conjunction with the board of directors and executive committee of the corporation.

Section 2037 must also be avoided:

IRC §2037 was used to include benefits in the estate of *Fried v. Comm'r*, 54 T.C. 78 (1970). Fried's employer was obligated to pay a death benefit to Fried's widow, and if he died without a surviving spouse, payment would be made to his legal representative. Since Fried's widow would receive the death benefit only if she survived him (and because of the relative ages of Fried and his wife, the reversionary interest he retained for his estate was in excess of 5 percent), the death benefit was includible in his gross estate. (This problem can be overcome by having the covered individual opt against retention of a reversionary interest.)

Edward Tully was a 50 percent shareholder in a corporation that agreed with Tully and his costockholder to pay each decedent's widow specified death benefits. Here, however, there was no provision that payments would be made to Tully's estate if his spouse predeceased him. Thus the Section 2037 argument by the IRS was ruled out. The IRS then attempted inclusion under Section 2038(a)(1). The court agreed with the IRS that, as in the Bogley case (below), there had been a transfer of a property interest but rejected the contention that Tully's 50 percent stock ownership gave him unfettered power to alter, amend or revoke the plan.

In Ltr. Rul. 7802022, the IRS included a death-benefit-only payment in the estate of a shareholder because the agreement stated that the benefit was payable to the decedent's estate if his wife did not survive him. This was a reversionary interest that was worth more than 5 percent of the value of the property. See Ltr. Rul. 7827010 for a favorable ruling under Section 2038.

Also in the list of cases in this area are *Est. of Bogley v. U.S.*, 514 F.2d 1027 (Ct. Cl. 1975), and *Est. of Tully v. U.S.*, 528 F.2d 1401 (Ct. Cl. 1976). Bogley neatly stumbled into all the requirements for inclusion under Section 2037. His corporation—by corporate resolution—agreed to pay his widow two years' salary. If his widow predeceased him, payments were to be made to his estate. The resolution constituted an offer to Bogley, which he accepted by remaining with the corporation until his death. Thus the contractual nature of the death benefit was a property interest Bogely possessed at his death. The court stated that he made a transfer of that interest to his wife when he signed the contract. That was the final link needed by the IRS. He transferred property (the death benefit) during his lifetime, his wife could possess or enjoy the interest only by surviving Bogley, and if his wife died first, payments would be paid to his estate. Rev. Rul. 78-15, 1978-1 C.B. 289, dealt with a similar case in which the death benefits, by contract, would be made to the employee's widow, if living, or to his estate if she predeceased him.

Even Section 2035 can cause inclusion of DBO plans:

IRC §2035 was used in the *Estate of Porter v. Comm'r*, 54 T.C. 103 (1970). The Tax Court held that a salary continuation plan entered into within the three years immediately before the decedent's death was a transfer of property rights in contemplation of death. Note that the Tax Reform Act of 1976 did away with contemplation of death, although it provided for the inclusion of all gifts within three years of death. The Economic Recovery Tax Act repealed the three-year pullback rule for most purposes, one of the exceptions being transfers of retained interests under IRC §§2036-2038; as shown these sections may apply in the case of DBO plans.

In Rev. Rul. 81-31, 1981 C.B. 475, the IRS stated its position that upon entering the plan with the employer the stockholder has made a transfer to the beneficiary that is completed and taxable at death (i.e., postdeath gift!). If the beneficiary is the surviving spouse and the transfer qualifies for the marital deduction, the IRS position should not prove troublesome; if the transfer is not deductible, however, the IRS may attempt to value and tax the "transfer." See GCM 39159 (1984). As anticipated by commentators, the Tax Court took a contrary view in *Estate of Anthony DiMarco*, 87 T.C. 653 (1986). The IRS has announced its acquiescence in the *DiMarco* case.

4. *Casale v. Comm'r*, 247 F.2d 440 (2d Cir. 1957).
5. IRC §§264(a); 101(a). Keep in mind, however, the impact of the corporate AMT.
6. IRC §101(b), employee's death benefit exclusion. This exclusion must be prorated. The DBO distribution and other classes of income received by beneficiaries as a result of the shareholder's death (e.g., distributions from a qualified plan) are added and then the exclusion is prorated between the total amount and between the various beneficiaries. Proposals currently in Congress would eliminate this exclusion in the name of "tax simplification." Treas. Reg. §1.101-2(c).
7. *Rubber Associates, Inc. v. Comm'r*, 335 F.2d 75 (6th Cir. 1964), held that continuation of a deceased officer's salary was deductible since payments were part of a plan to pay additional compensation for past services. See also *Fifth Ave. Coach Lines v. Comm'r*, 31 T.C. 1080 (1959).

Note that payments are sometimes considered nondeductible constructive dividends. *Lengsfield v. Comm'r*, 241 F.2d 508; *Barbourville Brick Co. v. Comm'r*, 37 T.C. 7 (1961); *Nickerson Lumber Company v. U.S.*, 214 F. Supp. 87. In *Hardin v. U.S.*, 461 F.2d 865 (5th Cir. 1972), postdeath payments to the widow of a shareholder's brother were found to be constructive dividends to the shareholder since payments were, in essence, for the shareholder's "benefit." A similar result was reached in *Montgomery Engineering Co. v. U.S.*, 230 F. Supp 838 (D.C. N.J 1964), *aff'd* 344 F.2d 996 (3d Cir. 1965), where a controlling shareholder was held to have received a dividend when his corporation made payments to the widow of a former shareholder "to right the wrong he thought done to the widow" by her husband, the deceased shareholder.

CHAPTER 24

Generating Premiums Through Charitable Contributions

Creative planners are learning that it is possible to achieve several estate planning objectives simultaneously. They are also finding out that there are times when the most creative and effective way to meet one client goal is to achieve another.

Tax law makes it possible for a shareholder in a closely held corporation to make a significant charitable gift and simultaneously bail out earnings and profits without incurring dividend income. For example, a charitable contribution of stock (or some other property) may generate an income tax deduction that in turn will save income sufficient to fund the premiums for a buy-sell.

It works like this:

Step 1. The shareholder donates stock to a charity.
Step 2. The donation generates an income tax deduction to the donor (but the amount of stock is relatively small, so there is no loss of control).
Step 3. The money that otherwise would have been paid in taxes and that is saved through the income tax deduction is used to fund premiums for the buy-sell.

Assume your clients are a father, son and daughter, each of whom owns a one-third interest in the FSD Corporation. The business is facing an accumulated earnings tax problem, the three stockholders are in high income tax brackets (assume 30 percent) and all three are charitably inclined. Even though the corporation is cash-rich, the shareholders—because of the demands of their high living standards—have a cash flow problem in personally funding their buy-sell agreement on a cross-purchase basis.

Their goals are to

- reduce or eliminate the accumulated earnings tax problem,
- provide a meaningful annual gift to charity and
- provide adequate insurance to fund a cross-purchase buy-sell.

Here is one way all three goals may be met: Each shareholder would contribute $10,000 worth of stock to one or more qualified charities each year. This in turn would generate a deduction of $3,000. In other words the charitable contribution will save each shareholder $3,000 that otherwise would have been paid in taxes, resulting in a net cost of $7,000 for the charitable contribution.[1] Each shareholder's $3,000 tax savings (a $9,000 total) can now be used for cross-purchase agreement premium payments.

What happens next? The charities now own stock in a closely held business—which they could sell to the FSD Corporation for $30,000. This eases or relieves the corporation's accumulated earnings tax problem by removing cash from the corporation. Thus all three objectives have been met.

Will the donor/shareholder be considered to have received a dividend because the corporation bought back the stock from the charity? The IRS will not treat a gift of stock to a qualified charity followed by a redemption of such stock as if the stock had been redeemed from the donor (i.e., it will not impose dividend treatment), even though there was an *understanding* that such redemption would take place, *unless* the donee/charity was *legally bound*, or could be compelled by the corporation, to have the stock redeemed. So no restrictions should be placed on the charity's use of the stock, nor should there be a commitment either for the charity to sell or for the corporation to buy the donated stock.

If a charity that will voluntarily agree to a subsequent redemption can be found, use of such a gift redemption can provide significant tax benefits and be a source of premium dollars.[2] It is possible to require the charity that wants to sell the stock to an outside party to offer it first to the corporation and then to its shareholders at fair market value. This first-offer requirement should not adversely affect the tax benefits of this technique.

One additional caveat: the appreciation in the stock in excess of the taxpayer's basis at the time the stock is donated to charity is an item of tax preference.[3]

Thus AMT could result from large contributions, or small contributions for taxpayers with other items of tax preference, reducing the tax savings generated by the gift. So each taxpayer's personal tax picture must be analyzed prior to planning along these lines.[4]

Endnotes

1. Note that as a result of the Revenue Reconciliation Act of 1990 the actual tax savings could be revised through adjustment to itemized deductions imposed on higher-income taxpayers.
2. Rev. Rul. 78-197, 1978-1 C.B. 83; *Palmer v. Comm'r*, 62 T.C. 684 (1974); *Carrington v. Comm'r*, 476 F.2d 704 (5th Cir. 1973); *Grove v. Comm'r*, 490 F.2d 241 (2d Cir. 1973). The requirements for success include the following: (1) bona fide gift to charity, (2) no requirement that charity sell stock and (3) no requirement that corporation buy stock.

   Detailed information on this technique can be found in Zaritsky and Leimberg, *Tax Planning for Life Insurance* (New York: Warren, Gorham, and Lamont, 1992), call 800-950-1210.
3. IRC §57.
4. IRC §55.

CHAPTER 25

Intentional Undervaluation

THE TYPICAL ARGUMENT

- "Why not save federal estate taxes by intentionally undervaluing the stock in setting the buy-sell price—and then make up the difference *outside* the buy-sell?"
- "What's the difference where the beneficiary gets the money as long as he or she gets the same *number* of dollars?"
- "If we do it this way, we can buy the outside insurance with before-tax corporate dollars (through a group insurance vehicle such as group term[1] or a split-dollar agreement[2])."

THE COUNTERARGUMENTS

1. IRS Not Bound by an Unreasonable Price

First, understand the distinction between lowering value in a buy-sell agreement to the lowest point where reasonable minds dealing at arm's length and with knowledge of all relevant facts could differ and intentionally lowering it *beyond* that point. A good test is to ask, "What is the lowest price you would accept for your interest if I made you an offer today?"

A price set in the buy-sell agreement that is less than that price would probably be beyond the reasonable limit. And the IRS undoubtedly will not consider itself bound by a price substantially below that "reasonable" price.

202

What's wrong with those arguments for intentional undervaluation? If the price in the buy-sell is set substantially below a reasonable price (the lowest point at which reasonable minds could differ), the IRS would not consider itself bound—even if the parties to the agreement are bound.

Technically, the IRS is never bound to accept a price set by the taxpayers. Historically, it would almost always honor the price set in an agreement if

- the estate was obligated to sell at a shareholder's death;
- the agreement prohibited a lifetime sale of the stock without a first offer to the other party (or parties) at no more than the "deathtime" contract price; and
- at the time the agreement was executed the price set was fair and adequate.

If those conditions are not met, the decedent shareholder's estate could be put in the interesting position of paying estate tax on an amount far greater than the amount it actually received.[3] The estate might even pay a tax exceeding the price it received for the surrendered stock.

Further complicating the matter is the yet-to-be-seen interpretation by the IRS of Chapter 14 gift tax valuation rules as they pertain to buy-sell agreements.[4] As previously discussed, not only will the existing case law remain applicable (except to the extent replaced by the new law), but Chapter 14 of the gift tax law has created a new "arm's-length" test and revised the interpretation of the "business purpose" and "device" tests. The final regulations to Section 2703 provide that an agreement among parties who are not the natural objects of one's bounty may not be subject to Chapter 14, but the authors believe this should not be interpreted as an invitation to undervaluation, because existing case law has always required a fair market price. Violation of these stringent tests will result in a significant gift tax cost.

Gift tax law now requires that, in the case of buy-sells between family members or the natural objects of the other's bounty, all three of the following tests be met for the price established in a buy-sell to be determinative of value (and to avoid unintended gift tax cost):

1. The agreement must be a bona fide business arrangement.
2. The agreement in totality must not be a device to transfer property to a member of the decedent's family for less than adequate and full consideration.

3. The terms must be comparable to similar arrangements between persons in an arm's-length transaction.

2. Lifetime Sale Price Cannot Exceed "Deathtime" Price

A second problem with intentional undervaluation is caused by the restriction that must be placed in the agreement forbidding a stockholder to sell during his or her lifetime at a price higher than the "deathtime" price.[5]

If the price at which stock is sold during lifetime cannot exceed the artificially low deathtime price because of this first-offer requirement, a potential tax mine field is armed. For example, consider (1) the shareholder who is not getting along with the coshareholders and wants to leave the firm, (2) the disabled shareholder who cannot perform services and needs the cash value of his or her capital interest or (3) the shareholder who would like to retire. If the intentionally undervalued price is $200,000—but should have been at least $300,000—that shareholder is legally entitled to only $200,000. A greater payment by the coshareholders is unlikely, but if it is made it could actually be considered a taxable gift.

3. High Income Tax Cost

If the difference between the actual value and the artificially lowered value is made up through a DBO plan, the entire amount of death benefit received by the deceased shareholder's family becomes taxable at ordinary income rates. If the shareholder was in a relatively low estate tax bracket (or if the income tax the family will pay exceeds the death taxes it would have paid), the savings through intentional undervaluation may be totally illusory. For instance, if the decedent/shareholder is survived by a U.S. citizen spouse, and stock and other property passes to that person in a qualifying manner, the unlimited federal estate tax marital deduction will eliminate the federal estate tax.

4. Possible Loss of Estate Tax Savings

If the difference is made up through group term insurance, there will be no estate tax savings if death occurs within three years of the time the additional coverage is purchased. An absolute assignment must be made more than three years prior to death to remove the proceeds from the insureds' estate.[6]

Such an assignment is potentially doubly costly to a noncontrolling shareholder: control over the coverage is lost immediately, and in the event of divorce the shareholder will be paying Table I costs for a policy that could be owned by his or her ex-spouse outright or, more likely, as a trustee. Every time the shareholder/employee receives a raise, that cost will increase. Group insurance as a funding vehicle has the further disadvantage that at the time an employee/shareholder retires, this coverage either ceases or drops substantially (perhaps when the stock has appreciated in value and the need for insurance has increased) and can be converted only at what may be a prohibitive cost to both the employer/corporation and the employee/shareholder.

5. Potential Loss of Benefit to Minority Shareholder

In the case of any corporate-provided or -subsidized "outside" funding for a minority shareholder, the controlling management could change or drop the employee benefit—an especially troublesome risk for the retired or disabled minority shareholder.

6. Disadvantage to Buyer

In a cross-purchase arrangement, although the seller might in fact be made whole, the buyer may be disadvantaged. One reason for using a cross-purchase agreement is to give the buyer an increased basis in the acquired stock. If the buyer underpays, the balance is made up by the corporation, so this tax benefit will be sacrificed to the extent of the "bargain."

7. Disadvantage to Shareholder's Family

Perhaps most important of all the factors is that a shareholder's family should receive the maximum financial security possible through the use of corporate dollars—in *addition* to a fair price for the decedent/shareholder's business interest.

8. Counterproductive Estate Tax Savings

To the extent a unified credit or the unlimited estate tax marital deduction is available, it may be counterproductive to try to "save" estate tax through an artificial means.

Endnotes

1. IRC §79 pertains to the taxation of an employee for the current economic value of group term life insurance provided by his or her employer. Under that section, generally an employee's income—for amounts of group term life insurance in excess of $50,000 (to the extent such cost exceeds payments made by the employee)—is "equal to the cost of group term life insurance," so long as the plan does not discriminate in favor of key employees.

   Deductions for group term life insurance are governed by IRC §162(a)(1) rather than IRC §79. IRC §162(a)(1) allows an employer to deduct group term insurance premiums as "other compensation for personal services actually rendered."

   Although a group life insurance plan may include an element of permanent cash value type of insurance, the favorable treatment afforded group term coverage does not apply to this portion of the total premium. The $50,000 tax-free element and Table I rates (a government uniform premium rate table used as a basis for determining income realized by the employee and computed on the basis of five-year age brackets) apply only to the term coverage.

   To the extent of any permanent coverage, the cost must be paid for by the employee. If the employer pays the costs of this element, that amount must be treated as additional compensation to the employee. If the permanent portion of the premium is—together with all other compensation—reasonable, it will be deductible by the employer as additional salary to the employee. Additionally, the corporation could give the employee a bonus to be used to pay premiums on the permanent portion. Again, the bonus could be deductible by the corporation subject to the "reasonable compensation" requirement.
2. Indirect funding may be accomplished through devices other than group insurance. Use of the DBO approach is one of a number of alternatives to providing death benefit dollars through group term/permanent insurance.
3. *Estate of Dickenson, Jr.*, 63 T.C. 771 (1975).
4. IRC §2703.
5. *Est. of Caplan v. Comm'r*, 33 T.C.M. 189 (1974); *Est. of Trammel v. Comm'r*, 18 T.C. 662 (1952); Rev. Rul. 59-60, 1959-1 C.B. 237. The agreement to fix the value for federal estate tax purposes must prohibit the owners from disposing of their interests during their lifetimes without first offering such interests to the other party or parties at no more than the contract price. A contract or option under which a party can dispose of an interest at any price chosen during lifetime will not be binding on the IRS for valuation purposes upon a shareholder's death.
6. IRC §2035(d).

CHAPTER 26

S Elections and the Buy-Sell Agreement

An S corporation (formerly known as a *subchapter S* or *tax option corporation*) is one that elects not to be taxed as a corporation.[1] Instead, for most purposes its tax attributes—including taxable income, deductions, capital gains and losses and credits—are passed through to its shareholders and picked up on their individual income tax returns. In this regard the S corporation is treated in a manner similar to a partnership.

EFFECT OF THE TAX REFORM ACT OF 1986

Prior to the Tax Reform Act of 1986 the S election was most commonly made by corporations experiencing losses, especially start-up enterprises. Using the pass-through characteristic, the S corporation's owners could apply corporate losses against their personal income. Subsequent to the 1986 act, however, the S corporation became a much more widely used tax-planning device. Many of its prior advantages remain viable, and TRA '86 made significant new benefits available:

1. Losses (to the extent of basis) may be passed through to shareholders to offset personal income from other sources.
2. Double taxation is avoided. Because S corporation income is taxed only once (to its shareholders as the income is earned), significant income tax savings may be realized over the normal double taxation of income to the owners of C corporation (where corporate earnings are taxed

as earned to the corporation and then again to the shareholders as dividends).

3. Individual federal and state income tax brackets may be lower than the corporation's rates, thus leading to lower overall taxation on the business's earnings.

4. Because each shareholder is taxed on his or her share of all corporate earnings, the "reasonable compensation" issue for the deductibility of corporate distributions disappears. In other words there is no accumulated earning tax problem with an S corporation.

5. Perhaps most dramatically, the favorable tax treatment often afforded the distribution of cash received upon a corporate-level sale of assets of a liquidating corporation no longer applies. In its place lies a dangerous potential tax trap: C corporations are now subject to tax on the sale of their assets. Then, when the cash proceeds of the sale are distributed, shareholders are taxed a second time on the liquidating distributions. But S corporations can often avoid this tax on "built-in gains."

6. S corporations are not subject to the corporate AMT, which can save them hundreds of thousands of dollars. For example, assume a C corporation purchased $1 million of life insurance on the life of its president and that it had already used up its $40,000 exclusion from the AMT upon his death. Upon the receipt of insurance proceeds the corporation would have to pay an AMT of about $150,000. This tax would not be levied if the business operated as an S corporation.

7. S corporation status makes additional flexibility possible if for no other reason than the failure to meet the major safe harbor tests of Section 302(a) (see Chapter 5) is to some extent irrelevant.[2] Distributions from an S corporation with no earnings and profits are, if the corporation has been an S corporation since inception, income-tax-free to the extent of the shareholder's basis. Amounts distributed to the shareholder in excess of basis are taxed as capital gains. This is the same result that would occur if the Section 302(a) tests had been met.[3] So there is no harsh penalty if a selling shareholder keeps some shares and continues to vote and otherwise participate in the corporation's management. Thus to a great extent, "there is more flexibility in planning installment payment redemptions in an S corporation than with a C corporation."[4] In the authors' opinion, however, a cross-purchase type buy-out will be indicated in most cases.

ELECTION REQUIREMENTS

An S election is, therefore, more valuable than ever. But the requirements for maintaining the election are quite stringent, and the S election can inadvertently be lost.[5]

An S corporation may not have:

- more than 35 shareholders (although spouses count as only 1 shareholder);
- a shareholder (other than an estate or certain qualifying trusts) who is not an individual (e.g., another corporation or a partnership);
- a shareholder who is a nonresident alien; or
- more than one class of stock, except for differences in voting rights, (i.e. preferred and common will not qualify, while nonvoting common and voting common will).[6]

The S election will be lost if a majority (shareholders owning more than 50 percent of the corporation's stock) vote to revoke the election or if a transfer is made in violation of the preceding requirements.[7]

A properly drawn buy-sell agreement may protect the election. The agreement could provide, for example, that

- shareholders be restricted from transferring shares to individuals or other transferees who are ineligible from being S corporation stockholders;
- transfers to a qualifying trust be conditioned on the beneficiary's filing an election to treat the trust as a qualified subchapter S trust (QSST);[8]
- if shares are transferred in a manner that would disqualify the election, those shares be subject to purchase by qualifying shareholders or redeemable by the corporation; or
- shareholders must prepare their personal estate plans in a manner consistent with preserving the S election (so, for example, shares not subject to the buy-sell that pass in trust must pass to a QSST).

In the appendix to this book is a specimen agreement that may be helpful for attorneys who have as clients C corporations that are going to elect S status. The specimen documents may also be useful for buy-sell agreements of existing or new S corporations.

FORM OF BUY-SELL AGREEMENT

As with a C corporation, while the cost of premiums for insurance to fund a redemption agreement remains nondeductible, the receipt of proceeds by an S corporation is tax-free (assuming no transfer for value, of course). Similarly, any gain realized upon surrender of the policy is passed through and taxed to the shareholders.

Receipt of the life insurance proceeds will have no corporate AMT consequences. Accumulated earnings tax concerns disappear upon distribution of the life insurance to shareholders, and the tax-free character of the proceeds is preserved.

Yet, according to some authorities, it may be more advantageous for the insurance to be acquired on a cross-purchase basis.[9] Why?

S corporation shareholders are taxed on the income of the corporation as it is earned. This tax is applied even on the corporate income used to acquire insurance on a nondeductible basis and even if the shareholders receive no cash distribution with which they may pay the tax. So S corporation shareholders may have a tax liability due to life insurance premiums but no cash to pay that tax.

A solution would be for the corporation to distribute a deductible bonus to its shareholders large enough so that—after their tax payments—they would still have enough cash to make premium payments.

Additional Disadvantages of Stock Redemption and S Corporation–Owned Life Insurance

In choosing between a corporate stock redemption type agreement and a cross-purchase plan, consider these ten points:

1. Premiums paid by the corporation are currently taxable to its shareholders in proportion to their stock ownership—rather than according to the insured's age or health. This may mean that the burden of premium payments is allocated unfairly.
2. Shareholders will pay tax on the premiums just as if they received a bonus and purchased the policy on their own. But they do not personally own either the policies or their cash values.

3. The surviving shareholders receive no step-up in basis when the S corporation redeems a decent/shareholder's stock (unlike the result if the policies were owned in a cross-purchase arrangement). The survivor's basis remains the same, despite having indirectly paid for a portion of the buyout with personal after-tax dollars.

4. As is the case with a C corporation, the higher the S corporation's earnings and profits, the more likely a distribution to a shareholder will be considered a dividend. But in an S corporation earnings and profits are inflated by the excess of policy cash values over net premiums paid and by the excess of death proceeds over policy cash values at death.

5. If the buy-sell price-setting formula is based on a multiple of earnings, that figure would not compare to a C corporation's before- or after-tax earnings since (with minor exceptions) there is no S corporation tax bracket. Earnings are passed through for tax purposes to the firm's shareholders.

6. Although the IRS has held that buy-sell agreements per se do not create a second class of stock, there is always the possibility that a stock redemption plan to which the corporation is a party could be held to create such a second class of stock.[10]

7. When a stock redemption is funded with life insurance, the premiums are paid with after-tax dollars. This has the effect of locking in income. Of course corporations with no inherited earnings and profits will not be deemed to have received earnings and profits merely because of life insurance.

8. The payment of life insurance premiums by the S corporation has a tax impact depending on whether they are charged to capital. Since the outlay for premiums is nondeductible in computing taxable income (and therefore not chargeable to capital), the expenditure decreases the basis of the shareholder's stock. For purposes of determining the accumulated adjustments account (AAA), this reduces the amount that in turn reduces the amount of potential tax redistributions to shareholders.

9. When the corporation receives tax-exempt income (i.e., life insurance proceeds), the income tax basis of the shareholder's stock increases. Only the excess of the proceeds over the premiums paid increases basis if premiums have been charged to capital. The receipt of tax-free life insurance should have no effect on the AAA account. The receipt of insurance proceeds increases the basis of not only the surviving shareholder's stock but also the deceased shareholder's stock. Since this was

already adjusted to the date-of-death value, redemption could result in a capital loss.

10. The actual redemption of the stock decreases earnings and profits. Although this would be advantageous when the S corporation has inherited earnings and profits, it would also be disadvantageous because the redemption reduces the accumulated adjustments account.

For these reasons many authorities suggest either a cross-purchase or a third-party ownership of the insurance. Proceeds could then be loaned to the corporation to enable it to redeem stock under IRC §303 when appropriate.

SPECIAL DRAFTING CONSIDERATIONS WHERE S STOCK IS INVOLVED

If an S corporation has more than one class of stock, the pass-through of taxes directly to the shareholders may be lost, and the corporation may become taxable as a separate entity.[11] It is extremely important, therefore, that the buy-sell agreement (as well as the corporation's other key documents) avoid giving shareholders varying rights to share in the firm's profits or in the proceeds of any sale or liquidation.

It is clear that the mere presence of special restrictions on stock issued as compensation to key employees will not, per se, be considered a second class of stock.[12] So in the authors' opinion, if the buy-sell provides some shareholders with differing buyback procedures or pricing formulas, a second class of stock is not an automatic result. However, if the parties intend to give some shareholders rights or obligations not given to others, the buy-sell should very clearly state that "each issued share of stock has an equal right to dividends, asset appreciation, and the proceeds of any sale or liquidation."

The draftsperson of an S corporation buy-sell should also consider the fact that the income tax liability of S corporation shareholders accrues on a day-by-day basis ratably throughout the year. This means that the selling shareholder will have an income tax liability for earnings of the business up until the date the stock is sold. This liability should be considered in establishing the formula for determining the purchase price of the stock.

Endnotes

1. IRC §§1361–1379.
2. See Emory, "More Flexibility Possible for Installment Redemption of S Corporation Shareholder." *Letter Ruling Review* 3, (No. 6, June 1991): 4 (Tax Analysts).
3. IRC §1368(b). Even if the S corporation had E&P, the same general result would occur—to the extent the distribution was not more than the firm's AAA. IRC §1368(c).
4. See Emory, "More Flexibility Possible for Installment Redemption of S Corporation Shareholder."
5. IRC §1361(b).
6. The IRS has ruled that provisions in a shareholders' agreement resulting merely in differences between shareholders as to voting rights and obligations do not create a second class of stock. PLRs 850611 and 9011055. Proposed regulations in this area affirm that if the only difference is the right to vote the stock will not be classified as more than one class.
7. IRC §1362(d). One person who owns more than half the stock can revoke the election.
8. IRC §1361(d)(2).
9. See Apfel and Wolfe, "AMT Increases Advantages of Cross-Purchase Arrangements over Redemption Agreements," *Taxation for Lawyers* (Jan/Feb. 1990), discussing how accounting methods affect the choice of agreement form and concluding that the cross-purchase arrangement is often desirable.
10. See O'Neil and Saubert, "Redemptions of S Corporation Stock as an Alternative to Stock Sales: An Update," *S Corporations Journal*, 3 (No. 4, Winter 1990–91).
11. IRC §1361(b)(1)(D).
12. Rev. Rul. 85-161, 1985-2 C.B. 191.

Cross-Purchase vs. Stock Redemption: A Summary

The fundamental differences between the cross-purchase and stock redemption plans must be applied to each corporation's particular circumstances. Weighing the following factors will facilitate a decision between the two.

Stock Redemption vs. *Cross-Purchase*

How It Is Arranged

The *corporation* contracts with the stockholders to purchase the stock of any deceased shareholder at an agreed-on price or according to an agreed-on formula. The corporation is applicant, owner, premium payer and beneficiary of a policy on the life of each stockholder in an amount needed to purchase the stock.	*Stockholders* agree among themselves that the survivor(s) will purchase the stock of a shareholder who dies, at an agreed-on price or according to an agreed-on formula. Each stockholder is applicant, owner, premium payer and beneficiary of the policy(ies) on the life of other stockholder(s).

Number of Shareholders

Where there are more than three shareholders, a stock redemption arrangement is indicated since only	When there are two or three shareholders, the group is usually small enough to minimize adminis-

Stock Redemption   *vs.*   **Cross-Purchase**

one insurance policy per stockholder is required. This can result in a cost savings for two
reasons: (1) larger policies often
result in a lower premium over
$1,000 of coverage; (2) each policy
has a built-in "premium adjustment factor," an annual charge
for paperwork ranging from $25 to
$40. Obviously a $1 million policy will cost less per year than ten
$100,000 policies. Also, a corpo-
rate premium payer and owner
would lead to administrative sim-
plicity and less chance of lapse.

trative problems. The formula for
the number of policies needed is
$N \times (N-1)$ where N is the number
of stockholders.

Amount of Insurance Needed

Slightly larger insurance amounts
may have to be carried because
when the first owner dies, and the
corporation receives the proceeds,
the value of the corporation's assets
jumps, and therefore the cost to
purchase a given interest may increase. (This can be avoided
through proper wording of the
agreement itself.) It may also be
argued that the value of the business is reduced by loss of the key
individual's services. Application of
the AMT could cause the amount
of insurance required to be increased by almost 20 percent.

No comparable problem exists. The
net worth of the corporation is
unaffected by the receipt by an individual shareholder of life insurance proceeds.

Differences in Ages

Each stockholder pays premiums in
proportion to ownership interest.

The youngest shareholder carries
the heavy burden of paying

Stock Redemption	*vs.*	*Cross-Purchase*

If, because of differences in age, the premiums are unequal (assume the premium on *A*'s life is $1,000 and the premium on *B*'s life is $2,000), and *A* and *B* each own 50 percent of the stock, *B* might feel the impact of the premium is inequitable because *B* is actually contributing $500 to the cost of the policy on his or her own life. (If this were a cross-purchase agreement, the cost would be only $1,000.)

premiums on the life of the older shareholder and usually being in the weakest financial position to pay these premiums. A split-dollar arrangement between the corporation and the employee/shareholder may provide the answer.

Differences in Ownership Interest

Since the corporation is premium payer, there is a pooling effect in the payment of premiums. The stockholders bear this cost in direct relation to their stockholdings. This works to the disadvantage of stockholders with larger holdings and to the advantage of those with small holdings. (Since stockholder *R* owns 80 percent of the corporation, *R* would be contributing 80 percent of the premium cost to purchase the costockholder's 20 percent of the business.)[1]

Each stockholder pays for what he or she may receive.

Certainty of Performance

The corporation cannot bind itself absolutely to buy its own stock (most states require that sufficient surplus funds be available and that the redemption not defraud creditors). Naturally, funding

Individuals can bind themselves absolutely to fulfill an agreement.

Stock Redemption	*vs.*	*Cross-Purchase*

with income-tax-free life insurance (subject, of course, to the AMT) alleviates—but does not necessarily eliminate—the problem.

Creditor's Rights

Since the policies are corporate assets, they are subject to claims of business creditors. Corporate creditors may make claims against policy cash values and proceeds of corporate-owned life insurance.[2]

Free from claims of the corporation's creditors since the life insurance is owned by individual stockholders on the lives of costockholders. Creditors of the shareholder who owns the policy may be able to reach cash values and proceeds of policies owned on the lives of others.

Deductibility and Taxation of Premiums

The corporation is allowed no deduction for premium payments. Premium payments are not considered constructive dividends to stockholders unless the purchase discharges a primary, unconditional and personal obligation of the surviving shareholders.

Shareholders receive no deduction. If the corporation gives the employees reasonable bonuses, these may be deductible by the corporation (and income to the employees) and used to purchase insurance on the lives of the other stockholders.

Income Taxation of Insurance Proceeds

The corporation will receive life insurance proceeds income-tax-free. The AMT may result in the receipt of the proceeds triggering an indirect income tax.

Shareholders/beneficiaries will receive life insurance proceeds income-tax-free.

Stock Redemption   *vs.*   *Cross-Purchase*

Ratio of Stockholdings

If the ratio of stock held by each shareholder previous to the redemption is desired to be retained *after* the redemption, this method is indicated. Surviving stockholders' percentage of stock ownership is increased pro rata by the amount of stock redeemed based on their previous ownership percentages.

If it is desirable to change the ratio of ownership, a cross-purchase is indicated because the agreement can specify and affect whatever new ratio of ownership is desired by the parties involved. This would be achieved by varying the amount of stock to be purchased from the decedent's estate by each shareholder. For example, *A* owns 60 shares, *B* owns 30 shares and *C* owns 10 shares. *A* now dies. With *equal purchases, B* would acquire 30 shares for a total of 60, and *C* would acquire 30 shares for a total of 40. With *proportionate purchases, B* would acquire 45 shares for a total of 75, and *C* would acquire 15 shares for a total of 25. If the survivors are to be *equal shareholders,* then *B* would acquire 20 shares for a total of 50, and *C* would acquire 40 shares for a total of 50.

Possible State Law Restrictions

A corporation may be restricted from purchasing its own shares absent sufficient surplus.[3] Local law and corporate charter and by-laws must be examined. This problem (that a corporation's purchase of its own stock is normally prohibited by state law except out of its own surplus) can be alleviated by having the stock

A cross-purchase arrangement is indicated if corporate law may create problems.

Stock Redemption	vs.	*Cross-Purchase*

purchase agreement provide that the surviving stockholders will cause the corporation to take such actions as it can to create a surplus; for example, the stockholders might vote to create a surplus by revaluing corporate assets or alternatively recapitalize and reduce the par value of the corporation's stock (thereby creating paid-in surplus—assuming it is unnecessary to make the purchase out of earned surplus).

Comparative Tax Rates[4]

Indicated if the corporate tax rate is lower than the individual tax rate, because the after-tax cost to pay premiums would be correspondingly lower.	When individuals pay premiums, only after-tax dollars are available. If the individuals are in lower personal income tax brackets than the corporation, and since life insurance premiums are not deductible by the corporation, the cost of funding by the cross-purchase method may be less. (Even if the salaries of the stockholders have to be increased to provide money for premium payments, as long as they are still in lower tax brackets than the corporation, this method would be indicated.)

Unreasonable Accumulation of Surplus

Until the total cash accumulated by the business—including cash value of these policies—reaches $250,000 ($150,000 in the case of professional corporations), there	No similar problem exists since corporate funds are not used.

| *Stock Redemption* | *vs.* | *Cross-Purchase* |

will be no adverse tax consequences in most cases. Accumulations in excess of that amount raise the tax issue of "reasonableness." Life insurance funding of a stock redemption type of agreement per se does not give rise to unreasonable accumulations problems. The key issue is: does the accumulation have a business- rather than stockholder-oriented purpose?

Surviving Shareholder's Cost Basis

Cost basis is important because it is subtracted from the amount realized in a sale and the result becomes the taxable gain (or loss). Under a corporate redemption, although the value of a shareholder's stock interest increases, the cost basis remains the same—even after the corporation redeems the decedent's stock. So if a surviving stockholder were to sell his or her share of the business later, the surviving shareholder would have to pay increased taxes because of his or her increased gain. This is because under stock redemption plans the surviving stockholder's cost basis is his or her original investment and is not increased by the insurance proceeds—since they were paid not by the stockholder but by the corporation.

A survivor receives an increase in cost basis for the shares purchased from a decedent/shareholder's estate. In the event of a sale during life, the taxable gain and, therefore, the tax to be paid on that sale are reduced. If there is a strong possibility that the stockholder will sell stock during life, a cross-purchase agreement is indicated. If the survivor does not sell the stock and still owns it at death, that stock together with all other appreciated assets will receive a stepped-up basis (This is also true in the case of a stock redemption.)

Stock Redemption	*vs.*	*Cross-Purchase*

Seller's Cost Basis

The seller (the shareholder/employee or his or her estate or beneficiary) uses cost (more technically, "adjusted basis") as the starting point for ascertaining gain or loss on a sale. The estate or heirs of a decedent take the federal estate tax value of the stock as their basis for computing gain or loss on a subsequent sale.

Same as for stock redemption.

Change of Nature of Agreement

If the agreement is originally of the stock redemption type, a later transfer of life insurance policies to parties other than the insured may generate a transfer-for-value problem.

A cross-purchase plan is indicated if the nature of the agreement might change in the future. If life insurance policies are transferred to a corporation in which the insured is an officer or shareholder, the proceeds will retain their income-tax-free status.

Transfer-for-Value Problems

The corporation continues to own the policies at the death of the stockholder, and no transfer is necessary at death. This eliminates the possibility of a transfer-for-value problem. Existing policies can be safely transferred by shareholders to the corporation to initiate the plan.

Where each stockholder owns a policy on the lives of the costockholders, and more than two stockholders exist, the possibility of a transfer-for-value problem exists. When one stockholder dies, his or her estate will usually wish to transfer (sell) the policies owned on the other stockholders to the survivors. Since transfer to a costockholder of the insured is not an exception to the transfer-

Stock Redemption	*vs.*	*Cross-Purchase*
		for-value rule, a serious tax problem could result with respect to the death proceeds of any of the transferred policies. The decedent/shareholder's estate can sell such policies only to the respective insureds, to the corporation if the insured is an officer or shareholder or to a partner of the insured (for example, if the surviving stockholders are also partners in a bona fide venture).

Family Corporations—Constructive Ownership Problems

In almost any family-owned corporation, any close relationship among stockholders may invoke the constructive ownership problem. For example: If a son is an estate beneficiary, the estate, though not an actual owner, would still be considered constructive owner of all remaining outstanding shares by virtue of the son's shares being attributed to the estate. Thus the purchase of the shares, not being a complete redemption that terminates the estate's interest in the corporation, would not qualify for treatment as a capital exchange for stock. The result is that the transaction could be considered a dividend distribution, and all the proceeds would constitute ordinary income to the estate. In some cases attribution may be waived and capital exchange treatment preserved.	No similar problem exists, because no redemption of stock is involved. Constructive ownership (attribution) problems are avoided.

| ***Stock Redemption*** | ***vs.*** | ***Cross-Purchase*** |

Estate Taxation of Insurance Proceeds

Assuming the corporation is the beneficiary of the entire proceeds, the proceeds will be considered in valuing the stock interest of a decedent/shareholder but will not be separately includable in the insured's estate as life insurance. If the agreement is binding during life, the estate is bound to sell for a reasonable price and the price agreed on was arrived at in an arm's-length bona fide negotiation, the agreed-on price may control for federal estate tax purposes where it is between unrelated parties. To be binding between family members, generally an agreement must meet the three IRC Chapter 14 tests.

Since each stockholder owns a policy on the lives of costockholders, the fair market values in the policies on the lives of surviving stockholders will be includable in the estate of a decedent/stockholder. Proceeds of any policies on the life of the decedent owned by his or her coshareholders will not be includable in his or her estate.

WHY A CROSS-PURCHASE MAY NOT BE WARRANTED

Although this book presents many reasons for favoring a cross-purchase plan over a stock redemption arrangement, that preference is not absolute. There are many reasons why a cross-purchase plan may not be indicated:

1. Psychologically—and for cash flow reasons—stockholders may prefer to have the corporation make premium outlays.
2. If the shareholders are in tax brackets higher than the corporation's bracket, it makes good business sense for the corporation to pay premiums.
3. If there are more than three shareholders, the cost (an annual charge is levied by an insurance company for each policy—the more policies, the more annual charges are involved) and administrative inconvenience is high. For instance, with ten shareholders, 90 policies would

be necessary initially. Every change in valuation would signal the need to consider the purchase of 90 additional policies.

The formula to compute the number of policies necessary under a cross-purchase agreement is

$$N \times (N-1)$$

with N being the number of shareholders. For example, the ten-shareholder cross-purchase agreement would be funded by $10 \times 9 = 90$ policies. Each time the business was revalued, 90 new policies would be required.

4. If an individual stockholder has a potential (foreseeable) creditor (or divorce) problem, receipt of insurance proceeds could be followed by attachment, making the insurance unavailable to fund the purchase. On the other hand, receipt of the proceeds by the corporation—assuming, of course, that it does not have its own creditor exposure—would avoid this problem.

5. If a cross-purchase agreement is underfunded and the shortfall is paid out in installments, the interest on the deferred payments is likely to be considered "investment" rather than "trade or business" interest. This would limit the deductibility of such interest and thereby increase the cost of the purchase stock considerably.

6. The absolute percentage of ownership of each shareholder in a corporation increases when a cross-purchase plan is used—a key consideration where the planner is representing a minority shareholder.[5]

Endnotes

1. This can be viewed in another way; it is true that the "big" shareholder is in essence funding his own buyout, but some might say that this is a small price to pay for retaining the minority (often younger) shareholder in the business and providing incentive for that person to work harder for the business (which enriches the "big" shareholder disproportionately). It is true, however, that where the interests of the parties are extremely disparate, a stock redemption may be inherently unfair. Consider the following example:

    The Lankford Bay Marina is worth $1 million (exclusive of life insurance). Doug owns 90 percent of the stock. Barbara, his friend, owns the remaining 10 percent. If the corporation buys $900,000 of insurance on Doug's life, at his death the corporation will be worth about $1,900,000.

    If the buy-sell does not take the insurance proceeds into account, at Doug's death his estate will be paid $900,000 (90 percent of only $1 million). If the buy-sell takes the entire $900,000 of insurance into account, at Doug's death his estate should be paid $1,710,00 (90 percent of $1,900,000). But that would strip the corporation of all but $190,000. That would be the value of what Barbara purchased under the buy-sell. Since Doug will end up with 90 percent of the proceeds if they are taken into account in valuing his interest, to provide Barbara with a business worth $1 million, the corporation would have to purchase $9 million worth of insurance. This is clearly an absurd and unintended result.

Wherever there is a wide disparity in ownership, the draftsperson must therefore consider the impact of the life insurance on the burden being placed on the buyer. A possible partial solution is to build in the right of the buyer to make installment payments. See Donald, "Corporate Buy-Out Agreements," 106-5th T.M.: A-5.

2. The other side to this is that the corporation has the policy cash values and could use that money for an emergency or an opportunity or could borrow it and invest it in the business if necessary.

3. Planners should anticipate the risk of the selling shareholder that payments from the corporation might not be legally permissible if the effect of the redemption is to leave the corporation with more liabilities than assets. A stock redemption type of buy-sell should anticipate such a contingency.

4. Corporate after-tax earnings are needed to pay premiums in a stock redemption plan, while personal after-tax dollars are required in a cross-purchase arrangement. In some cases the corporation should pay bonuses to shareholder employees or shoulder all or the bulk of the premium outlay through a split-dollar arrangement. The problem with the typical comparison of which party is in a lower tax bracket is complicated by the fact that the IRS could apply dividend treatment to what the corporation classified as a bonus. This would, of course, make corporate premium payments relatively less expensive than under a cross-purchase plan, because the double tax on earnings would be avoided.

5. In a stock redemption plan the proportion of each shareholder's "before and after" interest in the corporation will remain the same relative to other remaining shareholders.

C H A P T E R   2 8

Switching from Stock Redemption to Cross-Purchase

There are many reasons why the owners of a business might decide to switch to a cross-purchase agreement from a stock redemption arrangement. For example, if the amount of insurance is large, there may be a corporate AMT (alternative minimum tax) that may be as high as 15 percent of the policy proceeds. This tax can be avoided if the life insurance is owned on a cross-purchase basis.

Once the decision to switch has been made, the owner must determine what to do with existing corporate-owned life insurance. This is an important decision, because an improperly handled switch can have disastrous tax consequences. Various possible solutions are discussed in the following sections.

Transfer Corporate-Owned Policies on the Life of an Insured to Coshareholders. Although this might seem like the simplest solution, it invokes the insidious transfer-for-value tax trap. The result is that all or most of the death proceeds lose their income-tax-free status and become subject to ordinary income tax. Only the consideration (the price paid for the policy) plus premiums paid by the new policy owner(s) (the insured's coshareholders) after the transfer will be income-tax-free.

Transfer Corporate-Owned Policies First to the Insured and Then to Coshareholders. The second transfer would be made as a gift or in an exchange of policies. While a transfer to the insured is a safe harbor even if the transfer is for valuable consideration, three potential problems arise with this course of action:

226

1. The IRS would probably view the two transactions as one prearranged plan, tie the two together as one and tax it as a transfer for value regardless of the second-step "gift" (this is really a quid pro quo arrangement since none of the "gifts" would occur in the absence of other, similar gifts). The reciprocal exchange of policies, regardless of what it is called, is a transfer for valuable consideration.

2. If the transfer to the insured, followed by the second transfer to a coshareholder, is made within three years of death, the proceeds will be included in the insured's estate for tax purposes to the extent the insured cannot prove he or she received adequate consideration in money or money's worth.

3. If the insured's death occurs while the insured, rather than the intended owner, holds the policy, the policy will be included (in addition to the stock) in the insured's gross estate. Even worse, the intended owner, the insured's coshareholder, will still be legally obligated to purchase the stock but will not have the cash to make the purchase (while the insured/decedent's estate will have both stock and insurance proceeds).

Transfer Only the Term Insurance Portion of the Policy on the Life of the Insured to a Coshareholder. That is, make a split-dollar cross-purchase with the corporation continuing as policyowner and the insured's coshareholder as beneficiary for the proceeds in excess of policy cash values. The corporation enters into a split-dollar endorsement type of arrangement with the shareholders.

The problem here is that the pure risk (term) portion of the proceeds has been transferred to a coshareholder for consideration (each stockholder has tacitly agreed with the corporation that, in return for the corporation's interest-free outlay of premiums, a fringe benefit, he or she will continue in the corporation's employment). The same transfer-for-value problem can occur with a brand-new policy owned initially by the corporation.

A solution may be to have the coshareholder of the insured apply for the policy and then transfer to the corporation all rights except the right to receive his or her portion of the proceeds. A transfer to a corporation in which the insured is an officer or shareholder is a protected exception to the transfer-for-value rule.

Often the best solution is the purchase of new insurance using a collateral assignment technique in which each shareholder is the applicant, owner and primary beneficiary of policies on the lives of the coshareholders. The corporation's interest is protected by a collateral assignment from the shareholder/policyowner.

Terminate the Corporate Stock Redemption Agreement but Retain the Original Policies in the Corporation. These policies could be

- used to provide key employee protection for the business;
- used to fund a DBO plan;
- used to finance the employer's obligation under a nonqualified deferred compensation arrangement;
- made "paid up" or placed on "reduced term" status;
- continued as before with no change in the stock redemption plan (with further appreciation in the firm handled through a supplementary cross-purchase type of agreement with new insurance arranged in this manner); or
- used to effect a Section 303 stock redemption. New insurance, arranged on a cross-purchase basis, could be used to provide funds for surviving shareholders to purchase stock from the estate of a deceased shareholder.

Terminate the Stock Redemption Plan but Transfer Corporate-Owned Policies to the Insured. This transfer would be excepted from the transfer-for-value rule. Such a transfer can be accomplished with minimal cash outlays in several ways:

- Existing corporate obligations to shareholders (such as loans) can be offset by the "purchase price for the policy." (Note that the price paid must equal the fair market value of the policy. If only the cash value is paid, but the actual fair market value exceeds the policy cash value, the difference could be considered additional compensation or a dividend to the new policyowners.)
- An immediate loan of the policy's cash value can be made by the new owner to pay for the policy.
- In the case of an S corporation, value of the policy can be treated as a distribution against the shareholder's AAA account or otherwise undistributed (but already taxed) earnings for the current year.

Transfer Corporate-Owned Policies to Coshareholders Who Are Also Partners. A transfer to a partner of the insured is an exception to the transfer-for-value tax trap. For example, if the shareholders happen to be partners in a partnership that owns a parcel of real estate leased to the corporation, and the partnership is a bona fide venture, the distributed policy should not be subject to the transfer-for-value rule. The partnership should exist before the transfer occurs. The partnership should have a business purpose other than the acquisition and retention of the life insurance policies.

Transfer Corporate-Owned Policies on the Life of an Individual to a Partnership. The coshareholders in the corporation also must be partners in the partnership.[1]

Endnote

1. See PLR 9042024. See also Ben-Horin, "Use of Life Insurance to Fund Buy-Out Agreements," *NYU Tax Inst.* 28 (1970): 819, 824. See also Leimberg and Doyle, *Tools and Techniques of Life Insurance Planning* (Cincinnati: National Underwriter Co. 1992), call 800-543-0874; and Zaritsky and Leimberg, *Tax Planning for Life Insurance* (New York: Warren, Gorham and Lamont, 1992), call 800-950-1210.

CHAPTER 29

The Wait-and-See
Solution

Rapidly changing tax laws, as well as continual changes in clients' circumstances and objectives, make it difficult for members of the estate planning team to know whether to use the stock redemption or cross-purchase type of buy-sell. The solution to this dilemma is to "wait and see." That is, planners and their clients can postpone making a decision on the purchaser until the decision *must* be made and when much more is known. That time is the death of the shareholder.

HOW THE WAIT-AND-SEE WORKS

The Wait-and-See buy-sell[1] works like this:

1. A buy-sell agreement is drafted *immediately*.
2. The agreement provides for a price established by a realistic formula, meeting the criteria of Chapter 14's IRC Section 2703, to be paid for a decedent/shareholder's stock at one or more specified "triggering events" such as death, long-term disability, divorce, bankruptcy, termination of employment with the company or retirement.
3. The agreement *immediately* binds the terminating (deceased) shareholder's estate to sell.
4. Funding for the buyers' obligations is established *immediately*.
5. The agreement does not specify who the purchaser will be until a given period *after* the triggering event (such as the death of the shareholder).

Here's what happens when the triggering event occurs:

Stage 1. *Option:* Within a given number of days after the death of a shareholder the corporation must exercise the option to purchase all or any portion of the decedent's stock. This is the approach that will be taken if counsel believes a stock redemption is appropriate. At the discretion of counsel, the option can be set for 30, 60 or 90 days, starting on the occurrence of the triggering event.

Stage 2. *Option:* To the extent the corporation chooses not to exercise its option, surviving shareholders are given an option to purchase the decedent's stock in proportion to their current stock ownership (or, if desired, in any proportion they desire). If, in the opinion of counsel, a cross-purchase is the proper approach, the surviving shareholders will be the buyers. At the discretion of counsel the option can be set for 30, 60 or 90 days, starting at the termination of the corporation's option.

Stage 3. *Mandatory:* At this point, if unpurchased shares remain, the corporation must buy them. This phase is mandatory; the corporation must purchase any shares it has not already purchased (or that have not been purchased by the surviving shareholders). This guarantees the estate a purchaser for its stock according to the preestablished formula.

The order of this three-stage option approach is important. Recall that if the corporation relieves a shareholder of a binding obligation, a constructive dividend will result.[2] The shareholder legally obligated to purchase the stock is considered to have received a dividend to the extent the corporation has paid for the stock (i.e., to the extent it has satisfied his or her legal obligation). Conversely, options, not legally obligating the holder, avoid this problem.

HOW THE INSURANCE IS ARRANGED[3]

There are multiple alternatives for arranging the insurance under the Wait-and-See buy-sell:

Corporation as Owner

The corporation can purchase a policy on the life of each shareholder, becoming policyowner, premium payer and beneficiary. If, at the end of the option period, it was decided that the corporation should be the purchaser, it will use the insurance proceeds it receives to finance its purchase of stock from a decedent/shareholder's estate. It might also use the insurance proceeds to effect a Section 303 partial stock redemption. The balance of the stock can then be purchased by the surviving shareholders on a cross-purchase basis. (Note, however, that the AMT could still result from the receipt of the proceeds.)

If, at the end of the option period, it was decided that the surviving shareholders should be the purchasers (or to the extent stock remained to be purchased after the corporation's option expired), the corporation can lend the insurance proceeds to the shareholders. The loan will be fully secured (either by the purchased stock itself or by personal assets of the purchasing shareholders) and on the same terms as a commercial bank loan. The loan will be repaid within a reasonable period of time from bonuses or increased salaries.

Shareholders as Owner

The second possible means of arranging the life insurance will prove useful if counsel for any reason believes that the shareholders should own the insurance. Each shareholder purchases and pays premiums on a policy insuring coshareholders. When a shareholder dies, the surviving shareholder(s) receive the proceeds.

If a stock redemption is indicated, the surviving shareholders can lend the proceeds to the corporation (the reverse of the first approach) or make capital contributions to their corporation—thus increasing their cost basis.

Third-Party Owner

A third party—for example, an irrevocable trust—can purchase the insurance as a means of keeping the proceeds out of the purchasing shareholder's estate. Upon the death of the insured and the receipt of proceeds by the trust, the trustees can lend the proceeds (fully collateralized and at a rate of interest equal to or slightly better than the average bank rate in the area) to the purchaser on bona fide terms. The purchaser then acquires the decedent/shareholder's stock with that loan and eventually pays off the loan with after-tax earnings.

Variations

Many variations on these themes are possible:

1. Whole life policies can be purchased by the corporation, and low-outlay term policies can be acquired by the shareholders, or a split-dollar agreement may be utilized.
2. Some of the purchase price can be assumed by the corporation under the wait-and-see approach, with the balance paid for individually by the surviving shareholders.

ALTERNATIVE TO CLASSIC WAIT-AND-SEE APPROACH

Another way of accomplishing the wait-and-see objectives is through two agreements, one an option agreement held by individual shareholders and the second a binding stock redemption plan. The option agreement allows the surviving shareholders as individuals to purchase a decedent's stock within, say, six months of his or her death. The stock redemption agreement requires the corporation to redeem any stock of the deceased shareholder not purchased under the option agreement at the expiration of the six-month period.

Life insurance (perhaps under a split-dollar arrangement or Section 162 bonus plan) would be set up to fund a cross-purchase plan. To the extent the surviving shareholders chose not to exercise their option personally, they could make a capital contribution to the corporation. This would give the corporation cash for the redemption and give the shareholders an increase in basis equal to their respective capital contributions.

Endnotes

1. Copyright © 1991 by Stephan R. Leimberg. The text, The *Wait and See Buy-Sell* by Stephan R. Leimberg and Morey S. Rosenbloom, can be obtained for $10 from Financial Data Center, PO Box 1332, Bryn Mawr, PA 19010; 215-525-6957. This text explains the reasons for a buy-sell and the alternatives for funding it as well

as the details of the Wait-and-See buy-sell and includes a specimen document of a complete Wait-and-See buy-sell.

2. See *Daniel Gerson v. Comm'r*, T.C. Memo. 1989-52, 1989 where the shareholder was personally and unconditionally obligated to purchase the stock that was redeemed; See also *Jacobs v. Comm'r*, 698 F.2nd 850 (CA-6 1983); *Holsey v. Comm'r*, 258 F.2nd 865 (CA-3 1958) *rev'g* 28 T.C. 1962 (1957); *Wall v. U.S.*, 164 F.2nd 462 (CA-4 1947); *Stephens v. Comm'r*, 60 T.C. 1004 (1973).

3. See Christensen, " 'The Wait and See' Buy-Sell Agreement," *Trusts and Estates* (May 1981).

CHAPTER 30

Buy-Sell Agreements
and Divorce

Up to this point we have been discussing the relationships between the shareholders among themselves and the corporation, as reflected in the buy-sell agreement. Less frequently considered, however, is a potential additional party: a spouse in the process of divorce. Although not in fact a shareholder, this person could have a significant impact on the relationships of the shareholders and the business.

To what extent could a buy-sell agreement affect the division of property or be impacted itself by a court decree or settlement agreement between the parties?[1] Not only is the divorce rate incredibly high, but the impact of divorce on a business can be devastating when proper preparation has not been made. In the absence of a buy-sell an ex-spouse can become an owner; if the divorce contingency is ignored, the cash drain on the owners may be highly destructive. For these reasons defensive divorce planning before the fact is a skill that every planner must develop.

EQUITABLE DISTRIBUTION

Many states have adopted the concept of equitable distribution, which is used in the division of marital property when spouses divorce. Generally, under the concept of equitable distribution, property acquired by a husband and wife during the marriage is considered marital property, while property brought to the marriage by each party is considered separate property. Often the increase in the value of separate property during the marriage is considered marital property, as may be separate property used for the benefit of both husband and wife.

Upon a divorce a judge will provide (in the absence of an agreement) for the division of the marital property "equitably" between husband and wife. *Equitable* does not necessarily mean "equal." Moreover, in deciding what division is equitable, a judge will consider the amount and nature of the separate property of each party. Thus separate property may affect equitable distribution even if that property itself is not divisible.

The Problem

Let's say that Buddy and Ryan, two unrelated professional football coaches, each own one-half of the issued and outstanding stock of a company that owns a football team, the Beagles. Buddy and his wife, Norma, are in the process of getting a divorce and are unable to agree on a division of marital property.

The Beagles stock was acquired by Buddy and Ryan during the marriage of Buddy and Norma when the relationship was rosier. Now Norma's lawyer is demanding an equitable distribution of the value of Buddy's interest or, as an alternative, the actual stock itself.

Buddy and Ryan both know that to be in business with Buddy's ex-wife, Norma (and her husband and in essence their attorney) would be intolerable. The pressures a former spouse as a voting but nonworking owner could place on the working shareholders create a living nightmare that no sane business relationship would choose.

Effect of a Buy-Sell Agreement

If the court is inclined to grant Norma a division of the value of Buddy's interest, it might consider the buy-sell agreement. But even if it can be shown that there was an arm's-length negotiation between Buddy and Ryan in determining price and terms, and thus the agreement is given significant weight, it is unlikely to be absolutely determinative of the value and validity of Norma's claim.

Parties often seek to bind spouses to their buy-sell agreements by having them execute a joinder to the instrument. However, in at least one case the court ignored a spouse's execution of a joinder, because she did not work in the business, comprehend the agreement, have any financial background or have legal counsel.[2] Therefore conservative counsel and clients should consider adding to the joinder the spouse's acknowledgment that he or she had

1. complete availability of the books and records of the company,
2. knowledge of company practices,
3. advice by separate counsel (or chose to reject such advice) and
4. the expectation that the agreement would be binding on her with respect to the analysis of marital rights.

In the event a spouse does not sign such a joinder, Buddy and Ryan could consider agreeing on a lower buyout price, supplementing the death benefit difference with life insurance or lifetime benefits with qualified and nonqualified retirement plan funding. While such a step could have dramatic ramifications (and probably would not be binding for federal estate tax purposes), it might establish a lower stock value for equitable distribution purposes, at least as a starting point.

If the court believes Buddy will be unable to pay the equitable value to Norma in cash, it might actually grant her request for stock in the Beagles, despite the limitations on transferability of shares found in most buy-sell agreements. In anticipation of this problem, those drafting the agreement might provide that actions contrary to the agreement could result in an option to the other shareholder or the corporation to purchase the shares. Of course, this could have adverse cash flow and other ramifications and does not address the problem of where the buyer will obtain the funds to make the payments.

Finally, if neither Ryan nor the Beagles exercise the option, and Norma receives the shares, the buy-sell agreement could provide that the shares so transferred be held subject to a voting trust. While that vehicle would allow Buddy and Ryan to retain control as before, it is uncertain whether the court would uphold the trust, because the ex-spouse was not an original party to the buy-sell agreement.

Endnotes

1. The concepts in this chapter are derived from the interesting and informative article by Landsman, "Divorce Planning in the Closely-Held Business Context," *Trusts and Estates* (May 1984): 41–46.
2. *Suther v. Suther*, 28 Wash. App. 838, 627 P.2d 110 (Ct. App. Div. 1, 1981).

C H A P T E R   3 1

Section 303
Redemptions

IRC §303 establishes a way for a corporation to make a distribution in redemption (i.e., a payment in return for its stock) of a portion of the stock of a decedent/shareholder without taxation as a dividend. In other words a Section 303 redemption is a corporate purchase of its stock that makes exchange treatment possible even if the transaction would not meet the safe harbor rules of IRC §302.

A Section 303 (partial) redemption can be accomplished as part of an overall stock redemption plan or as a supplement to a cross-purchase buy-sell. It is particularly useful in cases where the redemption would not otherwise qualify for capital gains treatment, such as where the transaction would not be considered a complete termination of the selling shareholder's interest or where the family or entity attribution rules make it otherwise impossible to receive sale or exchange treatment.

Section 303 is often an ideal tool for a family corporation because it makes it possible for the family to retain control of the corporation while redeeming enough shares to furnish a deceased stockholder's estate with the cash to pay death taxes, funeral costs and allowable administration expenses. In addition, attribution (constructive ownership) rules specifically do not apply to a redemption under Section 303.

Section 303 prevents a distribution used to redeem stock from being classified as a dividend distribution to the extent it does not exceed specified limitations. This protection applies only if

1. the stock in the decedent/shareholder's estate exceeds a specified percentage of the estate (described later);
2. the ownership interest of the stockholder is reduced directly by the redemption; and
3. the distribution is made within a specified period of time after the stockholder's death.

WHAT STOCK QUALIFIES FOR REDEMPTIONS?

Only stock includable in the decedent's estate may be redeemed under Section 303.[1] Although apparently any heir owning such stock included in the decedent's gross estate may take advantage of Section 303, in most instances the estate's executor (who normally needs the cash for estate settlement) will be the seller. The IRS has ruled that any stock (common or preferred) includable in a decedent/shareholder's estate may also be redeemed under this provision.[2]

The protection of Section 303 applies to a distribution by a corporation only if the estate tax value of all the stock of such corporation included in the decedent's gross estate is more than 35 percent of the adjusted gross estate.[3] (Technically a Section 303 redemption is permissible if the value of the stock exceeds 35 percent of the excess of the value of the gross estate over the sum of expenses, indebtedness and taxes under IRC §2053 or amounts allowable as a loss under IRC §2054.)

For purposes of computing this percentage, stock that was the subject of a generation-skipping transfer[4] or that was transferred within three years of death[5] is included in the gross estate. If the decedent owned more than 20 percent of the stock of two or more corporations, they may be treated as one corporation in applying the percentage requirements.[6]

For example, if the stock owned by Bob LeClair was worth $360,000 and his gross estate less allowable expenses, indebtedness, taxes and losses was worth $1 million, it would qualify for a Section 303 stock redemption. But assume that when Bob died he owned 100 percent of Grad Corporation's stock and 20 percent of Money Book's stock. Assume the Grad Corporation is worth $850,000 and the Money Book stock is worth $750,000. Bob's gross estate less allowable deductions totals $2,500,000. Bob owns all the stock of the Grad Corporation. The Money Book corporation is worth a total of $4,600,000.

Standing alone, neither corporation's stock would meet the "more than 35 percent" test. The Grad Corporation would be 34 percent ($850,000/$2,500,000), and the Money Book Corporation would be 30 percent ($750,000/$2,500,000). However, the stock of the two corporations can be combined since the value of the stocks included in Bob's estate ($1,600,000) compared to the total value of the outstanding stock in both corporations ($4,600,000) is almost 35 percent ($1,600,000/$4,600,000), which is greater than 20 percent of the total stock value of both corporations. Therefore Bob's executor can combine the two values ($850,000 + $750,000) to see if the more-than-35-percent test is met. It is, since the combined value of the two stocks is 64 percent ($1,600,000/$2,500,000) of the test amount. This means the stock of either or both corporations can be exchanged in return for cash under the safety of Section 303 (up to permissible limits).

A Section 303 redemption is allowed only to the extent that the burden of paying off debts, expenses and taxes actually falls on the party whose stock is to be redeemed.[7] For example, suppose a surviving spouse wishes to take advantage of Section 303. If the stock was distributed as part of the marital share, then it generates no federal estate tax liability. Presumably Section 303 would not be available, since as part of the marital share it generates no federal estate tax.

If two or more shareholders exist, an apportionment may be required:

Assume Herb Garfinkle's tentative tax base is $1 million, and his estate qualifies for a Section 303 stock redemption. You have computed an estate tax liability of $290,000. The gross estate includes $700,000 of X-On stock plus another $250,000 of X-On stock held by a trust for his son but included in Herb's estate because he held a retained life interest, i.e., the right to income from trust assets for as long as he lived. If Herb's will is silent as to the payment of the tax, the trust's liability for the estate tax (and therefore the ability to sell stock under Section 303) is computed as follows:

$$\frac{\text{Value of Trust (\$250,000)}}{\text{Taxable Estate (\$1,000,000)}} \times \text{Federal Estate Tax (\$290,000)}$$

The result is that no more than $72,500 of stock can be sold by the trust to the corporation under Section 303. If the trust was not responsible for any of the estate tax liability under state law or was exonerated under the decedent's will, no stock could be redeemed under Section 303.

From an estate planning standpoint, if the facts reveal that assets other than stock of a corporation owned by the estate owner are so large as to make the stock value less than the required percentage of his or her estate, the owner may wish to make lifetime transfers of other property sufficient to bring the value of the stock up to the required percentage. (The gift must be made more than three years prior to the shareholder's death.) Or, in a marginal case, the value of the estate owner's stock may be increased by the purchase of corporate-owned key executive insurance.

A stockholder might even enter into a binding buy-sell agreement that fixed the value high enough to meet the more-than-35-percent test, or the executor of an estate may deliberately let the IRS examiner value the decedent's stock higher so as to qualify for a Section 303 redemption. This, of course, could have other income and estate tax consequences.

MAXIMUM DISTRIBUTION IN REDEMPTION UNDER SECTION 303

Distributions in redemption of stock qualified under Section 303 are protected from being taxed as dividends only in the aggregate amount of

1. the federal and state estate, inheritance, legacy and succession taxes (including interest thereon) imposed because of the deceased stockholder's death;
2. the amount of funeral and administration expenses allowable as deductions to the estate[8] (Note that if the executor elects to claim the administration expenses as deductions for income tax purposes, waiving deductibility on the federal estate tax return, the expenses may still be covered in a Section 303 redemption; the IRC speaks in terms of "allow*able*," not merely "allow*ed*."); and
3. generation-skipping tax resulting from a taxable termination or distribution, or direct skip, of stock.[9]

TIME LIMITATION FOR DISTRIBUTION

The distribution in redemption of stock under Section 303 must be made within three years and 90 days after the federal estate tax return is filed (i.e., four years after death in the usual case). Alternatively, if a timely petition for redetermination of federal estate tax is filed with the Tax Court, the distribution must occur within 60 days after the Tax Court's decision becomes final.

Finally, the IRC allows up to 14 years for the Section 303 redemption where the estate elects to defer estate tax payments under Section 6166.[10]

LIFE INSURANCE TO FINANCE REDEMPTION UNDER SECTION 303

Even though the principal owner knows that there is no danger that a purchase coming within the statute's terms will create a large income tax liability in his or her estate, the owner should set up definite plans in advance. If selling a part of the stock to the corporation at death appears to be the most advantageous estate arrangement, the principal owner should ensure that the corporation can carry out that plan. In nearly every state a corporation may purchase its own shares only out of surplus unless there is to be a reorganization of its capital structure. Therefore the corporation should own insurance on the principal stockholder's life payable to itself in the amount, at least, of the estimated combined death taxes, funeral and administration expenses that the deceased stockholder's estate will be called on to pay.

In addition, if the receipt of the insurance proceeds will result in the imposition of AMT, the corporation should acquire additional life insurance coverage to guard against a shortfall in net proceeds. This will place in the corporate treasury at time of death the funds necessary to acquire the amount of stock permitted under Section 303. Corporate life insurance for this purpose is recommended. Alternatively, some formal "outside" funding with insurance owned by a third party and loaned to the corporation should be established.

AGREEMENTS UNDER SECTION 303

Under the typical arrangement, where it is contemplated that a majority shareholder's shares will be redeemed under Section 303, an agreement between the shareholder and the corporation normally is not necessary. When a majority shareholder dies, the executor succeeds to a position of control and therefore is in a position to see that the redemption is carried out.

In certain situations an agreement would seem advisable. Obviously, if a minority shareholder's shares are to be redeemed under Section 303, an agreement lends certainty to the arrangement. In addition, if antagonism exists between majority and minority interests in a particular corporation, a preexisting agreement to redeem a majority shareholder's shares under Section 303 would deflect criticism by the surviving minority interest.

TAX TREATMENT OF THE REDEMPTION DISTRIBUTION

As already mentioned, a corporate distribution qualifying for a Section 303 redemption is treated as the purchase price paid in exchange for the stock. As such the distribution is eligible for capital gains tax treatment. Because the basis of the stock steps up to its estate tax value, the purchase price of the stock will usually equal the estate tax value, and there will in fact be no capital gain. To the extent the Section 303 requirements are not met, cash or other amounts paid out by the corporation will not be a capital transaction, the seller's basis will become irrelevant and the entire distribution will be taxed as a dividend (to the extent it did not qualify for favorable treatment under Section 303).

COORDINATING A SECTION 303 REDEMPTION WITH A SECTION 6166 INSTALLMENT PAYOUT

Under Section 6166,[11] the payment of estate taxes attributable to a closely held business can be extended over 14 years. Only interest on the principal (federal estate tax) is payable during the first four years. During the next (up to) 10 years, principal and interest are paid.[12]

To qualify under this installment election the closely held business must comprise more than 35 percent of the decedent's adjusted gross estate. The aggregation of business interests is permitted to meet this more-than-35-percent test if 20 percent or more of the value of *each* business is included in a decedent's gross estate.

The corporation could purchase a key executive insurance policy on the life of the employee/shareholder. At the shareholder's death the executor would make the installment election under IRC §6166. The installment payments under Section 6166 could be funded by a series of Section 303 redemptions. At the date of a decedent's death the corporation could redeem enough shares under Section 303 to enable the executor to pay the estate taxes attributable to the nonbusiness assets, plus the interest due on the unpaid balance of the estate tax. The corporation would then invest the remainder of the insurance proceeds.

Earnings on that money would be used to make further Section 303 redemptions equal to the interest payments in each of the next three years. In the fifth year, when principal payments of the federal estate tax are due (in addition to interest), the corporation could redeem the remaining stock. If the proceeds have produced a good rate of return, the result to the corporation could be a net gain.

The integration of Sections 303 and 6166 makes it possible for the corporation to purchase a "discounted policy" (a policy with a face value of less than the total allowable Section 303 redemption amount) because the corporation does not have to buy the entire amount of stock allowable under Section 303 at a shareholder's death. So it can invest the unused proceeds to produce sufficient funds to effectuate future redemptions.

Endnotes

1. IRC §303(a).
2. PLR 8946081.
3. IRC §303(b).
4. IRC §303(d).
5. IRC §2035(d)(3)(A).
6. IRC §303(b)(2)(B).
7. IRC §303(b)(3).
8. IRC §303(a).
9. IRC §303(b)(1)(C).
10. IRC §303(a).
11. See Leimberg et al., *Tools and Techniques of Estate Planning* (Cincinnati: National Underwriter Co., 1992), call 800-543-0874.
12. NumberCruncher Software (215-525-6957) does this calculation.

CHAPTER 32

Disability and
Buy-Sells

Few attorneys would allow clients operating a closely held corporation or partnership to be without a properly funded, binding buy-sell agreement. In fact an attorney who has served as longtime corporate counsel and fails to inform clients of the need for and desirability of a business continuation plan may even be considered guilty of malpractice. Yet few existing plans take into account the most threatening event that can disrupt and damage a business—the long-term disability of a working shareholder.[1]

THE NEED FOR A DISABILITY PROVISION

Out of three male shareholders, each aged 25, the chances that one will be *disabled* for 90 days or more are 49.4 out of 100 (see Table 32.1). If there are six shareholders, one long-term disability is a 75 percent probability!

Considering the high probability of this contigency, it is extremely important that measures be taken in advance to handle the consequences of disability. The following questions will need to be answered:

1. How will the business owners prevent fights and dissension between the disabled shareholder (who probably will want all or a portion of his or her salary continued) and the remaining shareholders? The nondisabled shareholders, working full-time in the business, will eventually tire of paying a salary to a nonproductive associate.
2. How can the business provide sufficient income to the disabled shareholder without dividend treatment?

TABLE 32.1   Probability of at Least One Long-Term Disability Prior to Age 65

| | Number of Owners | | | | |
| | 2 | 3 | 4 | 5 | 6 |
Age	Lives	Lives	Lives	Lives	Lives
25	36.5%	49.4%	59.7%	67.8%	74.4%
30	35.4	48.0	58.2	66.4	73.0
35	34.2	46.7	56.7	64.9	71.5
40	32.9	45.1	55.0	63.2	69.8
45	31.1	42.8	52.5	60.6	67.3
50	28.3	39.2	48.5	56.4	63.1
55	23.4	33.0	41.4	48.7	55.1

Source: 1985 Society of Actuaries DST Experience Table

3. How can the cord be cut from the necks of both the disabled shareholder (dependent on the business skill and success of the remaining shareholders) and the remaining shareholders (doing all the work but splitting profits and future growth with someone no longer generating revenues)? That is, how does the business remove and replace an unproductive individual?

4. How can the principals prevent an indefinite and potentially limitless cash flow drain on the business?

5. Once a buyout becomes inevitable, how can the business pay a price for the disabled shareholder's interest that is both fair to the buyer and adequate to allow the disabled shareholder's family to survive and maintain their standard of living?

How would you feel and what would you be inclined to do if a shareholder became disabled; you hadn't considered, discussed or anticipated long-term disability in the buyout; and:

1. You represented the disabled shareholder?
2. You represented the remaining shareholders?

HOW TO PROVIDE FOR DISABILITY

Planners should provide for the transfer of stock in the event of disability as part of a comprehensive overall buy-sell plan (death, retirement, disability, etc.) or in a separate disability buyout arrangement.

A mandatory stock transfer agreement triggered upon specified events that include long-term disability of a shareholder/employee facilitates corporate and personal financial planning because of its certainty and helps to preserve personal relationships. Alternatively, the permanent and total disability (however that is defined) of a shareholder for a specified period of time could give the disabled shareholder a put requiring the repurchase of his or her shares.

Planning Considerations

Here are some considerations for clients, consultants, counsel and other advisers:

Specify the Degree to Which a Shareholder Must Be Disabled To Trigger the Buyout. Use only "total disability" since lesser degrees of disability would be too complex to ascertain or monitor.

Establish a Waiting Period Between the Time Disability Occurs and the Time the Buyout Becomes Operative. This should be coordinated with the funding vehicle, as discussed in more detail later.

Consider the Pros and Cons of a Reversal Clause. The shareholder may recover after the buyout starts but before the full purchase price has been paid. This contingency should be addressed in planning (discussed in more detail later).

Allow for a Series of Illnesses or Injuries. Contingency plans should cover a string of debilitating events resulting in a series of disability periods—none of which lasts longer than the waiting period. Counsel may provide that subsequent periods of disability related in cause to a prior period of disability and occurring within a specified period of time (say 90 to 180 days) from the date of the first period of disability shall be considered together in computing the total amount of time the disability has continued. Be sure to correlate such a "connecting" clause with policy provisions (this is typically known as the *recurrent disability clause*).

A buyout triggered after, say, "12 months of continuing disability" discourages a disabled individual from returning to work because doing so means starting a whole new 12-month waiting, or elimination, period. A recurrent disability clause in both the buy-sell agreement and the insurance policy will alleviate this concern. Most carriers deal with the recurring disability issue by allowing gaps to exist between periods of disability as long as they are not separated by more than six months and are the result of the same or related causes. This approach both preserves the integrity of the elimination period and recognizes that even life-threatening illnesses are often halted by temporary remissions.

Make the Definition of *Total Disability* Effective from All Perspectives. Clients should understand it and feel it is equitable and at the same time practical under the given circumstances. The best approach is to incorporate by reference the definition in a disability policy (the same policy used to finance the buyer's obligation).

Use of insurance policy definitions has an interpretive history that increases the certainty of their scope and meaning. Potential for dispute is substantially reduced because an independent third party, the insurer, will determine the existence or nonexistence of total disability. This approach also ensures that policy benefits will be payable when the buyout is required by the agreement.

Draft a Fallback Definition. Such a definition will be useful when disability insurance is not in force or the policy definition is disputed for some reason. Possible alternatives include

- using the Social Security definition of disability;
- allowing the parties to agree among themselves that disability exists; or
- allowing the buyer and seller to each select one doctor who in turn will select one doctor between them and who will decide through a binding majority vote whether total disability exists.

Provide for a Specific Waiting Period of One to Two Years. This will be the period of time that total disability must continue before the buyout occurs. A premature buyout, where a disabled shareholder is obligated to sell despite a subsequently full recovery, will result in frustration, bitterness and unnecessary expense. This waiting or elimination period should be at least as long as the period provided for in the insurance policy funding the agreement.

The ultimate decision as to the *length* of the waiting period should be a *function* of

- the premium cost the parties are willing to pay;
- underwriting considerations (many insurers encourage the use of longer waiting periods by allowing higher coverage limits for longer periods); and
- the probability of recovery.

As Figure 32.1 illustrates, the longer a person is disabled, the less likely he or she is to recover. Conversely, the best chance of recovery is during the first 12 months.

At most ages, statistics show, the use of a waiting period in excess of two years merely postpones the inevitable; the probability of further disability or death approaches 100 percent.

Be sure the "trigger date" (the date on which the buyout obligation becomes contractually effective) is timed to coincide with the commencement of the disability policy's indemnity payments.

Consider What Should Happen if a Disabled Shareholder Recovers. Should the shareholder be given the right to return to the business? If so, on what terms? Some advisers feel that after the buyout has started it is inadvisable to reverse the process. Besides uncertainty that the "recovered" shareholder may not in fact be recovered sufficiently to function productively in the business, the following events may have occurred in the interim:

- Significant changes in the technologies involved in the business
- Changes in the customer or client relationships
- Hiring of replacements

Disability buyout policies are designed to provide for this last circumstance through presumptive disability provisions. Most providers will continue benefits even if a recovery occurs after a buyout has been exercised.

FIGURE 32.1 Probability of Recovery from Disability

Period of Time an Individual Has Been Disabled	Chance of Recovery Where Age at Disability Is:		
	Age 35	Age 45	Age 55
6 months	58%	44%	27%
12 months	34%	23%	11%
18 months	27%	18%	9%
24 months	23%	15%	8%
36 months	20%	13%	7%

Base the Purchase Price on Underwriting Requirements and Fair Market Value of the Stock Interest. Most insurers specify valuation methodology that must be used with their policy, but the insured is often given a choice of selected reasonable methods. The insured is generally required to provide financial statements in the underwriting process to verify the value insured. Where a death buy-sell plan is already in effect, the two agreements should be coordinated.

Be Aware That the Date on Which the Price Is Determined Is Extremely Important. Remember that a significant period of time will pass after the onset of the disability before the waiting period requirement is satisfied. So (in situations other than when a simple agreed-on price is specified) be sure the agreement spells out whether the date is the date on which total disability began or the date on which the buyout becomes operative. Most authorities feel the onset of disability is the better valuation date since the shareholder's active involvement ends at that point and all future gain or loss is appropriately allocable to the remaining active shareholders.

Decide Whether the Buyout Should Be in a Lump Sum or Installments. A lump sum seems attractive since it is simple and severs the relationship quickly. But the buyout may require a large amount of cash from a corporation that has just lost the services of a key person. The corporation may not be able to accumulate such large sums without accumulated earnings tax problems, and insurer participation limits and/or underwriting requirements may make it impossible to pay out the full amount through insurance. If a cross-purchase arrangement is used, shareholders may not have enough cash to fund the buyout in a lump sum.

The installment method reduces the cash flow drain on the purchaser. It may also reduce taxes paid by the selling shareholder because gain can be spread over more than one tax year. On the other hand, installment payouts require that the disabled shareholder incur a long-term risk and remain dependent on the financial future of the business.

The preferred approach, therefore, is to provide for a combination of insured benefits paid in installments and a lump sum paid out from lump-sum disability buyout insurance that may have to be supplemented by funds from corporate surplus.

Insurers provide for choices in the form of benefit in specialty buyout policies. Larger aggregate benefits (as much as double) are available if the insured chooses the installment plan. The installment alternative offers benefits over periods of up to 60 months following the elimination period.

Know the Tax Ramifications. Planners and clients should understand the applicable tax provisions:

- No tax deduction will be allowed to the buyers no matter how the stock is purchased; the price paid for the stock is nondeductible regardless of whether the corporation or the remaining shareholders purchase the stock.
- Remaining shareholders are not taxable on money paid to the disabled shareholder for stock through either insured benefits or corporate income. A purchase by the corporation is not considered a dividend and has no effect on their basis.
- When the corporation is the purchaser, regardless of whether the payment is in a lump sum or in installments, the disabled shareholder must meet stringent tests to avoid dividend treatment. For this reason, if the corporation is to be the purchaser, it is extremely important that counsel carefully study the impact of stock redemption and attribution rules, the waiver requirements and the implications of a return to business by a recovered shareholder concerning the waiver (one who relies on the waiver of family attribution rules cannot go back into the business within ten years without risking dividend treatment on the entire payout).
- Premiums paid on disability insurance to finance the buyout are not tax-*deductible*.
- When benefits from disability insurance are received (by either the corporation or the remaining shareholders), those dollars are income-tax-free.

Use Life Insurance Premiums in the Buyout. If corporate-owned life insurance also contains waiver-of-premium provisions, at the end of the six-month waiting period money previously used to pay life insurance premiums the corporation can use to help pay for the disabled shareholder's stock and help indemnify the corporation for its loss of a key person. For example, $10,000 of annual life insurance premiums could now be used to assist in the buyout.

Consider an Acceleration Clause. This would step up payments or convert installment payments into an equivalent lump sum if death occurs after installment payments have begun but before all payments have been made. Disability buyout policies provide for either a death benefit or the continuance of disability benefits if death occurs during the disability buyout. In addition, the corporate life insurance on the disabled shareholder should be continued to cover the risk of death prior to the completion of the buyout.

Consider a Specialty Disability Insurance Policy Designed Just for Disability Buy-Sell Funding. These policies pay a lump-sum cash settlement benefit of up to $1 million (if the business interest warrants such values) to fund the ownership transfer. If installment benefits are elected, the benefit amount can go up to $1.5 million. Generally the maximum benefits are increased if the insured elects a longer elimination period (e.g., 24 months are required by typical insurers for maximum coverage). Obviously the underwriting requirements include information about past and current income, net worth, debt, nondebt capital sources, ownership and possibly pro forma statements for the future of the business, in addition to the required medical information regarding the proposed insured.

Endnote

1. See Checkoway, "Insuring the Disability Hazard in the Small Close Held Corporation," *Life Insurance Selling* (April 1989); and Grinblatt, "Definitions Are Important in the Professional Disability Market," *Life Insurance Selling* (April 1989).

The "Leimberg Systems Approach" to Buy-Sell Planning

WHY A SYSTEMS APPROACH?

Although every buy-sell case involves new facts and new circumstances, planners will find tremendous advantages in systematizing and standardizing the method by which they work up a case. The following "systems" approach will make planning efforts more cost-effective, will highlight important facts that might otherwise be missed, will make key issues recognizable more quickly and will facilitate simple, understandable and therefore workable solutions.

THE PROCESS

There are eight steps in the Leimberg Systems Approach:

Step 1. Assembling the facts
Step 2. Framing the issues
Step 3. Stating the *what if*s
Step 4. Listing the objectives
Step 5. Valuing the interest
Step 6. Deciding on the type of buy-sell
Step 7. Selecting a funding mechanism
Step 8. Arranging the funding

Individual planners may decide to condense, expand, rearrange or otherwise change these steps to suit their own goals and method of operation. The key is to develop a system that works in an individual practice (and that can be transferred to and used by new associates).

Here's where to start:

Step 1. Assemble the Key Facts

As in any other estate or business planning case, the place to start in planning a buy-sell situation is with the facts. Obtain accurate and comprehensive information about everyone related to the business as well as those people or organizations they love or feel a responsibility for. Then write down, in short paragraphs, the operative and most essential facts.

Let's assume the following facts as an illustration.

The Business. Your clients are the owners of the Open and Shut Case Corporation. OSC is a closely held manufacturing business that makes (you guessed it) custom-made law cases (briefcases for short attorneys). The corporation has generated an average annual earnings over the last five years, after all expenses, debt service and salaries (each of the three employee/owners takes $200,000 out of the business), of $100,000. Capital currently invested in the business totals about $500,000. The business is highly leveraged with average debt of more than $4 million.

The Shareholders and Their Families. Three former law students—Barry Ster, Y. Zoldowl and Catchum Nappen—each own one-third of OSC. All three went into business directly out of law school, and—except for a short stint in the plumbing and air-conditioning business—all have invested their entire working lives in the case manufacturing business.

Although all three graduated cum laude ("from their parents"), none ever passed the bar examination.

Barry Ster, the chairman of the board, is 57. Barry has a serious blood pressure problem. Barry is married and has three grown children, Mon, Mas, and Mini. All of the children are financially successful, but none has any desire to work at OSC. Barry's wife, Cani, is very active in local politics but has no desire to be involved in the business. Barry is the founder and driving force of the business. His strong suit (case) is innovation. Two early inventions of his, the rock solid case and the patented "steel bagel security locks," have helped the company take a strong and early lead in the legal briefcase manufacturing field.

Y. Zoldowl, president of the company, is 50 years old. Although he is the youngest of the three shareholders, his foresight in investing and skill in managing the firm's cash flow and investments and his quality control of its manufacturing process are essential to OSC's continued success.

Y is divorced and has stated he is not likely to remarry. Y has two children, Hansel and Gretel. Hansel is a 25-year-old late-blooming "flower child" who feels capitalism is (like work) evil. He obviously is not interested in the business. Gretel, however, has had enough of the crumbs of life and has found her way back to the business. She is already a vice president of the firm and, given four or five more years of experience, could possibly run the business with proper backup and management support.

Catchum Nappen, the company's treasurer, is 54. He is married and has three children, two of whom are practicing orthopedic surgeons. His wife is a talented artist and the owner of a yarn shop. She has little interest in the OSC Corporation. Seldom Nappen, Catchum's son, is 30. Seldom, a CPA, worked for a "Big Eight" (then there were seven, six and now five) CPA firm since graduating from college. He now works for the OSC Corporation as its comptroller.

A planner working for OSC Corporation will want to learn much more about each of these individuals and how they feel about the business and how they relate to each other. This vital information should include

- income and capital needs of each person involved;
- personal as well as business objectives; and
- current as well as likely future interpersonal relationships should one or more die, become disabled or retire.

Step 2. Frame the Major Issues the Client Must Face

At this second stage the planner writes down, in an organized and concise manner, the client's answers to questions such as these:

1. What will happen to the business itself upon the death, retirement or disability of one or more of its shareholders?

2. If you haven't checked to see what would happen, how do you know what will?

3. What would—and what should—happen if . . . ? (It's amazing how few successful business owners have ever taken the time to analyze this contingency.)

4. If you die or become permanently disabled, what should (do you want to) happen to your business interest? (Many times the client will say, "My wife will take over the business" or "I want my (15-year-old) daughter to take over the business." This should prompt the next question.)

5. Is that "want" realistic? (The client often has not considered that the spouse may not want to run the business even if she could or know how to keep the business going until that child is legally, emotionally and intellectually ready to run a business. Often clients do not make the distinction between working in a business and running it.)

6. Should your interest be sold to a coshareholder? To an outsider?

7. If your business interest is to be sold, have you structured the sale to minimize taxes and assure your (or your family's) receipt of the maximum possible purchase price? Where will the cash to effect the buyout come from?

8. If one of your coshareholders dies, would you be willing to accept his or her heirs into the business as active participants?

9. Would those heirs be capable and experienced enough to carry their load as employee/managers?

10. Will you be able to get along with the heirs? Would you be willing to live with the heirs as inactive participants?

11. Will they want more dividends then you are willing to pay?

12. Will they need more income from the business than it can produce without their contributing to earnings?

13. Will they be cooperative and support your methods and ideas about how the business should be run?

14. If your coshareholders' heirs—or their guardians if they are minors— gain control of the business, what will happen to your position as an employee?

15. Would you be willing to work with an outsider who purchases the stock of a deceased coshareholder from his or her heirs?

16. Can that outsider work effectively with you and you with him or her? Will that person be an asset or a detriment to the business?

17. Would you consider selling out to the heirs of a deceased coshareholder? Could they afford to buy you out? What will you do after you sell yourself out of a job?

18. Would you want to buy out the heirs of a deceased shareholder? Where would you obtain the cash? What impact will that cash drain have on both you and the corporation?

The answers to these questions should give the planner a good idea of how the client is (or is not) thinking and what his or her goals are.

Step 3. State the *What Ifs*

Nothing is more important in planning for the estate of the typical business owner than arranging for the proper disposition of the family business. But the only way to fully understand the importance of this action is to write down, in short paragraphs, what happens if nothing is done:

- If the owner does nothing to create a market for his or her business interest, the business will likely be sold after death by the executor or the family members who inherit it.
- Assuming the family retains the interest, if family members do not (or cannot) take an active role in its management, they will have to rely mainly on the dividends paid on profits produced through the efforts of the remaining active owners of the business. This is an event that typically weakens the business and in the long run often leads to resentment on both sides.
- The end result of "doing nothing" is inevitably the realization of a lower value from the business than if the client had negotiated the terms at arm's length while alive and healthy.

Step 4. List the Client's General and Specific Objectives

At this point the planner writes down the major general goals that the *client* has (or should have) expressed. These may include the following:

1. Create a market for an (otherwise unmarketable) interest.
2. Provide a fair (and/or adequate) price.
3. Keep out inactive and potentially dissident stockholders.
4. Provide a smooth transition of management control.
5. Assure surviving shareholders that they—and no one else—will receive the fruits of their future labors.

6. Reduce the financial pressure on a decedent's heirs caused by death taxes and estate settlement costs.

7. Set the value of the business for federal and state death tax purposes and avoid expensive, time-consuming and aggravating litigation with the IRS and state tax authorities.

8. Assure employees, especially minority shareholder employees, that their jobs are secure even if one or more employee/shareholders die. (Consider the impact on a corporation if more than one shareholder dies within several years of another. Key executive coverage is essential to provide a shock cushion in this event.)

9. Protect an S corporation election.

Now the goals specific to the case at hand, gleaned from an incisive study of the facts and some of the issues that study has raised, are restated in the planner's own words. The planner should note potential solutions along the way.

For instance, particular consideration should be given to the following points in the case of OSC Corporation:

1. All three families have been receiving an income stream of $200,000 a year for several years. Do they expect the payment they will receive for a decedent's interest to be sufficient to continue a $200,000 annual income to each family? Do they anticipate a payment equal to, say, five or ten years' income? Either the buy-sell must take those expectations into account or the families of the three shareholders must be prepared psychologically and economically to accept a considerable reduction in income at the death or long-term disability of any of the three business owners.

2. At the death of any of the three shareholder/employees creditors will (justifiably) be very nervous. In fact Barry Ster's increased mortality and morbidity potential should make creditors demand life insurance coverage on his life (as well as the lives of both other shareholders). His coshareholders should also consider a fully funded disability buyout either as a separate agreement or as part of the normal buy-sell. Barry created the product that brought OSC its major sales success. Is he working on a new innovation that would further increase the corporation's loss at his death or disability?

3. Y. Zoldowl is considered essential to the continuing success of the business. Is the firm recruiting and training backup personnel? (What is it doing to solve its "5 R" problems of recruiting, retaining, retiring,

rewarding and reversing the tax law discrimination against such key people?) What would be the monetary impact on the firm of Zoldowl's death or disability? Can the firm continue as a viable economic enterprise without him? At the least, key employee life and disability coverage on Zoldowl should be obtained as an economic shock cushion for the firm.

On the personal level, careful trust planning is needed for Zoldowl's son, Hansel. Zoldowl's daughter Gretel, who is already a vice president of the firm, probably expects to obtain her father's stock at his death. Should a "one-way sub-buy-sell" be implemented requiring Gretel to purchase her father's stock at his death? The "master buy-sell" among the three current shareholders could provide for a purchase of the stock at the death of the survivor of Y. Zoldowl and his daughter.

4. Catchum Nappen wants to provide income for his wife, but like Y. Zoldowl, Catchum has a child in the business. Catchum's son, Seldom Nappen, the comptroller of OSC, may want to enter into a "one-way sub-buy-sell" similar to the one described for Gretel Zoldowl (Dad dies, son buys). Payments the son makes to his father's estate to pay for the stock can be used to provide income for his mother. The master buy-sell would provide that the stock of the survivor of father and son would be purchased at the second death.

Step 5. Value the Interest To Be Sold

The first line of the table in Figure 33.1 shows that, assuming an expectation that the owners will receive a 16 percent rate of return on an investment of $500,000, they should realize $80,000 a year. If in fact the business produces average annual earnings of $100,000, $20,000 of earnings are attributable to goodwill (intangible assets). If this amount is capitalized at 20 percent (i.e., divided by 0.20), goodwill has a total value of $100,000. The business would therefore have a total value of $600,000: $500,000 (tangible assets) plus $100,000 (goodwill). Under these assumptions a one-third interest would be worth approximately $200,000. Different assumptions (lines 2–5 in Figure 33.1) would, as shown, result in a different total value.

Simple valuation tools, such as the one illustrated in Figure 33.1, can provide useful and cost-effective valuation ranges. But without adjustments this computation would significantly understate the value of the OSC corporation because of the high salaries and large debt service it has been paying.

FIGURE 33.1 Going Concern Value

Average Annual Earnings...$100,000
Estimated Capitalization Rate...0.200
Average Annual Asset Value $500,000
Rate of Return on Tangible Assets 0.160

Return on Tangible Assets	Earnings from Tangible Assets	Earnings from Intangible Assets	Goodwill Value	Total Business Value
1 0.160	$80,000	$20,000	$100,000	$600,000
2 0.170	$85,000	$15,000	$75,000	$575,000
3 0.180	$90,000	$10,000	$50,000	$550,000
4 0.190	$95,000	$5,000	$25,000	$525,000
5 0.200	$100,000	$0	$0	$500,000

Computation courtesy of Number Cruncher Software. Call 215-525-6957.

Furthermore, the survivors would be devastated economically and psychologically if they received only $200,000 for a decedent's interest. That amount, equivalent to one year's salary, is probably far less than the survivors need and almost certainly less than their expectations. (A counterbalancing consideration is that at the death of any one of the three coshareholders the business will lose a vital factor in its success that, in turn, can wipe out much of the firm's goodwill value. Buy-sell planning must therefore consider what steps—beyond a mere restrictive agreement—are necessary to stabilize and maximize the value of the clients' business.)

In adjusting a corporation's earnings a planner should use a five-year average after-tax profit figure and

1. add back excessive salaries;
2. reduce earnings if salaries are too low;
3. add back bonuses paid to shareholder/employees;
4. add back excessive rents paid to shareholders;
5. reduce earnings if rents paid to shareholders were below what was reasonable in the market;
6. eliminate nonrecurring income or expense items or items that unreasonably distort the long-run situation;
7. adjust for excessive depreciation; and
8. adjust for major changes in accounting procedures, widely fluctuating or cyclical profits or abnormally inflated or deflated earnings.

In some situations—such as in this brief case—it may pay the parties to start with the largest amount of insurance they can afford and work backward to determine the value for a decedent's interest.

Once the parties have placed a value on the business that they are willing to live (or die) with, move to step 6.

Step 6. Decide On the Type of Buy-Sell To Use

Should the buy-sell take the form of a stock redemption or a cross-purchase?

A planner must consider many factors, such as these:

- The survivors' cost basis (cross-purchase is generally favored)
- Creditors' right to the life insurance (the favored approach depends on whose creditors are stronger)
- The ratio of ownership desired after the buyout (a cross-purchase allows the ownership ratio to be maintained or varied)
- Tax brackets of the owners and the corporation (premiums generally should be paid by the lower-bracket taxpayer)
- The number of shareholders (if more than three or four shareholders exist, a stock redemption is usually preferable)
- Differences in ages (a cross-purchase forces a younger shareholder to pay premiums on an older shareholder's life)
- Differences in stockholdings (in a stock redemption the larger stockholder is helping the lesser owner buy him or her out)
- Certainty of performance (state law may prohibit corporate purchase of its own shares if the corporation has an inadequate surplus)
- Unreasonable accumulation of surplus (favors a cross-purchase)
- Constructive ownership (attribution problems are totally avoided with a Section 303 stock redemption or cross-purchase plan)
- Corporate AMT (avoided with a cross-purchase)
- The type of entity (a cross-purchase is favored in an S corporation)

All of these and other factors must be considered (together with the clients' circumstances, objectives and priorities) by both the planner and the clients before deciding on the appropriate course of action.

Step 7. Select the Funding Mechanism

The best documentation is worthless paper unless the buyer(s) can afford to pay the purchase price under the buy-sell. Planners should examine the alternative funding possibilities and weigh the advantages and disadvantages of each:

1. *Cash:* the cost to obtain and retain a sufficient amount is high, and the date it will be needed is uncertain.
2. *Borrowing:* loans are expensive, and interest may not be currently deductible on a cross-purchase basis because of investment interest limitation rules.
3. *Installment payouts:* Massive earnings are required, as shown in Figure 33.2, and interest may not be currently deductible because of investment interest rules. If a corporate buyer netted 10 cents on each dollar of sales, it would require $4,506,920 of sales merely to make payments!
4. *Life insurance premiums:* The cash outlays are relatively low and highly predictable.

FIGURE 33.2   Cost to Buyer of 10-Year Installment Sale

(Assuming Interest Is Deductible)

Input: Interest Rate 0.130
Input: Purchase Price $200,000
Input: Buyer's Tax Bracket...0.35

Year	Principal Payment	Interest	Total Payment	Earnings Required
1	$20,000	$26,000	$46,000	$56,769
2	20,000	23,400	43,400	54,169
3	20,000	20,800	40,800	51,569
4	20,000	18,200	38,200	48,969
5	20,000	15,600	35,600	46,369
6	20,000	13,000	33,000	43,769
7	20,000	10,400	30,400	41,169
8	20,000	7,800	27,800	38,569
9	20,000	5,200	25,200	35,969
10	20,000	2,600	22,600	33,369
Total	$200,000	$143,000	$343,000	$450,692

Note that if interest is considered investment interest, no interest deductions may be currently available to a shareholder/purchaser. This would increase the cost of a cross-purchase installment buyout from $450,692 to $527,692, a $77,000 increase in cost, and require $770,000 in additional sales!

The ideal method to provide funds in the event of death or disability should have a relatively low cost, should not adversely affect the working capital or credit position of either the business or its owners, should be predictable (easy to work into cash flow planning), should be simple to understand and should be easy to administer.

Step 8. Decide on How To Arrange Funding

If life insurance is used (as it almost always should be if the shareholder is insurable), the factors in Step 7 can be used to determine whether the insurance should be owned by the corporation, the shareholders, or an outside third party.

In fact many variations on these themes are possible: A portion of the purchase price could be assumed by the corporation under the wait-and-see approach, and the balance could be paid for individually by the surviving shareholders. Life insurance could be set up on a split-dollar double-bonus basis (enough after tax to pay for both the premium and the tax on the bonus) to fund the purchase of the stock that will be bought by the survivors.

To the extent the surviving shareholders chose not to exercise their option, they could make a capital contribution of the proceeds to the corporation. This would give the corporation cash for the redemption and give the shareholders an increase in basis equal to their capital contribution.

A FINAL THOUGHT

If a planner attempts to handle the buy-sell in a vacuum, it will not fit into the client's overall estate plan. Attempts to solve each buy-sell case without a method and overall game plan will not be cost-effective; the planner will end up wasting a great deal of time trying to think of what to do next—and how. Having a systematic process for attacking any type of case streamlines the process, saving the planner time and the client money. The systems approach reveals problems that might otherwise be missed and helps the planners develop creative solutions that otherwise would have eluded them.

CHAPTER 34

Drafting
Considerations

The tax, insurance and other planning ramifications of the type of buy-sell agreement chosen and method of funding used are of paramount importance. Yet a well-constructed agreement must typically govern all types of transfers (voluntary or as a matter of law, inter vivos or testamentary) and address other concerns as well. And as with any business arrangement, although cooperation is anticipated among the parties, the agreement may last for a long period of time during which circumstances are likely to change through birth, marriage, divorce, nonformal estrangement, bankruptcy and other contingencies.

Planners and their clients can deal with various issues up front in the agreement to guard against future disagreement. Some of these provisions may be common to stock redemption and cross-purchase situations, while others may be unique to one or the other.

GENERAL CONSIDERATIONS

Role in Overall Planning

Coordinating the terms of the buy-sell agreement with the overall estate planning of the owners of the business is an essential part of the task that must be undertaken by the draftsperson. "Restrictions on the passing of closely-held stock may fail in the face of conflicting estate plans whether the buy-sell restrictions appear in the form of the corporation's articles of incorporation, its by-laws, or even a buy-sell contract to which the deceased shareholder is a signatory."[1]

For instance, where the terms of the shareholder's will are inconsistent with the terms of the buy-sell, the business associate may suffer since the courts may give precedence to the terms of the decedent's will over the terms of a buy-sell[2] or to the terms of a will over the provisions in a firm's bylaws restricting the transfer of stock.[3]

Planners should remember that the buy-sell document is *not* intended merely for funding or merely for tax purposes. It always has important estate and business planning implications.

A buy-sell can also be designed to accomplish multiple objectives. In one situation the goal was to balance a client's desire to safeguard a family business with the attainment of a QTIP restricted marital deduction. The corpus of the QTIP trust would consist entirely of family-controlled stock. The client wanted the business decisions made by an unrelated person but the economic gain from the business divided between his wife and his children. Two trusts were established, a QTIP trust and a "children's trust." Twenty percent of the stock went into the QTIP, and 80 percent went to the childrens' trust. The QTIP trustee was authorized to run the business and acquire and hold unproductive property—subject to a power to dispose of unproductive property on the spouse's request. But any sale of the stock was made subject to a 30-day right of first refusal by the children's trust to purchase the stock.[4]

Exceptions To Consider

Another estate planning area often overlooked in drafting a buy-sell agreement is the exceptions. Planners should ask their clients if any transfers they may want to make in the future should be excepted from the basic restriction (e.g., transfers by gift to a trust for children or grandchildren). Many children have been cut out of a business interest because the buy-sell did not take them into consideration.

In one instance known to the authors a CPA was working as comptroller for his father and uncle's firm for almost ten years when the father died. Each man wanted 50 percent of the business. The buy-sell required a total sale of the decedent's interest to the uncle (who had his own son whom he wanted in the business). The decedent/shareholder's son not only lost his right to the future growth of the business for which he had worked so long and hard; he soon found himself out of a job as well. Had the buy-sell established a master buy-sell and a sub-buy-sell allowing a sale between father and son (by excepting it from the general provisions) and then providing for a sale of the survivor of them to the uncle, the father's goal would have been accomplished.

Restrictions To Include

When a buy-sell is created, the draftsperson must review the reasons for a written[5] restrictive agreement and build in, to the extent appropriate, provisions that accomplish the clients' objectives in these areas. Essentially, most attorneys focus on four points:

1. Restrictions that give owners control over future "partners"
2. Restrictions that establish rules for operating the corporation
3. Restrictions that create mechanisms for future decision making
4. Restrictions that help to formulate plans for limiting uncertainty surrounding death, disability, divorce and retirement

Types of Restrictions. Creative planners can and should tailor the form to the facts and objectives of the parties. Here are some of the gradations of restrictions[6]:

1. Total prohibition against any transfer of stock[7]
2. Requirement that no transfer can be made unless the corporation and/ or other shareholders approve[8]
3. Limitation of transfers to within a specified class (such as the shareholder's close family members)[9]
4. Requirement that the stock must be offered to the corporation or the other shareholders before it can be offered to a third party[10]
5. Requirement that the estate sell and the corporation (in the case of a stock redemption) or surviving shareholders (in the case of a cross-purchase) buy[11] (a cross-purchase usually provides that shareholders must purchase in proportion to their current percentage of ownership to keep the relative percentage of ownership undisturbed[12])
6. One or more variations on these themes (perhaps allowing differences for lifetime sales as opposed to those that occur after death)

The most typical set of restrictions provides as follows:

1. A shareholder may not make a transfer of stock during lifetime without the consent of the corporation or other shareholders.

2. The corporation or other shareholders have the right of first refusal if a shareholder wants to transfer stock during lifetime.

3. In the event of an involuntary sale or transfer of a shareholder's stock (such as to satisfy a judgment, at a bankruptcy sale or in a marriage dissolution), the corporation or other shareholders have an option to purchase the shares from the transferee.

4. At a shareholder's death his or her estate must sell and the corporation must purchase all of the stock.

Defining the Client

In drafting a buy-sell agreement the attorney must ask a number of both practical and ethical questions before beginning to work:[13]

- Who *is* the client? (The client may be one or more of a group of several shareholder/owners,[14] all of whom could be separately counseled, or the attorney may represent all of the shareholders—and their families.[15]
- On which side of future litigation will the client be in the future? (This uncertainty is what creates the evenhandedness that characterizes a well-drafted buy-sell and helps to establish the fairness of the market value of the stock for federal and state death tax purposes.)
- What does the client bring to the bargaining table? (Money or creditworthiness? Expertise? Contacts? Immediate ability and willingness to work full-time? This in turn will dictate, to a large extent, how far the other parties will allow the attorney to go in securing those provisions necessary or useful to protect or enhance the client's interests.)
- Is the client in a minority or majority position? (A majority shareholder may want immediate cash to buy out a departing shareholder but the right to use a long-term payout. A minority shareholder will want to negotiate protection not otherwise available under state corporate law.)

What does an attorney who represents *all* of the parties do when the interests of some of the individuals are inconsistent with the interests of others or with the corporation's interests?[16]

Planners should *never* assume the parties are harmonious—even (especially) when all the parties are related. Parties must deal with each other on a multiplicity of levels, and a problem on one level almost always becomes a problem on other levels.

State Law Restrictions

State law must be examined in the drafting process. First, planners need to ascertain what will result if no buy-sell agreement exists and the client is an owner of a professional corporation or association where ownership of stock is particularly limited.[17]

A second area where state law must be considered in the drafting process pertains to "lawful restrictions" (e.g., "right of first refusal," mandatory corporate or other shareholder approval, prohibitions on transfer to a designated class of persons (assuming that designation is not unreasonable). What limits, if any, does state law place on the parties' rights to restrict the transfer of stock?[18]

Third, many states have statutes that specify the terms under which a corporation may purchase its own stock. The purpose of such "surplus" laws is to protect creditors as well as minority shareholders. Specifically, these laws prohibit shareholders from bailing out cash to the detriment of creditors or minority shareholders by requiring "sufficient surplus." Most states limit a corporation to purchases out of surplus—i.e., retained earnings only. If the corporation does not have sufficient surplus, it may not buy back its stock, regardless of what the buy-sell requires. (Planners should remember that the "net amount at risk"—excess of death proceeds over policy cash values—creates surplus from which the stock of a deceased shareholder may be purchased.[19]) Some states provide that the purchase must not render the corporation insolvent. Several solutions to this potential problem are covered later in this chapter.

PROVISIONS DEALING SPECIFICALLY WITH LIFE INSURANCE

Stock Redemption Agreements

The agreement should contain the following provisions and information:

1. It should include a schedule of policies acquired, or to be acquired, on the life of each shareholder, indicating the insured, the insurer, the policy number (if available) and, of course, the face amount of the policy.
2. It should recite that the corporation will be the applicant, owner, pre-

mium payer and beneficiary of the policy, consistent with the redemption approach.

3. It must permit the shareholders to demand proof from the corporation that premiums have been paid.[20]
4. It should authorize the shareholders to pay the premiums and receive prompt reimbursement from the company if the company has not already done so.[21]
5. It must permit the corporation to acquire additional coverage on the lives of any of its shareholders and to add a schedule to the agreement listing the new policies and making them subject to the terms of the agreement.[22]
6. It should give the corporation the right to replace existing policies.[23]
7. It should require the shareholders to cooperate, for example, by submitting to examinations and completing applications.[24]
8. It should consider the date at which the value of the corporation will be measured and the impact of the receipt of life insurance on value. (This is discussed in detail in Chapter 11.)

In a redemption context the corporation will be the policyowner, with the right to receive dividends, assign coverage, borrow against the cash value, designate the beneficiary and so forth, subject to its commitments in the agreement.

Since corporate actions may be controlled by its officers and/or majority shareholders, the protection of minority shareholders may be an issue to consider, as noted earlier. Each shareholder should be entitled to information regarding actions taken by the corporation with regard to these assets, both as a matter of law and by agreement. Counsel should also consider requiring the joint consent of all parties to protect minority shareholders from corporate action that they consider contrary to their interests at the time the agreement was executed.

Upon the sale by a shareholder of stock during lifetime to the corporation or another party, or upon termination of the agreement, the initial coverage may no longer be necessary. The agreement should provide for the disposition of coverage in such instances.

The suggested solution is—at that time—to authorize the shareholder to purchase the policy on his life for its current fair market value net of policy loans upon written notice that the corporation will no longer pay premiums and the policy has entered or is about to enter the grace period. Such a purchase would be a transfer for value but would not harm the tax-free character of the proceeds upon maturity, because the transfer would be to the insured, an exception to the transfer-for-value rule.[25]

Absent a purchase, the agreement could permit the surrender of the policy by the corporation, which would in turn receive the policy value. Finally, this right should not be construed as conferring on the shareholder an incident of ownership on the policy, resulting in additional inclusion in his estate.[26]

Some policies have a rider allowing a substitution of insureds, thus permitting the coverage to be extended to the life of an ongoing shareholder upon the withdrawal of the original insured. Caution should be exercised in this case, however, because the IRS has ruled that the substitution of insureds will be a taxable event. IRC §1035 provides that a policy may be exchanged for a new policy on the life of the same insured without causing a taxable event. Unfortunately, however, the IRS has ruled that the substitution of insureds on the same contract is deemed to be a surrender of the policy followed by the acquisition of a new policy. As a result the corporation would have taxable income to the extent the surrender value, at the time of the substitution, exceeds its basis in the policy—i.e., its total premiums paid.[27]

Cross-Purchase Agreements

As with stock redemption agreements, cross-purchase arrangements should include a schedule of policy coverage; however, the documents will set forth different provisions and information:

1. Which shareholder owns the policy on the life of the coshareholder(s) (each shareholder should apply for, own and be the beneficiary of the policies owned on the life or lives of other shareholders)
2. Provisions regarding the acquisition of additional coverage (typically addressed as in a stock redemption agreement)
3. A mechanism that enables coshareholders to discover whether premiums insuring their respective lives have been paid[28]
4. An authorization of the corporation to pay the premiums if the policy-owner does not, with a deduction of that outlay from the shareholders' compensation[29]
5. Authorization of the insured to pay the premium on behalf of the policyowner and require prompt reimbursement by the latter in the event the premium is not timely paid

6. The requirement that the insurer provide information to the insured (not just the owner) upon request, to inform the insured of the status of the policy

Consistent with individual policy ownership, each coshareholder will be able to exercise all ownership rights with respect to the policy owned on the life of the other shareholder. Again, control over activities concerning the policies may be more limited when the policies are owned individually rather than corporately. As a result the agreement should restrict the exercise of these rights absent adequate notice to the insured.

As with redemption arrangements, the agreement should discuss the disposition of the policies upon a shareholder's sale of stock or termination of the contract. In a cross-purchase arrangement, however, a deceased shareholder's estate will own a policy on the life of the surviving shareholder, and that must be disposed of. In all instances the insured may be given the right to purchase the policy on his or her life without tainting the income-tax-free nature of the coverage. But consider the estate tax implications of providing a contractual right to the insured to make that purchase. The proceeds of the policy will be included in the insured's estate because that right to purchase the policy will be deemed an incident of ownership.

UNINSURABLE SHAREHOLDER PROVISIONS

What provisions should be made to cover the situation where a shareholder is uninsurable or insurance is inadequate? Consider the alternatives:

- Buy back the shares in a lump sum.
- Let the stock fall into a family member's hands and avoid the problem of raising cash to buy the stock.
- Buy the stock in installments.
- Pay for the stock in installments.[30]
- Give the remaining shareholders or the corporation the right to buy the stock, but grant the estate a put if they do not. This is similar to a wait-and-see approach. It allows the surviving shareholder an opportunity to see if he or she is comfortable with the decedent's heirs as "partners" while giving those heirs the ability to obtain cash for their interest.

SPECIAL PROVISIONS IN DRAFTING BUY-SELLS FOR PROFESSIONALS

When a triggering event occurs, the parties to a buy-sell consisting of a professional practice often "uncover distressing differences in how the practice and its value are viewed, especially if the members vary widely in age."[31] Furthermore, laws dealing specifically with professional corporations typically severely restrict who can own such stock and often require the repurchase of that stock by the corporation or other shareholders within a relatively short period of time.[32] So when reviewing or drafting[33] a buy-sell for professionals, the draftsperson should anticipate and consider solutions to the following problems:

Problem: When a professional leaves the practice voluntarily before normal retirement age, who takes the patients or clients?

Solution: Provide in the agreement that those clients brought in by each practitioner remain with that professional. Stipulate that those clients who entered the practice after the joint practice was formed be allowed to decide which professional they will go with. The precise wording of the patient or client notification should be contained in the agreement as well as a statement that all necessary records for each patient be transferred to the appropriate professional.

Problem: When a professional leaves the practice voluntarily before normal retirement age, how are the real and personal assets of the practice to be valued and split? For instance, what happens to the office, furniture, equipment and accounts receivable?

Solution: Specify that an independent appraiser be used to do the valuation and who will keep the office and telephone number (or who has a first option on them). Specify how much the departing professional will be paid for his or her share of the building, furniture and equipment. Consider stating that accounts receivable go into a separate account to be apportioned between the former owners according to their respective interests and paid out over a limited period of time (such as one to two years, after which they are probably worthless).

Problem: When a professional leaves the practice voluntarily before normal retirement age (for instance, to take a job someplace else or start his or her own practice), what happens to his or her share of the firm's value?

Solution: The firm or the remaining professionals should have an option (but not a requirement) to purchase the interest of a departing professional. Some agreements penalize such a person by discounting the value of the departing practitioner's interest as much as 25 percent. More commonly the option to buy back the interest is almost always coupled with the right to pay for the interest over a fairly long period of time, in some cases as much as 10 or 15 years.

Problem: A professional who chooses to leave prior to normal retirement age—or even one who retires at or after that point—could injure the firm by setting up a competing practice close enough to the firm to draw patients or clients.

Solution: Almost every buy-sell should contain a restrictive covenant, a non-competition clause that forbids the selling shareholder from competing with the buying shareholder. Such a provision will be upheld only if it is reasonable in terms of both geography and time. It should also spell out the specific damages to be paid if the agreement is breached.

Problem: When the group of practicing professionals grows large, the probability of disability of one or more of them prior to normal retirement grows rapidly. Will the firm continue salary during that time? For how long? What percentage of salary will be continued? At what point should a buyout be triggered?[34]

Solution: Most firms provide full or partial salary for up to one year to an owner, but at that point a disability buyout is triggered. The term *disability* must be defined in the agreement. The agreement should state that a professional who returns to work before the buyout begins must be able to perform at the same level of competency as before the accident, sickness or other institutionalization (a large number of disabilities are due to emotional, alcohol or drug problems). Such provisions should give the purchasing owners the right to extend payments for as long as five or ten years (with sufficient interest payable on the unpaid balance so that the "imputed interest" rules will not be applied by the IRS).

Problem: As ironic as it sounds, some buy-sells do not make a special provision for a buyout at normal retirement age.

Solution: A separate and specific provision should detail what is to happen upon the attainment of normal retirement age. It should distinguish between departure at normal retirement age and voluntary departure before that date (especially if the later event triggers a penalty for "abandoning the firm").

Give the retiring professional the right to any individual disability or health insurance coverage owned by the practice. Consider a provision allowing a retiring professional to purchase from the firm any life insurance on his or her life, but restrict the terms so that it will not be includable in his or her estate as an incident of ownership.[35] Provide that no purchase can occur unless the professional has reached normal retirement age and the firm has also given notice that it will no longer pay premiums and the policy has entered the grace period. Include a restrictive covenant with reasonable noncompetition provisions.

Problem: Most professional practices have little value relative to the accounts receivable. So when a professional dies, how can the decedent's estate realize a meaningful payment for his or her contributions?

Solution: The buy-sell agreement should require full funding through life insurance if possible. It should also require a lump-sum payment if there is sufficient insurance at the professional's death to enable the buyout. But the agreement should also require that, if the insurance is inadequate, a down payment of, say, 10 to 20 percent be made immediately for the stock, yet allowing installment payments of the balance over, say, five to ten years. Interest (at a rate high enough to block the IRS from imputing interest) should be payable on the unpaid balance.

The promissory note could be backed by a security agreement pledging both office assets and accounts receivable and further collateralized by requiring personal guarantees from each of the surviving professionals (and their spouses).

Problem: If a departing professional is not fully vested in a retirement plan, voluntary departure can result in a windfall to the remaining practitioner.

Solution: Consider providing that a departing practitioner will be compensated more generously than the retirement plan would allow. One way is by stating that upon such a departure the practitioner will be given amounts from accounts receivable equal to the value in the practitioner's retirement account.

Problem: Malpractice coverage must be continued for some period of time even if a group of practitioners is no longer working together. But who should pay the premiums?

Solution: Contact the malpractice carrier and find out how much a "tail" costs. Consider requiring a departing professional (who is leaving voluntarily for reasons other than disability or retirement) to pay the entire cost of malpractice tail coverage. Alternatively, the firm should pay a specified percentage.

Problem: What happens if—for any reason—a professional loses his or her license to practice or board specialization certification?

Solution: Insert a provision in the buy-sell giving the remaining professionals a call on the other's stock at a prearranged price.

MISCELLANEOUS PROVISIONS: PROBLEMS AND SOLUTIONS

Here are some potential problems that should be anticipated—and the potential solutions that can be built into the provisions in the buy-sell.

Problem: What is to be done if the corporation does not have adequate cash (even considering life insurance) to fund a buyout when a shareholder dies?

Solution: Obviously the textbook solution is to review the formula each year and purchase enough insurance to keep the plan fully funded. But there are a number of reasons why the amount on hand may still be inadequate. (What liability, if any, does the insurance agent who established the plan have if relied on by the parties to revalue and reassess need?) Attorney Howard Zaritsky[36] states: "If the agreement values stock by formula, the corporation should be required to have its accountant value the stock annually under the formula, and report the most recent value to the corporation and the stockholders. The corporation should then be required to obtain any additional insurance needed to cover this potential liability."

The buy-sell should permit a note for the excess of the purchase price over the available proceeds.

Problem: What should be done if the amount of insurance proceeds exceeds the value payable for the stock?

Solution: Provide that any excess goes to the corporation.

Problem: What happens to the life insurance policy on the life of a shareholder who terminates employment and sells stock back to the corporation?

Solution: Provide (carefully) for the disposition of any unneeded policies. The buy-sell may be able to give the insured the right to purchase the policy without causing inclusion of the policy in the insured's estate if the insured cannot initiate cancellation of the policy or control it in any way and therefore has no incidents of ownership in the policy. State in the buy-sell that the insured stockholder has no right to purchase a policy on his or her life from the corporation except upon written notice by the corporation that it will not continue the policy in force and that the policy is in the grace period. Require the insured to pay the full fair market value of the policy at the time of purchase (essentially interpolated terminal reserve plus unearned premium in the case of whole life policies and unearned premium in the case of term policies).

Problem: How can minority shareholders be assured of a market for their stock at a fair price? How can a deadlock in positions that is crippling the corporation be resolved?

Solution: Attorneys sometimes draft what is known as a *Russian roulette clause.* This provision (also often called a *slice of the pie*) states that any shareholder's offer to buy another shareholder's shares—or sell his or her own shares to another shareholder—is deemed to be an offer *both* to buy and to sell, at the price and terms at which the initial offer is made.

The idea is that the stockholder initiating the Russian roulette must offer a fair price, because if it is set too low, the initiator may be bought out by the other shareholder(s). (Of course, this may have been the intention.) It is also the ultimate deadlock-breaking procedure and may be necessary where state corporate law deadlock-breaking provisions are impractical or are not economically viable.

Assume there are two 50 percent shareholders, Ajax and Bjax. Ajax sends an offer to purchase Bjax's 10,000-share interest for $1 million. Bjax, the recipient of the offer, could choose to sell for that price or could demand 10,000 shares from Ajax for $1 million.

Problem: The Russian roulette clause typically favors the shareholder with the most wealth.[37] But a "trigger-happy" or hot-tempered shareholder may employ this technique as an alternative to reasonable compromise on various corporate positions. How can the shareholder without great wealth be protected?

Solution: Use a Russian roulette clause only when the parties have approximately equal resources. Both parties should have enough cash to effect a full buyout or be able to obtain third-party financing. This clause could be highly disruptive and destructive if one party had most of the essential business skills, contacts or capital, because control of the company would be worth more to that person than to a client who was essentially an investor/shareholder. The stronger-positioned party would therefore be willing to pay a premium that the other shareholder could not afford.

Problem: You represent a group, but not all of the shareholders in the corporation. They want to maintain control within that group but want flexibility and the ability to perpetuate control vis-à-vis the other shareholders.

Solution: Consider exempting transfers from within that group from the general restrictions on transfer outside the present stockholders.

Problem: In the typical buy-sell the corporation and/or shareholders are given a right of first refusal[38] that requires a selling shareholder to offer stock to them at an agreed-on price before offering it to an outsider. But must *all* of the selling shareholder's stock be purchased by other shareholders (or the corporation?) If this provision is *not* included in the buy-sell, the marketability of the seller's stock is limited. The other shareholders and/or the corporation could purchase just enough to make the seller's remaining stock a minority (unappealing) interest to outsiders. If the third party's (outsider's) offer is based on acquiring control (or equalizing voting rights), that offer may be withdrawn, or the price offered might be substantially lowered.

Solution: With an "all or nothing" right of first refusal, *all* of the selling shareholder's stock must be purchased by other shareholders (or the corporation) at the agreed-on price or under the agreed-on formula.

Problem: When the typical "right of first refusal" provision is used and the client is a minority shareholder or the other shareholders are cash-poor, that common clause may be worth little or even be counterproductive. Why?

According to the American Law Institute–American Bar Association's *Practical Lawyer*: "Minority shareholders rarely receive an offer from a third party because of the lack of a market for the shares" and "Cash poor shareholders may not be able to exercise their right of first refusal."

Solution I: The "take me along" (tag along) clause: provide in the buy-sell that when a third party makes an offer to one shareholder, the shareholders who did not receive one can demand that the third party also buy their shares (under the same terms and conditions) as a condition to buying *any* shares. This gives the minority shareholder or the cash-poor shareholder an option (i.e., a put) to receive a fair price for his or her stock even if that shareholder cannot otherwise prevent a third party from buying in.

Solution II: The "put it to the big boys" clause: provide, on behalf of minority shareholders, the right to demand that majority shareholders or the corporation itself buy the stock upon a given lapse of time and/or upon a specified event such as a third-party purchase of stock from a majority shareholder.

Solution III: The "long time a-comin' " clause: provide, on behalf of cash-poor shareholders, the time to finance the exercise of a right of first refusal or use the earnings of the corporation to pay off a stock purchase obligation by inserting long payment terms.

Problem: General corporate law prohibits a controlling shareholder from "oppressing" minority shareholders. But this fiduciary duty does not prevent the majority shareholder from selling stock to a third party that the minority client cannot work with or dislikes. As noted, absent a provision in the buy-sell, the majority shareholder has no duty to help minority shareholders "bail out" when the majority shareholder sells out.

Solution: A "take me along" provision can ensure that the minority shareholder will be bailed out if the majority shareholder decides to pull the plug. This protection is particularly important where the minority shareholder's job, in addition to the marketability of his stock, is at stake. The majority owner cannot sell unless the buyer buys the minority interest as well.

Problem: Some clients (often against the advice of counsel) offer employees small numbers of shares of stock in their corporations. Often this is done to solve a "5 *Rs*" problem.[39] But the mere presence of minority shareholders is often burdensome because recent case law has significantly broadened the fiduciary duty the majority shareholder owes to minority shareholders. Minority shareholders, no matter how few shares they own, have state law rights to:

- inspect the corporation's books, and
- receive timely notice of all board of directors' meetings and bring constant ("nuisance") suits against majority shareholders alleging a breach of fiduciary duty.

As a result, S corporation status may be jeopardized, and minority shareholders may make it more difficult for a majority shareholder to work, run the business or even sell stock (since any assignees will take stock subject to the same problems.)

Solution I: The best solution in most situations, if there is any choice, is not to offer a key person stock. Instead, give the key employee a fringe benefit such as nonqualified deferred compensation, split-dollar insurance, Section 162 coverage or a percentage of profits in lieu of stock. This provides incentive without the trouble and complication of a minority shareholder.

Solution II: Suggest that the client consider nonvoting common stock (even an S corporation can make this offer without jeopardizing its status as long as the shares are identical in every way except voting rights).

Solution III: Consider a "come along" provision requiring the minority shareholder to sell all stock to a third party offering to buy out the majority shareholder. The price and terms would be the same as for the majority stockholder. This provides a premium for the minority shareholder and makes the stock more attractive to potential buyers.

Solution IV: Build a call provision (the right to buy stock from the corporation, other shareholders or both) into the buy-sell. A call can be used to protect a majority shareholder from dealing with the constant disruption, dissent and annoyance of minority shareholders and also to protect against deadlocks. (The holder of the call could buy out the dissenting minority stockholders in the case of a deadlock).

The agreement could give the majority shareholder a call on the minority stockholder's shares. This would enable the majority shareholder to quickly smother any significant dissent and consolidate control. A call could also be used where the client holds only a bare majority if the client wants to be sure a merger, acquisition or other desired major transaction cannot be blocked. Often the mere threat of exercising a call is enough to positively affect the votes of minority shareholders.

Problem: You represent two out of three shareholders. Your two clients together hold a majority interest (e.g., each owns 26 shares) vis-à-vis the third shareholder. But if either of your clients dies or receives an offer from an outsider or from the third shareholder, the typical shareholder agreement would result in half of the decedent/shareholder's stock going to your remaining client and half of the stock going to the minority shareholder (or outsider). The problem is that your client loses control.

Solution I: Provide in the agreement that the selling shareholder's stock must be offered first to your other client at death or some other triggering event and then to the minority shareholder (or outsider) to the extent your client elects not to purchase the shares.

Solution II: Exempt transfers within the shareholder group you represent from general transfer restrictions. This enables your clients to keep the corporation close but retain flexibility.

Problem: Assume you represent Uncle Mutt, who owns 80 percent of the voting stock in a furniture company. He gets along very well with his niece, Henrietta, who owns the remaining 20 percent and works with him in the business. A buyer approaches Mutt with an offer, but when the buyer meets Henrietta, the two don't get along. The buyer is about to withdraw his offer.

Solution: A "tag along" provision built into the buy-sell requires the minority shareholder to sell at the same time the majority shareholder sells. The "tag along" provision enables the majority shareholder to sell and the outsider to buy without present or future interference from the minority shareholder.

If a "tag along" provision is used, be sure it deals with any side agreements, employment contracts, consulting agreements or nonqualified deferred compensation agreements. If these are to be taken away from the selling shareholder/employee, the seller must be given a comparable benefit of equivalent economic (after adjustment for tax differential) value.

Problem: Your client owns a minority interest in a corporation and is afraid actions will be taken without his knowledge against his interest.

Solution: Require formal notice. Be sure the agreement provides the following:

- That all notices and exercises of options of any type must be made in writing, be addressed to the corporation and all shareholders and be sent by certified mail
- When option periods begin and end
- That restrictions on transfers are conspicuously noted on each certificate (or the restriction may not be enforceable against bona fide purchasers)
- That any transfer to a third party is conditional on the party agreeing in writing to be bound by the terms of the shareholder agreement

Problem: Most buy-sells preclude the use of closely held stock as collateral. Although this appears to be a simple, effective way to prevent a third-party creditor from levying on the stock and obtaining it in the event of a default, it also forecloses a large potential source of credit.

Solution: Condition the shareholder's right to pledge stock on the creditor's agreement to give the corporation, the other stockholders or both the right to buy back the stock if the shareholder defaults on payments. This allows shareholders to leverage their corporate-encapsulated wealth and at the same time assures creditors of being able to regain their capital by foreclosing on the shares for at least the amount of the debt. It also assures other shareholders that stock will not fall into the hands of outsiders through a default if the stock is encumbered.

Problem: A bankruptcy court can find a buy-sell agreement executory and therefore subject to rejection by the trustee in bankruptcy. What if a shareholder goes bankrupt? What if the corporation goes bankrupt?

Solution: The trustee in bankruptcy does *not* have to reject the buy-sell. The fairer the purchase price is, the more likely it will not be rejected. The answer is to set the price or establish the formula in the buy-sell under arm's-length terms and keep it as fair as possible to all parties.

Problem: Any shareholder can petition a court for the involuntary dissolution of the corporation if the acts of the directors or those otherwise in control are fraudulent or oppressive. This course of action is becoming increasingly popular as an avenue of relief for minority shareholders and is available in most states. Will the buy-sell be allowed to stand in spite of a petition for such a proceeding?

Solution: A truly fair buy-sell will stand up against such an attack. The more fair and adequate the buy-sell terms and price, the more likely the shareholders' agreement will override a shareholder's right to evoke such a dissolution.

Problem: If the corporation has borrowed money from a bank, the loan agreement may forbid the corporation's purchase of its stock until the loan is repaid.

Solution: If possible, a waiver of this loan provision from the bank or other lender should be obtained before the stock redemption agreement is adopted— or a cross-purchase form of buy-sell should be used. The Wait-and-See buy-sell approach will help solve this problem.[40]

Problem: A majority shareholder will not want a minority shareholder (e.g., a family member) who is fired or who quits because of a business or family dispute to continue to hold stock and be able to exercise the rights given to all shareholders under state law. The other side of the problem is that a minority shareholder who has been fired or who quits will not want to (in the long run) hold a piece of paper that cannot force dividends, has little value as collateral and is difficult to sell.

Solution: Provide in the agreement that fired employees must sell their stock back to the corporation in the event of discharge for any reason (or "discharge for cause" to minimize the trauma to related employees). In essence this gives the majority shareholder an option to purchase another shareholder's stock at any time by firing him or her and then purchasing the shares.

A "discharge solely for specified cause" provision is more likely to survive judicial scrutiny tests for fairness and mutuality of obligation.

Problem: Assume your clients are running a business in which a specific professional license is required (e.g., a professional corporation or association) and one or more associates—for whatever reason—lose their license to practice.

Solution: Restrictions dealing with termination of employment should also cover what should happen if a professional loses his or her license. The agreement should specifically cover the procedures for the purchase of the stock and the purchase price.

Problem: The parties to a buy-sell want the selling shareholder to be required to sever all ties to the corporation upon the sale of stock.

Solution: Provide that complete termination requires resignation as director, officer and employee and termination of any employment agreement. Also provide for a required repayment of any loan between the shareholder and the corporation. Allow the corporate purchaser of stock to deduct (or add) the unpaid balance of the loan from (or to) the purchase price. Provide for disposition of life insurance on the life of the departing shareholder. (Do the parties want to continue the policy on the life of the terminating individual?)

Problem: Most states restrict a corporation's purchase of its stock to the extent of surplus or earned surplus. In no state can a corporation buy back its stock if the purchase would render the corporation insolvent.

Solution: Add a provision allowing shareholders and the corporation (to the extent permitted by state law) to reflect assets or appreciation in assets not recorded on the books in a surplus account. In other words, give surviving shareholders whatever rights are necessary to create the necessary surplus. Some states' laws allow a corporation to reduce the par value of the corporation's stock or revalue corporate assets to correspond to present fair market values.[41]

Counsel should also consider an "escape valve" that requires individual surviving shareholders to purchase any stock that the corporation is forbidden to buy because of an "insufficient surplus" state law.

Problem: If a shareholder can vote on the corporation's purchase of stock under an option, there may be a conflict of interest vis-à-vis the other shareholders.

Solution: If a conflict of interest is a perceived or even remotely possible problem, disqualify the selling shareholder from voting (as shareholder, director or officer) on that decision.

Problem: A client wants a child to succeed to ownership of the business, but the child is too young or too inexperienced to work in the business or run it.

Solution: A "buy time" buy-sell between the client and a key managerial (non-family) employee would provide that upon the client's death the employee purchases some of the decedent's stock at an agreed-on price. This equity interest in the business will tie the employee in with enough stock to encourage him or her to stay and yet retain control in the client's family. Insurance on the client's life (paid for by split dollar or executive bonus) would be owned by and payable to the key employee, who would use that money to purchase the employer's stock. The agreement would require the employee to sell back the stock to the corporation upon the occurrence or nonoccurrence of specified events or automatically sell the stock back after a given period of time (when the client's children should be old and experienced enough to run the business).

Problem: Most states permit a shareholder to file for an "involuntary dissolution." This is a form of statutory relief for minority shareholders when the acts of directors or others in control are fraudulent or oppressive.[42] How can the buy-sell be written so that it will stand up to such a proceeding?

Solution: Protection of minority shareholders (and the rights they will claim regardless of what is said in the agreement) must always be considered in the drafting of a buy-sell.[43] The success of a buy-sell agreement will depend in large part on how fair its terms and purchase price are as well as the wording of the statute. The shareholders' agreement probably will stand if it is fair and reasonable.

RESTRICTIONS ON TRANSFER INCIDENT TO DIVORCE

Because of the high incidence of divorce in this country, counsel should ask the following questions of each shareholder and build into the buy-sell appropriate protective provisions:

- What would be the impact on the corporation and its shareholders if a former spouse concluded a divorce with stock in the corporation?
- What would result if the employment of an ex-son-in-law or ex-daughter-in-law were terminated—but the fired employee (former family member) still owned stock in the corporation?
- What would be the impact on the family if a parent's corporation continued to employ a former son-in-law or daughter-in-law?

- How would the knowledge that the earnings due at least partially to his or her efforts would end up in the hands of his or her ex-spouse affect on the productivity of a working child?

Do general restrictions on sales and transfers found in the typical buy-sell agreement avoid the reach of an ex-spouse in a divorce decree or under a state's equitable distribution statute?

The trend is that the typical buy-sell drafting will *not* prevent a former spouse from acquiring shares in a family corporation (presumably because the prohibition on transfers contemplated under the usual buy-sell agreement covers only voluntary sales).

The solution is for the buy-sell to state, clearly and precisely, that transfers incident to divorce as well as any other involuntary transfers are covered under the same prohibition that applies to voluntary transfers.

COMMUNITY PROPERTY ISSUES AND ANSWERS

Community property is a concept under which (with a few exceptions) both spouses share equally in the income and capital of either spouse obtained during the marriage while living in a community property state. This means that one spouse cannot arbitrarily dispose of the other spouse's community interest. Therefore, in a buy-sell agreement where any of the parties are domiciliaries of a community property state, the agreement should contain:

- the written consent of both spouses to the terms of the agreement;
- a provision invalidating any attempted testamentary transfer of either spouse's interest to someone other than the surviving spouse in the event one predeceases the other and giving the survivor a right of first refusal on the stock; and
- wording dealing with the disposition of the stock in the event the couple becomes divorced or separated and requiring a mandatory offer of the stock to the corporation or other shareholders before it can fall into the hands of the spouse who did not work in the business.

PROTECTING THE PASSIVE STOCKHOLDER

An attorney who represents children or other passive shareholders must ask—and build into the buy-sell the responses to—these questions:

- How do I protect a family member who has retired, is no longer drawing a salary from the business and depends mainly on dividends from the business?
- How do I protect children who are too young or inexperienced but who own stock in the business and rely on that stock to provide dividend income for financial needs?
- How do I protect an older stockholder who, in a recapitalization designed to freeze an estate, received noncumulative preferred stock?
- How do I assure passive stockholders in an S corporation of at least enough income to pay taxes on the income taxable to them whether or not they receive actual dividends?
- How do I assure a minority shareholder's job if there is a change in management or control? (For instance, suppose at the retirement of the president and majority shareholder of a business, the minority shareholder employee, your client, cannot get along with the successor president—perhaps an outsider or family member who never worked in the business before.)
- How do I protect a client from the control problem if one of the 40 percent shareholders sold out to the other? (Suppose your client owned a 20 percent interest in a business, and the other 80 percent was held, 40–40, by two shareholders who were unrelated to each other.)

The solution to many of these types of problems is a put, which gives a stockholder the legal right to require that the corporation and/or the other shareholders repurchase some or all of his or her stock. This provision, incorporated into the buy-sell document, may allow the forcing of a buyback upon the occurrence (or nonoccurrence) of a specified event and could last either for the holder's life or for a limited period of time. So, if the corporation fails to pay dividends at a given level for a given period of time, or if dividends fall below a given level, the put becomes operative.

Likewise, the put could be triggered at the termination of employment, for any reason, of your client. It would enable your client to require the purchase of his or her interest at a stated price or according to a predetermined formula.

A put could protect a 20 percent minority stockholder from the tyranny of a 40 percent shareholder who suddenly becomes an 80 percent shareholder. Your client, the minority shareholder, could liquidate his or her interest at will rather than be stuck with stock with no realizable value or voting strength.

Puts can be designed so that they are exercisable against

- only the other shareholders,
- only the corporation or
- both the other shareholders and the corporation.

PROTECTING THE S ELECTION

An S election is easily lost if the stock is transferred into prohibited hands (e.g., an alien or a nonqualifying trust).

One answer is to preclude transfers of S stock to any party that does not meet IRC rules and provide that any transfer to an ineligible shareholder is ineffective (subject to prohibitions on alienability under state law). Another solution is to use a call. Holders of larger blocks of S stock can have a call on the interests of minority shareholders. Typically the call is exercised with payment on an installment basis.

Endnotes

1. See Hunsberger, "Owners and Estates: A Buy-Sell Primer," *Journal of the American Society of CLU & ChFC* (Sept. 1991): 48.
2. See *Lane v. Albertson*, 79 N.Y.S. 947 (1903); and *Storer v. Ripley*, 178 N.Y.S.2d 7 (1958).
3. *Globe Slicing Machine Co. v. Hasner*, 333 F.2d 413 (2nd Cir. 1964), *cert. denied* 379 U.S. 969 (1965).
4. PLR 8931005; IRC §2056(b)(7); and Reg. §20.2056(b)-5(f)(4), which states that a trust will qualify for the marital deduction even if there is no income-producing property in the trust if the surviving spouse has the right to make it income-producing.
5. A buy-sell must be in writing to be considered a contract to sell securities. See UCC (Uniform Commercial Code) §8-318. See also UCC §8-204, which requires that restrictions on the transfer of shares be documented on the security itself or that are not effective against subsequent transferees without actual notice.
6. Donald, "Corporate Buy-Out Agreements," 106-5th T.M. The validity of a given

restriction is measured by state law, which of course will vary considerably. Generally, if the restriction is "reasonable in the light of the facts," it will be upheld.

Courts typically look at these factors:

- Size of corporation (the more closely held, the more likely the court will uphold a restriction)
- The restraint to be placed on transferability (the lesser the degree of restriction, the more likely it will be upheld)
- The length of time the restriction will last (the shorter the term, the more likely it will be upheld)
- The likelihood the restriction will work in the best interests of the entire enterprise (the more it promotes the survival of the business as opposed to protecting or enhancing the interests of specific shareholders, the more likely it will be upheld)

7. Few courts will allow such restrictions—especially if there is no time limit. See *Bloomingdale v. Bloomingdale*, 177 N.Y.S. 873 (S.Ct. 1919).
8. Courts tend to uphold such agreements only if it can be shown that the power must or has been exercised reasonably and in good faith. See *Penthouse Properties, Inc. v. 1158 Fifth Ave. Inc.*, 256 App. 685, 11 N.Y.S.2d 417 (1939). The advantage of this provision is that current shareholders can exclude others without the need to tie up corporate funds in anticipation of a purchase. Of course this puts the potential seller at a disadvantage; no sale can be made without the consent of the other shareholders. This may result in expensive, aggravating and uncertain litigation even where the withholding of consent is eventually found by a court to be unreasonable.
9. The problem with a provision that limits transferability to a restricted class is that within that class there may still be individuals who are incapable of carrying their load as employees of the business or are undesirable as business associates to the present owners for some other reason such as inexperience, poor judgment or quarrelsome nature. Worse yet, it is impossible to predict who will belong to that group in the future since the composition of the group itself is likely to be dynamic.
10. "First offer" provisions are almost always upheld as long as they are reasonable. See *Evans v. Dennis*, 203 Ga. 232, 46 S.E2d 122 (1948). This is a very common method of restricting transferability and keeping a closely held business "close" and is often appropriate for lifetime buyouts.

However, a first-offer provision does not guarantee a market for a shareholder's stock (or the funding to pay for it) and therefore does not equate to estate liquidity. Where the corporation or surviving shareholders are the most likely buyers, by refusing to exercise an option to buy, the survivors have the decedent/shareholder's family over the proverbial barrel. The estate has an asset-generating estate tax but is not creating the cash to pay that tax. The estate as a potential seller can be "frozen out" until it is willing to sell under the terms and conditions and at the price dictated by the surviving shareholders. This problem is obviously exacerbated where the decedent was a minority shareholder.

11. The total buyout is the most popular of the restrictive agreements, and courts

have almost universally allowed such agreements where triggered at the death or disability of a shareholder. See *Greater New York Carpet House, Inc. v. Herschmann*, 258 App. Div. 649, 17 N.Y.S.2d 483 (1940).

12. The agreement will usually provide that if a shareholder does not purchase the amount of stock to which he or she is entitled, other shareholders can buy the remaining stock according to their percentage interests.

13. See Scott, "How To Draft a Shareholder Agreement," *The Practical Lawyer* 36 (No. 1): 63, for some excellent ideas on the problems and solutions in this area.

14. Suppose your clients were two out of three equal shareholders. As compared to the third, your clients had control. What would they want to happen if one of them died or received an offer from the third party? Under the typical wording the decedent's shares would be offered one-half to your remaining client and one-half to the third shareholder. The problem is that your remaining client would no longer have a controlling vote—unless the agreement provided that upon the occurrence of a triggering event it must first be offered to your remaining client and then to the third shareholder.

15. When representing all of the parties, the planner must keep in mind the ethical issues, because the interests of some of the parties will almost inevitably differ from those of others or be inconsistent with those of the corporation. The psychology and dynamics of family relationships must also be considered.

16. See Leimberg et al., *Tools and Techniques of Estate Planning*, appendix chapter on "Ethics: What the Estate Planner Must Know." (Cincinnati: National Underwriters Co., 1992), call 800-543-0874.

17. Each state has its own laws that sometimes distinguish between closely held corporations and others and are usually more liberal with respect to restrictions on transferability in the former than the latter. See MacMillan *Model Statutory Close Corporation Supplement to the Model Business Corporation Act* (Englewood Cliffs, N.J.: Prentice-Hall). Special separate laws cover professional corporations and associations.

18. See Scott, "How To Draft a Shareholder Agreement," *The Practical Lawyer* 36 (No. 1): 66, for a review of these restrictions.

19. See Blough, *Practical Applications of Accounting Standards*, (Salem, N.H.: Ayer Co. Pubs., 1981), 214–15.

20. Each shareholder has a financial interest in being certain that the corporation has maintained the policies by paying premiums when due. The shareholder would be concerned that the premiums on the policy on his or her own life are paid so that on his or her death there is a source of funds to buy out that interest.

Additionally, the shareholder would want to make sure that premiums on the life of a coshareholder are paid so that on the coshareholder's death he or she is able to cause the corporation to carry out the terms at the agreement without undue burden on the company's financial future.

21. Even with typical closely held corporations these provisions are important because some shareholders may have less participation than others in the day-to-day financial management of the company. The premium information should be readily available for the corporation to inform the shareholders, and the latter under state law would typically be entitled to review the corporate records.

22. Buy-sell agreements are generally expected to have long lives, and the price to be funded at inception may be insufficient at a later time.
23. This provision helps address changing circumstances or when a more appropriate policy becomes available with a new insurer or a downgrading of the financial rating of an existing insurer suggests a change in insurers.
24. To assist the corporation in obtaining additional or replacement coverage
25. IRC §101(a)(2)(b).
26. See Zaritsky, "Forgotten Provisions in Buy-Sell Agreements," *Institute on Estate Planning* 185: Chapter 6, 6-26. See also *Estate of Smith v. Comm'r*, 73 T.C. 307 (1979), and 1981-1 CB 1, where the IRS acquiesced in the decision, although not the Tax Court's analysis. See also PLR 9128008 and PLR 9127007, where the insured's right to repurchase the policy required inclusion of the proceeds in his gross estate. The suggested method should avoid an IRS attack.
27. Rev. Rul. 90-109.
28. Since the individuals will be the policyowners, it will be their personal obligation to pay policy premiums. The coshareholders will again desire some comfort that the premiums on the policies insuring their respective lives have been paid. Review of the records of their coshareholders will not be as readily available as review of corporate records in the redemption arrangement.
29. Premium payments will be nondeductible whether paid by the corporation or the shareholders, so in this event the shareholders must report the premium payments by the corporation on their behalf as taxable income; the corporation will receive a deduction to the extent the premiums are paid from compensation, provided the degree of compensation is reasonable. IRC §162(a)(1).
30. If installments are to be allowed, the agreement should specify:

    * the amounts payable and the dates on which payments are to be made,
    * the interest rate on any unpaid balance and
    * the type of security and terms of any escrow account to be required until payments are completed.

31. For an excellent and highly practical article in this area, see Hodes, "Why You Need a Buy-Sell Agreement Now," *Medical Economics* (November 26, 1990): 172.
32. See *Model Professional Corporation Supplement to the Model Business Corporation Act*.
33. As was mentioned in the beginning of this book, the authors intended that it be written mainly for and marketed to life insurance agents, financial planners and clients. Of course, we recognize that *only an attorney should draft a buy-sell*. But attorneys die or become unable to work themselves or sometimes have not reviewed buy-sell documents for many years. We also expect that nonattorneys be aware of the terms of buy-sell documents and feel their knowledge and insight can provide invaluable advice in this area—even with respect to what should or should not be considered by a competent attorney who will be doing the drafting. For these reasons the authors have included this extensive discussion of drafting provisions and the specimen documents.
34. These issues are covered in detail in Chapter 32.
35. PLRs 9128008 and 9127007.

36. See Zaritsky's excellent article, "Forgotten Provisions in Buy-Sell Agreements," *Miami Tax Institute on Estate Planning* (1985): 6-1.
37. But a stockholder without a "deep pocket" can often manage to obtain from a third party the funds to effect a buyout.
38. A typical right of first refusal provides:

    If a shareholder receives a bona fide offer for any of his stock from a third party, he must first offer the stock to his coshareholders (typically on a pro-rata basis) or to the corporation (or to both) (at a predetermined price, according to a predetermined formula, or at the price offered by the third party when the reason for the transfer is that party's offer) BEFORE the stock can be transferred to the third party.

    The purchase price is payable

    (1) under the terms of the agreement;
    (2) in accordance with the third party's offer.

39. See Leimberg, "Meeting and Beating The '5R' (Recruiting, Retaining, Retiring, Rewarding, and Reversing the Discrimination Against Those Who Add the Most to Profits) Problem." Reprints of this client-oriented brochure are available from Financial Data Center; 215-525-6957.
40. See Chapter 29.
41. Of course, if the corporation's ability to purchase its own stock is a major issue, the problem can be avoided totally by setting up the buy-sell on a cross-purchase basis.
42. See Thompson, "Corporate Dissolution and Shareholders' Reasonable Expectations," *Wash. Univ. L.Q.* 66 (1988): 193, 226–28.
43. See *Pupecki v. James Madison Corp.*, 376 Mass. 212, 382 N.E. 2d 1030 (1978), where a majority shareholder sold substantially all the assets of the corporation and in return was provided with payments under a noncompetition agreement and employment agreement. The minority shareholder successfully alleged that the agreements were in reality mechanisms for diverting part of the purchase price for the corporation's assets to the majority shareholder. The court permitted the claim against the majority shareholder based on allegations of breach of fiduciary duty and fraud.

C H A P T E R 3 5

Conclusions

When all is said and done, it seems that the classic methods, devoid of gimmickry, provide the best potential for planning the ultimate tax results with the most accuracy. Individuals can try "new-fangled" funding approaches to obtain current and future supposed tax advantages or financial bargains, but it is the basic approaches that are most dependable and likely to provide the desired results.

Thus the basic straightforward cross-purchase agreement will get the job done if each individual bears his or her weight. Without life insurance the individual probably would end up paying more on the same basis. A stock redemption agreement is probably called for when there are more than three stockholders, unless it is a closely held family situation and attribution rules cannot be overcome or the AMT exposure is too costly.

In those cases where family members are involved, where there is potential dividend treatment for noncomplete or nonsubstantially disproportionate redemptions, another approach should most likely be sought—possibly a Section 303 redemption combined with a bequest of stock to indicated family members or a cross-purchase buyout of any balance. The wait-and-see approach will often provide the ideal blend of the cross-purchase and stock redemption methods and afford the maximum in tax and financial planning flexibility.

It is clear that the only way to guarantee that the plan is fully funded at the proper time is by using life insurance. It is also clear that the type of plan selected—cross-purchase or stock redemption—dictates the proper owner and beneficiary for the insurance. Several factors determine which approach is the best to use; however, the factors that determine the best plan can change over time. Bearing that in mind, the best plan to start with might be a cross-purchase, if only because it allows the flexibility to switch to stock redemption that may not be available the other way around.

It is necessary to look at the potential benefits as well as the costs involved. If the shareholder's family is in need of funds for liquidity or family income, where or how the money comes in is immaterial. If the value is slightly out of date, this too is immaterial if it is sufficient for the existing purposes.

If the family of the deceased shareholder is able to receive enough money, net after taxes and expenses, relatively quickly to pay all of the debts and taxes of the estate and provide itself with adequate support, the main purpose for the establishment of an agreement has probably been met, and the substance of the agreement is immaterial. Unfortunately, there are pitfalls that make the substance of the agreement important indeed if the net desired results are to be achieved.

It is hoped that this publication has helped illustrate methods to fulfill the tax and business disposition intentions of both corporate business owners and heirs.

APPENDIX

Sample Buy-Sell
Agreements

- Cross-Purchase Agreement (Common-Law States)
- Stock Redemption Agreement (Common-Law States)
- Cross-Purchase Agreement (Community Property States)
- Stock Redemption Agreement (Community Property States)
- Specimen Shareholder's Agreements—Protecting S Election

This appendix contains sample cross-purchase agreements and stock redemption agreements for common-law and community property states. These agreements are for illustration only. A BUY-SELL AGREEMENT, LIKE ANY OTHER LEGAL DOCUMENT, CAN BE PREPARED ONLY BY AN ATTORNEY.

CROSS-PURCHASE AGREEMENT

(Common-Law States)

The agreement that follows is a cross-purchase plan. Under this type of buy-sell agreement, the shareholders individually agree to purchase the interest of the deceased shareholder. And the estate of the deceased shareholder is bound to sell the interest directly to the surviving shareholders. The corporation is not a party to this agreement. Each shareholder owns, is the beneficiary of and pays for insurance on the life of each of the other shareholders in amounts totaling his or her share of the purchase price. When a shareholder dies, the insurance on his or her life owned by each of the surviving shareholders provides them with the purchase price to carry out the terms of the agreement.

AGREEMENT by and between _____ and _____ (hereinafter called the Shareholders).

WITNESSETH:

WHEREAS, the Shareholders own the capital stock of _____Company, a corporation with its principal place of business at _____ (hereinafter referred to as the Company), _____ owning _____ shares of the stock of the Company, and

WHEREAS, the Shareholders believe that it is to their mutual best interests to provide for continuity and harmony in management and the policies of the Company; and

WHEREAS, the purposes of this agreement to provide for the purchase by the other Shareholder of one Shareholder's stock in event of his or her death, or in event he or she desires to dispose of any of his or her stock during his or her lifetime, and to provide the funds necessary to carry out such purchases;

NOW, THEREFORE, in consideration of the mutual agreements and covenants contained herein and for other valuable consideration, receipt of which is hereby acknowledged, it is mutually agreed and covenanted by and between the parties to this agreement as follows:

ARTICLE 1.

Restriction on Sale of Stock—Neither of the Shareholders shall, during their joint lives, assign, encumber or dispose of any lives, assign, encumber or dispose of any portion of their respective stock interests in the Company, by sale or otherwise, unless he or she first gives written notice to that effect to the other Shareholder. The other Shareholder shall have the right to purchase such stock at any time within 30 days after such notice at the price and under the mode of payment determined by Articles 4 and 5. If the offered stock is not purchased within the above period, the offering Shareholder may dispose of his or her shares in any lawful manner, except that he or she shall not sell any shares to any other person without giving the other Shareholder the right to purchase them at the price and on the terms offered by or to such other person. Upon the consummation of purchase, the selling Shareholder shall deliver the certificates to the purchasers.

ARTICLE 2.

Sale of Stock at Death—Upon the death of a Shareholder, the survivor shall purchase and the estate of the decedent shall sell the stock interest now owned or hereafter acquired by the Shareholder who is the first to die. The purchase or sale price and the mode of payment for such stock shall be determined in accordance with the provisions of Articles 4 and 5 of this agreement.

ARTICLE 3.

The Insurance Policies—In order to assure that all or a substantial part of the purchase price for the shares of the deceased Shareholder will be available immediately in cash upon his or her death, the Shareholders have procured insurance upon each other's lives as follows:

_____ is insured under life insurance policy No. _____ issued by the _____ Insurance Company in the face amount of $ _____, and _____ is the applicant, owner and beneficiary thereof.

_____ is insured under life insurance policy No. _____ issued by the _____ Insurance Company in the face amount of $_____, and _____ is the applicant, owner and beneficiary thereof.

Each Shareholder hereby authorizes the Company to pay the premiums on the policies owned by him or her and made subject to this agreement as such premiums become due and to charge his or her salary or other account therefor. In case any premium is not paid within twenty days after its due date, the insured shall be entitled to pay such premium as agent of the owner, and the owner agrees to reimburse him or her promptly for any such payment. The insurance company is hereby authorized and directed to give the insured, upon his or her written request, any information about the status of any policy on his or her life subject to this agreement.

Each Shareholder shall retain possession of the policies procured by him or her on the life of the other Shareholder. He or she may not, however, exercise any of the policy rights (without first having given the insured thereunder thirty days' written notice of the contemplated exercised, unless he or she has obtained from the insured a written waiver of such notice). Notwithstanding any other provision of this agreement, any dividends payable upon the policies prior to maturity by the death of the insured shall be paid to the owner in cash or disposed of as such owner may direct. This agreement shall extend to and include all additional life insurance policies issued pursuant to this agreement, such additional policies to be listed in Schedule B attached hereto and made a part hereof.

ARTICLE 4.

Transfer of Deceased Shareholder's Stock—Upon the death of a Shareholder, the surviving Shareholder shall proceed immediately to collect the proceeds of the policies on the deceased Shareholder's life which are subject to this agreement. Upon collection of all such proceeds and the qualification of a Legal Representative of the decedent's estate, the surviving Shareholder shall pay to the Legal Representative an amount equal to such proceeds, which amount shall constitute payment on account, in full, as the case may be, for the stock of the deceased Shareholder.

If the purchase price set forth in Article 5 exceeds the proceeds of life insurance, the balance of the purchase price shall be paid in _____ consecutive (monthly) (quarterly) (semiannual) (annual) payments beginning _____ months after the date of the decedent's death. The unpaid balance of the purchase price shall be evidenced by a series of negotiable promissory notes made by the surviving Shareholder to the order of the estate of the deceased with interest at _____ % per annum. Said note shall provide for the acceleration of the due date of all unpaid notes in the series on default in the payment of any note or interest thereon and shall give the maker thereof the option of prepayment in whole or in part at any time. All of the stock of the decedent covered by this agreement shall be pledged with the decedent's estate as security for the payment of said notes; provided, however, that the surviving Shareholder shall be entitled to exercise all rights of ownership in such stock prior to default in the payment of any note or interest thereon.

ARTICLE 5.

Purchase Price of Shares—The Shareholders agree that the present value of their stock is $ _____ per share. Within sixty days after the end of each fiscal year, or as soon thereafter as possible, the Shareholders, acting unanimously, shall redetermine the value per share of their stock and shall indicate such value by endorsement with their signatures upon Schedule A attached hereto and made a part hereof. If the Shareholders fail to redetermine the price agreed upon within twenty-four months following the end of the (fiscal) (calender) year, the value of a deceased Shareholder's stock shall be agreed upon by the representative of the decedent and the surviving Shareholder. If the representative of the decedent and the surviving Shareholder do not agree upon the value within _____ days after the death of a Shareholder, the value of the deceased Shareholder's stock shall be determined by arbitration as follows: the surviving Shareholder shall name one arbitrator. If the two arbitrators do not agree upon the value of the stock of the deceased Shareholder within _____ days of their appointment, they shall appoint a third arbitrator and the decision of the majority shall be binding.

For the purpose of this agreement the price at which the stock shall be sold and purchased during the life of a Shareholder shall be the same as the price established immediately above.

ARTICLE 6.

Disposition of Insurance Policies on Death or Termination—The surviving Shareholder shall have an option exercisable within a period of _____ months from the date of death of the deceased Shareholder, to purchase from his or her estate any or all of the policies owned by the deceased upon the survivor's life subject to this agreement on paying for each a price equal to the amount of (1) the cash surrender value thereof, if any, calculated on a prorated basis to the date of the transaction exclusive of any dividend, dividend accumulations, cash value of any paid-up insurance additions or policy loans, plus (2) the pro rata portion of any premium paid prior to such date which covers a period extending beyond the date of the transaction, and less (3) any policy loan plus interest then due. Any such policy not acquired by the survivor within the above option period may be surrendered to the insurance company by the deceased Shareholder's estate for its cash surrender value, or it may be held or disposed of in any lawful manner which the estate deems advisable.

In the event of the termination of this agreement from any cause other than the death of a Shareholder, each Shareholder shall have an option, exercisable within thirty days after such termination, to purchase any or all policies on his or her own life subject to this agreement on paying for each a price calculated on the basis prescribed in the preceding paragraph.

ARTICLE 7.

Termination of Agreement—This agreement shall terminate on

1. The written agreement of the Shareholders, or
2. The dissolution, bankruptcy or insolvency of the Company, or
3. The death of both Shareholders simultaneously or within a period of _____ days, or
4. The transfer of the stock of a deceased Shareholder to the surviving Shareholder, or the sale by a Shareholder during his or her life of all of his or her stock to someone other than the other Shareholder as herein provided.

ARTICLE 8.

Agreement To Be Bound by Contract—The executor, administrator or personal representative of a deceased Shareholder shall execute and deliver any documents or legal instruments necessary or desirable to carry out the provisions of this agreement. The agreement shall be binding upon the Shareholders, their heirs, legal representatives, successors or assigns.

ARTICLE 9.

Amendment or Alteration—The agreement may be amended or altered in any provision and such change shall become effective when reduced to writing and signed by the Shareholders who are parties hereto.

ARTICLE 10.

Liability of Insurance—Notwithstanding the provisions of this agreement, any life insurance company which has issued a policy of life insurance subject to the provisions of this agreement is hereby authorized to act in accordance with the terms of such policies as if this agreement did not exist. The payment or other performance of its contractural obligations by any such insurance company in accordance with the terms of any such policy shall completely discharge such company from all claims, suits and demands of all persons whatsoever.

ARTICLE 11.

State Law Governing—This agreement shall be subject to and governed by the laws of the State of _____, irrespective of the fact that one or more the parties now is or may become a resident of a different state.

ARTICLE 12.

Endorsement of Stock Certificate—Upon the execution of this agreement, the above designated stock certificates shall be surrendered to the Corporation for the affixation of the following endorsement thereon, to wit:

"This certificate is transferable upon compliance with provisions of a certain Agreement dated _____, 19_____ by and between _____, and _____, a copy of which is on file in the office of the Secretary of the _____ Corporation."

Following endorsement of the certificates as above provided, such certificates shall be returned to the Shareholders. Any stock issued to a Shareholder subsequent to the date of this agreement shall carry the same endorsement.

ARTICLE 13.

Binding Effect—This agreement shall be binding upon and inure to the benefit of the parties hereto and their respective heirs, executors, administrators and assigns.

SCHEDULE A

The undersigned mutually agree on this _____ day of _____, 19____, that for the purposes of this Stock Purchase Agreement each share of the Company has a value of $_____.

_____

_____

SCHEDULE B

Schedule of life insurance policies to Stock Purchase Agreement

Name of Company	Policy Number	Face Amount	Signature of Shareholders

STOCK REDEMPTION AGREEMENT

(Common-Law States)

Under the Stock Redemption Agreement that follows, the corporation owns, pays for and is the beneficiary of policies on the lives of the shareholders. Under this arrangement, the corporation becomes a party to the buy-sell agreement. The policies are in amounts equal to each shareholder's interest in the corporation. When a shareholder dies, the life insurance proceeds are paid to the corporation, which in turn uses them to buy the decedent's stock from his or her estate. Any life insurance proceeds paid by reason of the insured shareholder's death will be received income-tax-free by the corporation but may result in the imposition of alternative minimum tax.

The validity of an agreement between the corporation and its shareholders for the redemption of a deceased shareholder's stock depends mainly on state law. Generally, state statutes and court decisions favor the legal authority of a corporation to purchase its own stock. However, there are various restrictions on this power. For example, in most states the corporation can purchase the stock if there is earned surplus, or from capital surplus if the shareholders approve or if it is so provided in the articles of incorporation. However, since the rules do vary from state to state, the validity of a stock redemption plan in any given circumstances must be ascertained.

Properly arranged, the complete redemption of a shareholder's interest in a close corporation will be treated as a capital transaction. As such, the estate of the deceased shareholder will normally not incur any income tax liability, since the amount received by the estate will be equal to the value set for federal estate tax purposes.

However, especially in family-held corporations, the so-called attribution rules may come into play. These rules may cause the decedent to be considered the "constructive" owner of stock actually owned by family members and/or beneficiaries of the estate. Caution should be exercised in this area, and the statutory requirements closely followed.

AGREEMENT made this _____ day of _____, 19_____, by and between _____, _____ and _____ (hereinafter referred to as "Shareholders"), and the _____ Company, Incorporated (hereinafter referred to as the "Company"), created and existing under the laws of the State of _____.

WITNESSETH:

WHEREAS, _____, _____, and _____ are the only Shareholders of the Company, _____ owning _____% and _____ owning _____%; and

WHEREAS, the parties to this agreement believe that it is in their mutual best interests to provide for the continuity and harmony in management and the policies of the Company; and

WHEREAS, the purposes of this agreement are (1) to provide for the purchase by the corporation of the shares of any Shareholder in the event of his or her death, (2) to provide for the purchase of the shares of a Shareholder who during his or her lifetime desires to dispose of any of his or her stock, and (3) to provide the funds necessary to carry out such purchases;

NOW, THEREFORE, in consideration of the mutual agreements and covenants contained herein and for other valuable consideration, receipt of which is hereby acknowledged, it is mutually agreed and covenanted by and between the parties to this agreement as follows:

ARTICLE 1.

Disposal of Stock during Lifetime—During his or her lifetime, no Shareholder shall transfer, encumber or dispose of any portion or all of his or her stock interest in the Company except that if a Shareholder should desire to dispose of any of his or her stock in the Company during his or her lifetime, he or she shall first offer to sell all of his or her stock to the Company at a price determined in accordance with the provisions of Article 2. Any shares not purchased by the Company within 30 days after receipt of such offer in writing shall be offered at the same price to other Shareholders, each of whom shall have the right to purchase such portion of the remaining stock offered for sale as the number of shares owned by all the other Shareholders excluding the selling Shareholder. Provided, however, that if any Shareholder does not purchase his or her full proportionate share of the stock, the balance of the stock may be purchased by the other Shareholders equally. The mode of payments for the stock shall be in accordance with the provisions of Article 3. If the stock is not purchased by the remaining Shareholders within thirty days of the receipt of the offer to them, the Shareholder desiring to sell his or her stock may sell it to any other person but shall not sell it without giving the Company and the remaining Shareholders the right to purchase such remaining stock at a price and on the terms offered to such other person.

ARTICLE 2.

Purchase Price of Shares—Unless and until changed as hereinafter provided, the value of each share of stock of the Company held by each Shareholder shall be $_____. This price has been agreed upon by the Shareholders and the Company as representing the fair value of the interest of each Shareholder, including his or her interest in the goodwill of the corporation. The respective Shareholders hereby mutually agree to sell the stock standing in their names and subject to this agreement at the value herein stipulated, or at the value stipulated in any proper amendment of this agreement. The Shareholders and the Company agree to redetermine the value of the Company and their respective interests therein within sixty days following the end of each fiscal year. The value so agreed upon shall be endorsed on Schedule A attached hereto and made a part of this agreement. If the Shareholders and the Company fail to make a redetermination of value for a particular year, the last previously stipulated value shall control, except that if the Shareholders and the Company have not so redetermined the value within the twenty-four months immediately preceding the death of a Shareholder, then the value of the Shareholders' interest shall be agreed upon by the representative of the deceased Shareholder and the Company through its surviving Shareholders. If they do not agree upon a valuation within 120 days after the death of a Shareholder, the value of the deceased Shareholder's interest shall be determined by arbitration as follows: The Company through the surviving Shareholders and the representatives of the estate of the deceased Shareholder shall each name one arbitrator; if the two arbitrators cannot agree upon a value within thirty days, they shall appoint a third arbitrator and the decision of the majority shall be binding upon all parties. In any determination of value made after the death of a Shareholder, the value of the insurance proceeds in excess of the policy's cash surrender value at the time of the decedent's death shall not be taken into account.

ARTICLE 3.

Upon the Death of a Shareholder—Upon the death of any Shareholder, the Company shall purchase, and the estate of the decedent shall sell, all of the decedent's stock in the Company now owned or hereafter acquired. The purhcase price of such stock shall be computed in accordance with the provisions of Article 2 of this agreement.

If the purchase price exceeds the proceeds of the life insurance, the balance of the purchase price shall be paid in _____ consecutive annual payments beginning _____ months after the date of the Shareholder's death. Such unpaid balance of the purchase price shall be evidenced by a series of negotiable promissory notes executed by the Company to the order of the estate of the deceased with interest at _____ per annum. Such notes shall provide for the acceleration of the due date of all unpaid notes in the series on default in the payment of any note or interest thereon and shall provide that upon the default in the payment of interest or principal, all note shall become due and payable immediately and shall give the Company the option of prepayment in whole or in part at any time. Provided, however, that the Legal Representative shall have the option to demand in cash an amount at least equal to _____ % of the agreed purchase price. Upon failure of the surviving Shareholder to comply with such demand, then this agreement may be terminated at the option of the Legal Representative.

ARTICLE 4.

The Insurance Policies—The Company, in order to help fund its obligations under this agreement, has procured and made subject hereto insurance on the lives of the Shareholders as follows:

(1) _____ is insured under life insurance policy No. _____ issued by the _____ Insurance Company in the face amount of $ _____, and the Company is the applicant, owner and beneficiary thereof.

(2) _____ is insured under life insurance policy No. _____

issued by the _____ Insurance Company in the face amount of $ _____, and the Company is the applicant, owner and beneficiary thereof.

(3) _____ is insured under life insurance policy No. _____ issued by the _____ Insurance Company in the face amount of $ _____, and the Company is the applicant, owner and beneficiary thereof.

The Company shall pay premiums on the insurance policies taken out pursuant to this agreement and shall give proof of payment of premiums to the Shareholders whenever any one of them shall so request such proof. If the premium is not paid within _____ days after its due date, the insured shall have the right to pay such premium and be promptly reimbursed therefor by the Company. The Company shall have the right to purchase additional insurance on the lives of any or all of its Shareholders; such additional policies shall be listed in Schedule B, attached hereto and made a part of this agreement, along with any substitution or withdrawal of life insurance policies subject to this agreement. In the event that the Company decides to purchase additional life insurance on any Shareholder, each Shareholder hereby agrees to cooperate fully by performing all the requirements of the life insurer which are necessary conditions to the issuance of life insurance policies. The Company shall be the sole owner of the policies issued to it, and it may apply any dividends toward the payment of premiums. Upon the joint agreement of the Shareholders, other policies may be substituted for any policies made subject to this agreement or any policies subject hereto may be withdrawn. The Shareholders agree, however, that if at any time there should be no insurance subject to this agreement on the life of a particular Shareholder a party hereto, of if such insurance made subject to this agreement is impaired in value so that it would not provide at any time proceeds at lease equal to _____ % of the face amount of such insurance, such Shareholder may at that time elect to declare this agreement terminated by giving written notice to that effect to the other Shareholders. Any addition, substitution or withdrawal of policies shall be endorsed on Schedule B, attached hereto and signed by the Shareholders.

ARTICLE 5.

Purchase of Nonmatured Policies by the Insured—If any Shareholder withdraws from the Company during his or her lifetime or if this agreement terminates before the death of a Shareholder, then such Shareholder shall have the right to purchase the policy or policies on his or her life owned by the Company by paying an amount equal to the (cash surrender value) (aggregate net premiums paid) as of the date of transfer, less any existing indebtedness charged against the policy or policies. This right shall lapse if not exercised within _____ days after such withdrawal or termination.

ARTICLE 6.

Execution of the Agreement—A duly authorized officer of the Company and the executor or administrator of the deceased Shareholder shall make, execute and deliver any documents necessary to carry out this agreement. This agreement shall be binding upon the Company and the Shareholders, their heirs, legal representatives, successors and assigns.

ARTICLE 7.

Amendment of Agreement—This agreement may be altered, amended or terminated by a writing signed by the Company and all Shareholders.

ARTICLE 8.

Termination of the Agreement—This agreement shall terminate on the occurrence of any of the following events:

  (a) the written agreement of the Shareholders to that effect.
  (b) the exercise of a Shareholder's election to terminate this agreement pursuant to Article 4, or the exercise of a similar option by the Legal Representative pursuant to Article 3.
  (c) Bankruptcy, receivership or dissolution of the Company.
  (d) Death of two or more Shareholders simultaneously or within a period of thirty days.
  (e) When there remains only one Shareholder a party to the agreement.

ARTICLE 9.

Liability of Insurer—No insurance company which has issued or shall issue a policy or policies subject to this agreement shall be under any obligation with respect to the performance of the terms and conditions of this agreement. Any such company shall be bound only by the terms of the policy or policies which it has issued or shall hereafter issue and shall have no liability except as set forth in its policies.

ARTICLE 10.

State Law Governing—This agreement shall be subject to and governed by the laws of the State of _____, irrespective of the fact that one or more of the parties now is or may become a resident of a different state.

ARTICLE 11.

Effect of Bar Against Stock Redemption—If the Company is unable to make any purchase required of it hereunder because of the provisions of the applicable statutes or of its charter or bylaws, the company agrees to take such action as may be necessary to permit it to make such purchases, and the Shareholders who are parties to this agreement agree that they will also take such action as may be necessary for the Company to make such purchases.

ARTICLE 12.

Endorsement of Stock Certificates—Upon the execution of this agreement, the above designated stock certificates shall be surrendered to the Corporation for the affixation of the following endorsement thereon, to wit:

"This certificate is transferable only upon compliance with provisions of a certain Agreement dated _____, 19_____ by and between _____, _____ and _____, a copy of which is on file in the office of the Secretary of the _____ Corporation."

Following endorsement of the certificates as above provided, such certificates shall be returned to the Shareholders. Any stock issued to a Shareholder subsequent to the date of this agreement shall carry the same endorsement.

ARTICLE 13.

Binding Effect—This agreement shall be binding upon and inure to the benefit of the parties hereto and their respective heirs, executors, administrators, successors and assigns.

IN WITNESS WHEREOF the parties hereunto have executed this agreement at _____, in the County of _____, State of _____, on this _____ day of _____, 19____.

_____ Company, Inc.

By: _____

_____
Shareholder

_____
Shareholder

_____
Shareholder

SCHEDULE A

The undersigned mutually agree on this _____ day of _____, 19_____, that for the purposes of this Stock Redemption Agreement each share of the Company stock has a value of $_____.

_____

_____

SCHEDULE B

Schedule of life insurance policies subject to Stock Redemption Agreement

Name of Company	Policy Number	Face Amount	Signature of Shareholders

CROSS-PURCHASE AGREEMENT

(Community Property States)

THIS AGREEMENT is made by and among _____,
_____ and _____ (hereinafter called the
"Stockholders").

Recitals

A. The stockholders are owners of all of the outstanding capital stock
of _____ (hereinafter called the "Corporation"), such stock
being held by them as follows:

Stockholder	Shares
_____	_____
_____	_____
_____	_____

As used in this agreement, the term "Stock" shall include such shares and all
other shares of the capital stock of the Corporation of any and all classes, now
owned or hereafter acquired by any Stockholder whether by gift, inheritance, purchase, split, dividend or otherwise.

B. The Stockholders own and are the beneficiaries of policies of life insurance on one
another's life as listed in Exhibit "A" annexed hereto.

C. The parties hereto intend by this agreement to provide a market for the Stock of
any Stockholder whose death shall occur. It is further intended that, by means
of restrictions on the transfer of Stock, the Stockholders shall have the benefit
of continued control of the Corporation.

THEREFORE IT IS AGREED:

1. Death of a Stockholder

(a) **Sale of Stock**—In the event of the death of a Stockholder, the decedent's
personal representative shall sell, and the surviving Stockholders shall buy,
the decedent's Stock (including any interest his or her spouse may have in
such Stock through community property).

(b) **Ratio of Purchase**—Each surviving Stockholder shall make the purchase
required in subsection (a) in the same ratio to the whole thereof that his or her
shares of Stock bear to the total shares of Stock of all surviving Stockholders.

(c) **Purchase Price**—The purchase price shall deliver to the decedent's personal
representative, within ninety days following the date of his or her death, the
proportionate part of the price payable by each as follows:

(1) A cash down payment equal to the lesser of the full purchase price or the insurance proceeds receivable by the purchaser through policies on the decedent's life listed on Exhibit "A."

(2) For the balance, if any, a negotiable promissory note is substantially the form annexed hereto as Exhibit "C," made payable to such personal representative. The number of installments shall be at the election of the purchaser but shall in no event exceed sixty and shall in any event commence not later than _____ days after delivery of the note.

(d) **Delivery of Stock**—Upon receipt of such down payment and note, the personal representative shall deliver certificates to each purchaser representing the shares sold.

2. Survivorship

In the event of the death of all Stockholders within a single period of thirty days, then the provisions of Section 1 shall not apply and this agreement shall terminate.

3. Insurance Policies

The Stockholders may take out additional insurance on the life of any other Stockholder whenever, in their opinion, such insurance would be necessary or useful in helping them to carry out their obligations under this agreement. Such additional insurance shall be listed on Exhibit "A."

(a) **Purchase of Policies**

(1) In the event of any termination of this agreement, either as a whole or with respect to any Stockholder, then each Stockholder with respect to which the agreement has terminated shall have the right to purchase from the others any and all policies of insurance listed on Exhibit "A" on his or her own life. Such right shall be exercisable only by a written notice of intent delivered to such other Stockholders within 180 days following the date of such termination and accompanied by the full purchase price.

(2) In the event of the death of any Stockholder, all policies of insurance listed on Exhibit "A" owned by the decedent on the lives of the surviving Stockholders shall be sold to the Corporation, which shall buy them.

(b) **Purchase Price**—The purchase price of each policy of life insurance shall be its interpolated terminal reserve, increased by the amount of unearned premium and reduced by the amount of any loans secured by it.

4. Transfers during Life

(a) **Offer to Corporation**—In the event that any Stockholder wishes to make a transfer of his or her Stock during his or her lifetime, then he or she shall first offer it to the Corporation. The Corporation shall have ninety days following receipt of such offer in which to elect to accept it. Such election shall be by action of the Board of Directors on the issue of which neither the transferor nor his or her spouse shall be entitled to vote.

(b) **Offer to Other Stockholders**—If the Corporation does not accept the offer within the time specified, then such offer shall automatically extend to the other Stockholders.

(1) Each such other Stockholder shall have the right to elect to buy that number of the offered shares which bears the same ratio to the whole thereof as his or her shares bear to the total shares of Stock held by all such other Stockholders.

(2) Such election to purchase must be made within fifteen days of the expiration of the offer to the Corporation. Any Stockholder making the maximum purchase available to him or her is a "maximum purchaser" and any shares remaining unpurchased at the end of such fifteen days are "unpurchased shares."

(3) For a period of five days following the expiration of such fifteen-day period, each maximum purchaser shall have the right to purchase that number of unpurchased shares which bears the same ratio to all unpurchased shares as his or her shares [prior to application of this subsection (b)] bear to the total shares of Stock [prior to application of this subsection (b)] held by all maximum purchasers.

(c) **Contents of Offer**—The offer described in subsections (a) and (b) shall contain:

(1) The name and address of the prospective transferee and the price and terms of the intended transfer.

(2) An offer to sell the subject shares under the same price, terms and conditions as set forth in Section 1 for the purchase of a deceased Stockholder's Stock, except that the date for the offer shall replace the date of death as provided therein.

(d) **Offer Not Accepted**—If the Corporation and the other Stockholders fail to purchase all of the offered shares within the time prescribed, then the transferor shall be free (with respect to shares not so purchased) to make the transfer described in such offer and the transferee shall take such shares free of this agreement. If the transferee does not take all of such shares, then those shares remaining in the hands of the transferor shall be free of this agreement.

5. **Disposition by Spouse**
In the event that the spouse of a Stockholder predeceases him or her and makes a testamentary disposition of his or her community interest in the Stock, then:

(a) **Transfer to Surviving Spouse**—To the extent that such disposition is to his or her surviving spouse, or to a trust or trusts of which he or she is sole trustee, the transfer shall not be subject to the offer requirements under this agreement, but the interest so transferred shall, in the hands of the transferee, be subject to this agreement fully as if still owned by the Stockholder. This includes, but is not limited to, the duty of the transferee to sell such interest to the other Stockholders, and their duty to purchase it, on the Stockholder's death.

(b) **Transfer to Others**—Except as provided in subsection (a), no such disposition by such spouse shall be effective without him or her first offering such interest as follows:

(1) To his or her surviving spouse, the entirety thereof on the same terms

and for the same proportionate price as applies to a transfer by a Stockholder during his or her lifetime under Section 4, but without any prior offer to the Corporation or to the other Stockholders.

(2) If his or her surviving spouse fails to accept such offer, then to the other Stockholders, the entirety thereof on the same terms and for the same proportionate price as applies to a transfer by a Stockholder during his or her lifetime under Section 4, but without any prior offer to the Corporation.

6. Corporation Liabilities

If, at the time of his or her death, any Stockholder and/or his or her spouse shall be guarantors of any liabilities of the Corporation, the surviving Stockholders shall hold the decedent, his or her estate, his or her spouse and his or her heirs harmless from any and all such liabilities in the event of a default by the Corporation.

7. Endorsement on Stock Certificates

(a) **Endorsement**—Upon execution of this agreement, all certificates of Stock shall be endorsed by the Secretary of the Corporation as follows:

"This certificate is transferable only upon compliance with the provisions of an agreement dated _____, 19_____, among _____, _____ and _____, and which provides, in substance, that prior to transfer the shares represented hereby must be first offered to the other Stockholders at a price set forth in such agreement. A copy of such agreement is on file in the office of the Secretary of the Corporation."

Certificates representing Stock becoming subject hereto after the date hereof shall be similarly endorsed.

(b) **Removal of Endorsement**—In the event that the Stock represented by any certificate ceases to be subject to this agreement, then, upon delivery of such certificate to the Secretary of the Corporation, endorsed for cancellation, a new certificate for a like number of shares shall be issued to such holder without such endorsement.

8. Applicable Law

This agreement is executed in and is to be construed under and governed by the laws of the State of _____.

9. Binding Effect

This agreement shall be binding on the parties, their executors, administrators, spouses, heirs and assigns.

IN WITNESS WHEREOF the parties have signed their names this _____ day of _____, 19____.

_____

_____

_____

CONSENT OF SPOUSES

We, the undersigned spouses of the Stockholders, hereby acknowledge that we have read the foregoing agreement and consent to its terms, to the disposition made therein of any interest we may have in the Stock of the Corporation as community or separate property, and to the price now or hereafter determined by the Stockholders.

Date _____, 19____   _____

Date _____, 19____   _____

Date _____, 19____   _____

EXHIBIT "A"

Life Insurance

Insured	Owner	Amount	Insurance Company	Policy No.
_____	_____	$_____	_____	_____
_____	_____	$_____	_____	_____
_____	_____	$_____	_____	_____
_____	_____	$_____	_____	_____
_____	_____	$_____	_____	_____
_____	_____	$_____	_____	_____

EXHIBIT "B"

Purchase Price

Amount   *Date Reviewed*   *Signatures of Parties*
$_____   _____, 19____

_____

_____

_____

EXHIBIT "C"

Installment Note

$_____   Dated _____, 19____

For value received, _____ promises to pay to _____, or to his or her holder, the sum of $ _____ in equal consecutive monthly installments (including principal and interest) commencing _____, 19____, and continuing until the final payment on _____, 19____, with interest on the unpaid balance at the rate of _____% per annum.

If any installment is not paid when due, then the entire unpaid balance of principal and accrued interest shall become immediately due and payable at the option of the holder. If suit is made to collect any part hereof, the maker agrees to pay such attorneys' fees as the Court may assess. This note may be prepaid in whole or in part without penalty.

_____

STOCK REDEMPTION AGREEMENT

(Community Property States)

THIS AGREEMENT is made by and among _____ (hereinafter called the "Corporation") and _____, _____ and _____ (hereinafter called the "Stockholders").

Recitals

A. The capital stock of the Corporation consists of one class of shares, common, and there are on the date of this agreement _____ shares outstanding, held as follows:

Stockholder	Shares
_____	_____
_____	_____
_____	_____

As used in this agreement, the term "Stock" shall include such _____ shares of common stock and all other shares of the capital stock of the Corporation, of any and all classes, now owned or hereafter acquired by any Stockholder whether by gift, inheritance, purchase, split, dividend or otherwise.

B. The Corporation owns and is beneficiary of policies of life insurance on the lives of the Stockholders as listed in Exhibit "A" annexed hereto.

C. The parties hereto intend by this agreement to provide a market for the Stock of any Stockholder whose death shall occur. It is further intended that, by means of restrictions on the transfer of Stock, the Corporation shall benefit by a continuation of its present management.

THEREFORE IT IS AGREED:

1. Death of a Stockholder

(a) **Sale of Stock**—In the event of the death of a Stockholder, the decedent's personal representative shall sell, and the corporation shall buy, the decedent's Stock (including any interest his or her spouse may have in such Stock through community property).

(b) **Purchase Price**—The purchase price shall be in the amount set forth on Exhibit "B" annexed hereto.

(c) **Terms**—The Corporation shall deliver to the decedent's personal representative, within ninety days following the date of his death:

(1) A cash down payment equal to the lesser of the full purchase price or the

insurance proceeds receivable by the Corporation through the policies on the decedent's life listed on Exhibit "A."

    (2)   For the balance, if any, a negotiable promissory note in substantially the form annexed hereto as Exhibit "C," made payable to such personal representative and guaranteed by all Stockholders then living. The number of installments shall be at the election of the Corporation but shall in no event exceed 60 and shall in any event commence not later than _____ days after delivery of the note.

(d) **Delivery of Stock**—Upon receipt of such down payment and note, the personal representative shall deliver certificates representing the purchased shares to the Secretary of the Corporation for cancellation.

(e) **Insufficient Surplus**—If at the time the Corporation is required to purchase Stock hereunder its surplus is insufficient for such purpose, then (1) the entire available surplus shall be sued to purchase part of such Stock; (2) the Corporation and its Stockholders shall promptly take all required action to create surplus through recapitalization of its Stock; and (3) the Corporation shall then purchase the balance of such Stock.

2. Survivorship

In the event of the death of all Stockholders within a single period of thirty days, then the provisions of Section 1 shall not apply and this agreement shall terminate.

3. Insurance Policies

In addition to the policies of life insurance listed on Exhibit "A," the Corporation may take out additional insurance on the life of any Stockholder whenever, in the opinion of the Corporation, such insurance would be necessary or useful in helping it carry out its obligations under this agreement. Such additional insurance shall be listed on Exhibit "A."

(a) **Purchase of Policies by Insured**—In the event of any termination of this agreement, either as a whole or with respect to any Stockholder, then each Stockholder with respect to whom the agreement has terminated shall have the right to purchase from the Corporation any and all policies of insurance listed on Exhibit "A" on his or her own life. Such right shall be delivered only by a written notice of intent to an officer of the Corporation within 180 days following the date of such termination and accompained by the full purchase price.

(b) **Purchase Price**—The purchase price of each policy of life insurance shall be its interpolated terminal reserve, increased by the amount of any loans secured by it.

4. Transfer during Life

(a) **Offer to Corporation**—In the event that any Stockholder wishes to make a transfer of his or her Stock during his or her lifetime, then he or she shall first offer it to the Corporation, as follows:

    (1)   A written offer shall be delivered to any officer of the Corporation other than the transferor and his or her spouse. Such offer shall contain:

        (A) The name and address of the prospective transferee and the price and terms of the intended transfer.

(B)   An offer to sell the subject shares to the Corporation under the same price, terms and conditions as set forth in Section 1 for the purchase of a deceased Stockholder's Stock, except that the date for the offer shall replace the date of death as provided therein.

(2)   The Corporation shall have ninety days following receipt of such offer in which to elect to accept it. Such election shall be by action of the Board of Directors on the issue of which neither the transferor nor his or her spouse shall be entitled to vote.

(3)   If the Corporation fails to accept such offer within the time prescribed, then the transferor shall be free to make the transfer described in such offer and the transferee shall take such stock free of this agreement. Provided, however, that if such transfer is not effected within ninety days following expiration of such offer, then such Stock shall be subject to this agreement, including but not limited to reapplication of this Section 4.

(b)   **Gifts of Stock**—The provisions of subsection (a) to the contrary notwithstanding, any Stockholder may from time to time transfer Stock by inter vivos transfer to his or her spouse, his or her lawful issue or to a trust or trusts for such persons, without the offer described in subsection (a). Provided, however, that the Stock so transferred shall, in the hands of the transferee, be subject to this agreement fully as if still owned by the transferor. This includes, but is not limited to, the duty of the transferee to seek such Stock to the Corporation, and the Corporation's duty to purchase it, on the Stockholder's death.

5.   Disposition by Spouse

In the event that the spouse of a Stockholder predeceases him or her and makes a testamentary disposition of his or her community or separate interest in the Stock, then:

(a)   **Transfer to Surviving Spouse**—To the extent that such disposition is to his or her spouse, or to a trust or trusts of which he or she is the sole trustee, the transfer shall not be subject to the offer requirements under this agreement, but the interest so transfered shall, in the hands of the transferee, be subject to this agreement fully as if still owned by the stockholder. This includes, but is not limited to, the duty of the transferee to sell such Stock to the Corporation and the Corporation's duty to purchase it, on the Stockholder's death.

(b)   **Transfer to Others**—Except as provided in subsection (a), no such disposition by such spouse shall be effective without his or her first offering such interest as follows:

(1)   To his or her surviving spouse, the entirety thereof on the same terms and for the same proportionate price as applies to a transfer by a Stockholder during his or her lifetime under Section 4.

(2)   If his or her surviving spouse fails to accept such offer, then to the other Stockholders, the entirety hereof on the same terms and for the same proportionate price as applies to a transfer by a Stockholder during his or her lifetime under Section 4. In such event each other Stockholder shall be entitled to purchase the number of shares which bears the same ratio to the number offered as his or her shares bear to the total shares held by all other such Stockholders.

6. Corporation Liabilities

If, at any time of his or her death, any Stockholder and/or his or her spouse shall be guarantors on any liabilities of the Corporation, the surviving Stockholders shall hold the decedent, his or her estate, his or her spouse and his or her heirs harmless from any and all such liabilities in the event of a default by the Corporation.

7. Endorsement on Stock Certificates

(a) **Endorsement**—Upon execution of this agreement, all certificates of Stock shall be endorsed by the Secretary of the Corporation as follows:

"This certificate is transferable only upon compliance with the provisions of an agreement dated _____, 19____, among the Corporation and _____, _____ and _____, and which provides, in substances, that prior to certain types of transfer the shares represented hereby must be first offered to the Corporation in redemption. A copy of such agreement is on file in the office of the Secretary of the Corporation."

Certificates representing Stock becoming subject hereto after the date hereof shall be similarly endorsed.

(b) **Removal of Endorsement**—In the event that the Stock represented by a certificate ceases to be subject to this agreement, then, upon delivery of such certificate to the Secretary of the Corporation, endorsed for cancellation, a new certificate for a like number of shares shall be issued to such holder without such endorsement.

8. Applicable Law

This agreement is executed in and is to be construed under and governed by the laws of the State of _____.

9. Binding Effect

This agreement shall be binding in the Corporation and its successors by consolidation, merger or otherwise, and on the Stockholders, their executors, administrators, spouses, heirs and assigns.

IN WITNESS WHEREOF the parties have signed their names this _____ day of _____, 19____.

_____

_____

_____

_____

By: _____

By: _____

CONSENT OF SPOUSES

We, the undersigned spouses of the Stockholders, hereby acknowledge that we have read the foregoing agreement and consent to its terms, to the disposition made therein of any interest we may have in the Stock of the Corporation as community or separate property, and to the price now or hereafter determined by the stockholders.

Date _____, 19____   _____

Date _____, 19____   _____

Date _____, 19____   _____

EXHIBIT "A"

Life Insurance

Insured	Amount	Insurance Company	Policy No.
_____	$_____	_____	_____
_____	$_____	_____	_____
_____	$_____	_____	_____
_____	$_____	_____	_____
_____	$_____	_____	_____
_____	$_____	_____	_____

EXHIBIT "B"

Purchase Price

Amount
$_____

Date Reviewed
_____, 19____

Signatures of Parties
_____

By_____

_____

_____

EXHIBIT "C"

Installment Note

$_____   Dated _____, 19____

For value received, _____ promises to pay
to _____, or to his or her holder, the sum of
$ _____ in equal consecutive monthly installments (including prin-
cipal and interest) commencing _____, 19____, and continuing
until the final payment on _____, 19____, with interest on the
unpaid balance at the rate of _____ % per annum.

If any installment is not paid when due, then the entire unpaid balance of principal
and accrued interest shall become immediately due and payable at the option of the
holder. If suit is made to collect any part hereof, the maker agrees to pay such attorney's fees as the Court may assess. This note may be prepaid in whole or in part
without penalty.

_____

By_____

We, the undersigned Stockholders of the above Corporation, for good and sufficient
consideration, do jointly and severally guarantee payment of the above note when and
as due, both as to principal and interest.

Date _____, 19____   _____

Date _____, 19____   _____

SPECIMEN SHAREHOLDERS AGREEMENT

Protecting S Election

THIS SHAREHOLDERS AGREEMENT is made and entered into as of _____, 19_____ by and among _____, a _____ corporation (the "Company"), and each of the shareholders of the Company (collectively, the "Shareholders" and individually, a "Shareholder"), whose names appear on the signature pages hereto.

WITNESSETH:

WHEREAS, the Shareholders have delivered to the Company written consents to, and the Company has executed and will file with the Internal Revenue Service, an election (the "S Election") to treat the Company as an "S Corporation" under Sections 1361-1379 of the Internal Revenue Code of 1986, as amended (the "Code"), for the taxable year beginning _____ (the "Effective Date");

WHEREAS, in order to establish and preserve the S Election, the Company and the Shareholders desire to obtain certain representations and warranties from the Shareholders and to provide for certain restrictions on the transfer of any shares of any class of capital stock of the Company (the "Shares") owned by the Shareholders;

WHEREAS, the Company and the Shareholders desire to provide for the distribution to the Shareholders for each taxable year of the Company of a portion of the net income of the Company to enable the Shareholders to pay taxes payable by them with respect to the taxable income of the Company;

NOW, THEREFORE, in consideration of the premises and the mutual promises herein made, the parties agree as follows:

1. Each Shareholder hereby represents and warrants to the Company and each other Shareholder that: (i) such Shareholder owns the number of [common shares, without par value] of the Company set opposite such Shareholder's name on the signature pages hereto, (ii) such Shareholder is the only owner of any legal or beneficial interest in such Shares and that no other person has any rights in or to such Shares whatsoever (including, without limitation, by virtue of any community property law or other rights arising out of marriage), (iii) such Shareholder is either a United States citizen or a resident alien in the United States filing United States income tax returns, and (iv) all of the information set forth on such Shareholder's written consent to the S election as delivered to the Company is correct.

2. No Shareholder shall enter, transfer, assign, convey, encumber, pledge, hypothecate or otherwise dispose of, voluntarily, involuntarily or by operation of law, with or without consideration, or otherwise, including, without limitation, by way of gift, bankruptcy, receivership, levy or execution or other seizure and sale by legal process, any of the Shares, or any right, title or interest therein or thereto, now or hereafter owned, held or acquired by such Shareholder, without first obtaining the written consent of

the company or an opinion of legal counsel acceptable to the Company stating that the proposed transfer of the Shares will not have the effect of postponing the Effective Date of, revoking, or otherwise affecting the validity of, the S Election, or of disqualifying the Company from or terminating its S Corporation status. Any transfer or attempted transfer shall be null and void, not be recognized by the Company, and have no effect on the Company or the other Shareholders unless and until such consent or opinion has been obtained. The cost of such opinion shall be borne by the Shareholder proposing or attempting to transfer Shares. Whenever the term "transfer" or any variation thereof shall appear in this Agreement, either as a verb or a noun, it shall mean and include any and all of the aforesaid acts unless the context clearly requires otherwise. In order to enforce the restriction on transfer contemplated by this paragraph 2, the Company shall have the right to purchase any Shares attempted to be transferred in violation of this paragraph 2 on terms substantially similar to those of the proposed violative transfer.

3. The Company and each Shareholder agree not to take any action or fail to take any action which would have the effect of postponing the Effective Date of, revoking, or otherwise affecting the validity of, the S Election, or of disqualifying the Company from or terminating its S Corporation status. Any such act or failure to act shall be null and void, not be recognized by the Company, and have no effect on the Company or the other Shareholders.

4. For so long as the Company shall be an S Corporation, the Shareholders shall vote their Shares in such a manner as will cause the Board of Directors of the Company to cause the Company to distribute, and the Company shall distribute, to the Shareholders pro rata with respect to their Shares cash in an aggregate amount in each taxable year of the Company equal to not less than the federal taxable income of the Company for such taxable year *multiplied by* the Tax Rate. The "Tax Rate" shall be a percentage equal to the sum of: (A) the highest marginal federal income tax rate under the Code applicable to individuals for the taxable year of the Company (not including marginal rates designed as surtaxes to eliminate the benefit of lower tax bracket rates), *plus* (B) the highest marginal state income tax rate applicable to the fewest number of Shareholders holding a majority of the Shares for the taxable year of the Company if under the income tax laws of such state such Shareholders must pay income tax on such Shareholder's proportionate share of the Company's taxable income regardless of the amount of distributions to such Shareholder by the Company. Such amount of cash for a taxable year shall be distributed on or before the tenth business day following the date on which the federal income tax return for the Company for such taxable year is filed, or in the discretion of the Board of Directors of the Company more often to facilitate the periodic payment of estimated taxes.

5. The certificates representing any Shares subject to the terms and provisions of this Agreement shall bear substantially the following legend (or if such certificates already bear another legend such other legend shall be revised to include the substance of the following legend):

> "The shares represented by this certificate are issued and held subject to the restrictions on transfer contained in a certain Shareholders Agreement dated as of _____, 19____, by and among the Corporation and its shareholders, which is on file at the office of the Corporation. Transfer of said shares cannot be made except upon compliance with such provisions, of which

notice is hereby given. The Corporation will mail to any person affected by said Agreement a copy thereof, without charge, within five (5) days after receipt of written request therefor."

Upon execution of this Agreement, certificates for Shares presently held by Shareholders shall be surrendered to the Company and such certificates shall be endorsed with said legend and returned to the appropriate Shareholder, and hereafter the Company shall cause the legend to be placed on all certificates issued by it which represent any of the Shares.

6. If by unanimous written consent of the Shareholders, or if by a vote of more than _____ percent (_____%) of the Shares represented at a duly held meeting of Shareholders, the Shareholders determine to terminate the Company's status as an S corporation, and thereafter each Shareholder is provided with written notice of such determination, within sixty (60) days after the giving of such notice, each Shareholder, if requested, will execute a consent to such revocation in the form prescribed by the Internal Revenue Service and shall deliver such consent to the Secretary of the Company.

7. In the event of a termination of the Company's status as an S corporation, if the Company and Shareholders representing more than _____ percent (_____%) of the Shares desire that the Company's status as an S corporation be continued, the Company and such Shareholders agree to use their best efforts to obtain from the Internal Revenue Service a waiver of the terminating event on the ground of inadvertency. The Company and such Shareholders further agree to take such steps, and make such adjustments, as may be required by the Internal Revenue Service pursuant to Section 1362(f)(3) and (4) of the Code. The Shareholder who caused the terminating event to occur shall bear the expense of procuring the waiver, including the legal, accounting and tax costs and expense of taking such steps, and of making such adjustments as may be required.

8. Any Shareholder who breaches or otherwise fails to comply with the terms of this Agreement shall indemnify and reimburse the Company and the other Shareholders for any loss cost, expense or liability, including without limitation, any additional federal, state and local income tax, plus any interest accrued thereon or penalties applicable thereto, incurred or paid by the Company and the other Shareholders resulting from the postponement of the Effective Date, or the revocation or invalidation, of the S Election, the disqualification of the Company from or termination of its S Corporation status, or any other failure by such Shareholder to comply with the terms of this Agreement.

9. If and to the extent any of the provisions of this Agreement conflict with or are in addition to the provisions of any other agreement among the Company and any of the Shareholders, the provisions of this Agreement shall control.

10. This Agreement shall be governed by and construed in accordance with the laws of the State of _____.

11. This Agreement may be executed in one or more counterparts and each of such counterparts shall for all purposes be deemed to be an original but all of such counterparts shall constitute one and the same Agreement.

12. This Agreement shall be binding upon and inure to the benefit of the parties hereto and their respective heirs, successors and assigns.

IN WITNESS WHEREOF, the parties hereto have executed this Agreement as of the date first above written.

Index

ABOUT THE AUTHORS

STEPHAN R. LEIMBERG

Stephan R. Leimberg is professor of taxation and estate planning at The American College. He has been granted a BA degree by Temple University and a JD by the Temple University School of Law and holds the CLU designation. Mr. Leimberg is an adjunct professor of law in the Tax Masters Program of Temple University School of Law.

Professor Leimberg, the author of more than 40 books and the cocreator of four software packages, is the editor and publisher of *Think about It*, a monthly newsletter on income, estate and gift taxes relating to insurance, business and estate planning, published by many associations of life underwriters, CLU chapters and insurance companies; and a number of client-oriented brochures on estate, financial and business succession planning.

Professor Leimberg has been a main platform speaker at both the Million Dollar Round Table annual meeting and the Top of the Table and has appeared before numerous estate planning councils, life underwriters' associations, life insurance companies and CPA societies.

Professor Leimberg has also spoken at the NYU Tax Institute, the Southern California Tax and Estate Planning Forum, the Notre Dame Law School Estate Planning Institute, the Duke University Estate Planning Conference, the annual meeting of the National Association of Estate Planning Councils and the

Advanced Financial Planners Annual Meeting of the American Institute of Certified Public Accountants.

MOREY S. ROSENBLOOM

Morey S. Rosenbloom is a principal in CMS Companies, a Philadelphia-based personal investment banking firm. Prior to his joining CMS, Mr. Rosenbloom was a partner in the Philadelphia law firm of Blank, Rome, Comisky & McCauley. He graduated from Temple University School of Law and served as a legal assistant to the then chief justice, John C. Bell, of the Supreme Court of the Commonwealth of Pennsylvania.

Mr. Rosenbloom is an adjunct professor of law at the Temple University School of Law and has been an instructor of The American College advanced estate planning course. He is presently the chairman of the Real Property, Probate and Trust Law Section of the Pennsylvania Bar Association.

He has lectured at numerous seminars on the topic of estate and business planning to various legal, banking, insurance and estate planning groups throughout the country.

Mr. Rosenbloom has coauthored many publications and articles, including *Practical Will Drafting, Computing the Federal Estate Tax* and *The Wait-and-See Buy-Sell.*

JOSEPH M. YOHLIN

Joseph M. Yohlin is a partner in the tax and estates department of the Philadelphia-based law firm of Blank, Rome, Comisky & McCauley. His practice emphasizes estate planning and administration, taxation, and business and corporate law. He is a graduate of the University of Pennsylvania and has received a law degree and master's of law degree in taxation from Temple University School of Law.

Mr. Yohlin is listed in *Who's Who in American Law* and has published a number of articles on estate planning. He has lectured extensively for the Pennsylvania Bar Institute, Mid-Atlantic States Bank and Trust Tax Association, Villanova University School of Law, Pennsylvania and Philadelphia Bar Associations, the Pennsylvania Institute of Certified Public Accountants, and many other legal, accounting and professional groups.

Mr. Yohlin currently serves as president of the Philadelphia Estate Planning Council and chairman of the Probate Section Taxation Committee of the Philadelphia Bar Association, and is a member of the Governing Council of the Probate Section of the Pennsylvania Bar Association.